Resisting Gender

D0162421

Gender and Psychology
Feminist and Critical Perspectives

Series editor: Sue Wilkinson

This international series provides a forum for research focused on gender issues in – and beyond – psychology, with a particular emphasis on feminist and critical analyses. It encourages contributions which explore psychological topics where gender is central; which critically interrogate psychology as a discipline and as a professional base; and which develop feminist interventions in theory and practice. The series objective is to present innovative research on gender in the context of the broader implications for developing both critical psychology and feminism.

Sue Wilkinson teaches social psychology and women's studies at Loughborough University. She is also Editor of *Feminism & Psychology: An International Journal*.

Also in this series

Resisting Gender

Twenty-Five Years of Feminist Psychology

Rhoda K. Unger

SAGE Publications
London • Thousand Oaks • New Delhi

First published 1998

SAGE Publications Ltd
6 Bonhill Street
London EC2A 4PU

SAGE Publications Inc.
2455 Teller Road
Thousand Oaks, California 91320

SAGE Publications India Pvt Ltd
32, M-Block Market
Greater Kailash – I
New Delhi 110 048

British Library Cataloguing in Publication data

A catalogue record for this book is available from the British Library

ISBN 0 8039 7824 3
ISBN 0 8039 7825 1 (pbk)

Library of Congress catalog card number 98–61048

Typeset by Mayhew Typesetting, Rhayader, Powys
Printed in Great Britain by Biddles Ltd, Guildford, Surrey

Contents

Acknowledgements

Members of my family, friends, and colleagues have been very helpful in the writing of this book. In particular, I would like to thank my husband, Burt Unger, for his insightful comments and felicitous phrasing. I thank Sue Wilkinson for her incisive editing (of several drafts) and her constant reminders about avoiding ethnocentrism. I would also like to thank (in no particular order): Michelle Fine, Arnold Kahn, Martha Mednick and Joan Saks Berman, who read and commented on various chapters. Joan Berman and Joann Evansgardner also provided valuable historical information about some of the forgotten early feminist psychologists. This book is dedicated to all of us – to those whose contributions have been recognized; to those whose accomplishments have been overlooked; and to those who have given up in frustration and left the field.

The author acknowledges with thanks permission to reproduce the material in the following Readings: Reading 1, Unger 1982, *Psychology of Women Quarterly*, 7, 5–17; Reading 3, Unger, 1979c, *American Psychologist*, *34*, 1085–1094; Reading 4, Unger, 1983, *Psychology of Women Quarterly*, *8*(2), 9–32; Reading 5, Unger, 1990, Yale University Press, 122–131, 135–141; Reading 6, Unger, 1989b, Springer-Verlag, 17–24, 29–32.

1

Names/histories/names

What this book is – and isn't

This book contains the most difficult writing I have ever done. There have been several long hiatuses during which I decided I would never be able to finish it. I have been forced to reconsider many aspects of my research and my professional and personal life. And, I have had difficulty explaining to myself as well as to others just why I am writing it at all.

I have, however, been involved with the field of the psychology of women[1] since it emerged as a recognizable part of the discipline. I have, moreover, been involved with it as a researcher, teacher, text author, and organizational leader since its inception. Many of the issues with which I have been concerned have been of interest to the field as a whole. I believe the parallels between the issues in which I have been interested and similar questions pursued by others in the field have been the result of a synthesis of collective history and personal experience. Neither one nor the other is sufficient to illustrate the complexity of how the field developed in the way it did. This is my story of how it happened.

The psychology of women did not develop as a result of the work of any one 'great woman', but from the work of a critical mass of women who shared both an intellectual tradition and the constraints of being marginalized within that tradition. From this perspective, it appears almost inevitable that certain questions would be addressed.

Some of these questions had been asked once before – during the first wave of feminism in both the USA and Europe. But the women who challenged sex differences and women's place in society were forgotten and their studies disappeared because they did not become part of the formal institutional structure of psychology. They did not write their own histories and were written out of most histories of the field. My generation of feminist psychologists had to reinvent the wheel. Thus, part of the reason for this book is to leave a record for future generations. But it is also an attempt to understand how we can avoid forgetting and repeating the past.

I believe we can do so by means of a socio-structural analysis of the relationship between personal, political, and professional agendas. This time around, the psychology of women has been institutionalized as part of legitimate psychology. But this kind of structural change did not come easily and not all the women who fought for the psychology of women have survived. They can easily be omitted from the ceremonial history which is often written by the survivors. This story is about them as well as about some of my friends and distinguished contemporaries such as Carolyn Sherif, Barbara Strudler Wallston, and Nancy Datan who died before they could fully tell their stories.

Finally, this is a story about the way paradigm shifts actually take place. The official prescription for research states that hypotheses proceed logically from theory and from the results of earlier research. This recipe is followed in the formal introduction and procedures presented in research articles. It has not been my experience, however, that many research questions are actually generated in this way. This is especially true for the first research question in a series or one which offers a new paradigm for research. These questions require that the originator violate previous assumptions about how things work. They often invert figure and ground.

Where do such questions come from? Sometimes they are generated from ideas in other disciplines, but this only moves the problem one step further back in what could be an infinite regress. Rather, some of these questions illustrate the way the personal becomes professional. The researcher attempts to deal with an issue that has become salient in her own life or one that her experience has taught her does not work the way formal methodology and theory say it should. Thus, we must know about the researcher's life circumstances. It was no accident, for example, that Naomi Weisstein studied constructivist processes in both her studies of gender and her research on the neurology of perception (Unger, 1993b). Nancy Datan (1986) was consciously aware of such processes when she discussed what questions about midlife transitions she would have asked as she approached her own midlife as compared to the questions she had asked when she was a young mother (cf. Unger, 1995b).

I developed my Attitudes About Reality Scale partly because I was interested in my own epistemology and wondered whether or not it resembled that of some of my feminist colleagues. Feminist leaders in Division 35 and the Association for Women in Psychology (AWP) come from a variety of disciplines and backgrounds and I was curious to see if we had anything in common. It was only later that I realized that I could use positivist methodology to challenge some of the positivist assumptions within psychology, especially the idea that the observers' ideology had no impact on their research.

The comments in the previous paragraph help to explain why this book is a partly a memoir, partly history, and partly an analysis derived from a sociology of knowledge perspective. The personal, political, and professional aspects of each researcher's life are inextricably intertwined. This book represents an attempt to show how they influenced each other in the person I know best – myself. However, the development of the psychology of women is also an example of the collective nature of knowledge building. Organizational structures, fueled by the political activism of the late 1960s and early 1970s provided a place where like-minded women could meet, discuss ideas, and, later, provide a venue for their legitimization. Thus, this book is also the story of the growth of a field.

Because of the complexities of these issues and their intertwined nature, this book is not a linear narrative. First, I will introduce myself and other women in the emerging field and attempt to explain how we got there. Next, I will examine several areas of major concern in the psychology of women: discrimination against women; power and social control; critique of theory and content in psychology; and epistemology in terms of the personal lives of researchers, their institutional environment, and professional/political factors. Finally, I will look at the stages through which the field has moved and compare these to other, newer fields that focus on ethnic minorities and sexual orientation.

This book is not an official history of the psychology of women. Others have already provided much information about our past (cf. Mednick, 1978; Walsh, 1985; Mednick and Urbanski, 1991; Tiefer, 1991; Russo and duMont, 1997). It is, instead, a reflexive, more personal and social history. But, such a personal framework inevitably introduces biases and permits omissions.

I am writing from the perspective of an experimental psychologist who has been very involved in the leadership structure of the Division of the Psychology of Women of the American Psychological Association (APA). This explains why some people who were important in the early development of the psychology of women are relatively absent from this narrative. Some, such as Phyllis Chesler, were very involved in the creation of the AWP during a period when I was having children and did not go to many professional meetings. Chesler (1995) later wrote many popular books and became more a part of women's studies as a whole. Others, such as Sandra Bem and Carol Gilligan, made significant theoretical contributions, but have never been involved in women's organizations in psychology. As an experimentalist, I have also had less contact with clinical developments which occurred in parallel with the issues I have identified as important to the field. I invite others to tell these stories too.

Setting the professional stage

I never planned to study women or gender. Most of the women in my generation did not. There were no courses, no journals, and little history. Most of us had forgotten that there had ever been a first wave of feminism in the 1920s and, if we remembered, considered it irrelevant to our lives and work.

Looking back, it is hard to remember how lonely I felt in most academic/professional contexts. I started college in 1956, graduate school in 1960, and my professional career (my first full-time position) in 1966. There are figures about the percentage of women who participated in APA's annual conventions at these times – 10.8 percent in 1956 and 13.9 percent in 1966 (Mednick, 1978). But I am not sure these numbers convey the isolation of women psychologists both within the university environment and, especially, when we ventured into the 'outside world' of conferences and conventions.

During conferences women were invisible except as potential sexual partners for men. I was very naive when, as a graduate student, I attended regional and national conventions. During such a meeting I had a long conversation with one of the more famous faculty members at Harvard about the state of my dissertation. I was flattered that he was so interested and did not have an excuse ready when he invited me to his room for more 'in-depth' conversation. I got away before I blurted out what was on my mind: 'Dr —, you're much too old!'

Invitations for dinner at these meetings (even when one paid for oneself) seemed to be taken as invitations for sexual trysts afterwards. Organizations such as the AWP got started because of discrimination against women in job interviews and hiring (Tiefer, 1991). But many of us got to know each other, in part, because we banded together to have someone to go to dinner with who would not make a pass.

While we were visible as potential sexual partners for men, we were completely invisible as professional colleagues. In 1966 I went to an Eastern Psychological Association meeting with my husband Burt (who is not a psychologist) just after getting married. I was also on the job market at the time. We became involved in a number of conversations in which senior men asked my husband what I did (I was right there at the time). Burt was even offered a position at a prestigious university because he was a good listener for the distinguished professor who was holding court during a hotel party. Needless to say, when he indicated he wasn't professionally qualified, the position was not offered to me.

Most of the feminist psychologists who were professionally active during this period have their own 'war stories' (see, for example, Chesler, 1995; Lott, 1995; Crawford, 1997). But most of us were socialized to believe that personal history was irrelevant for us as objective social scientists. Some, like myself, have internalized that belief and it is only recently that I have begun to reveal myself in my scholarly papers (Unger, 1993b). I am still very uncomfortable in doing so. Nevertheless, I am convinced that some of the ways in which the psychology of women has developed reflects our particular experiences (this is, of course, also true for psychology as a whole) and that these stories should be told.

Throughout the years I have met many women psychologists. I have always tried to figure out why some of them became interested in the study of women (and later gender); why some of them became relatively successful in the field whereas others (just as bright and articulate) have disappeared; and why some became and remained social activists and others did not. I have also tried to answer these questions with myself as the object of scrutiny (although I recognize that my recollections are reconstructed from the framework of my own past history and current context).

A brief personal history

The first personal comments I ever made in a biographical statement seemed to me quite revealing at the time.

> Rhoda Kesler Unger regards herself as having been marginal throughout her professional career. She was the only woman in her year in the Experimental Psychology program at Harvard from which she received her Ph.D. She is a Professor of Psychology at Montclair State College and an active researcher in a primarily teaching institution. She is a feminist married to her first and only husband, with whom she is rearing two teen-aged daughters. . . . She believes that marginality explains her scholarly concerns as well as expanding their perspective. (O'Leary, Unger and Wallston, 1985, p. xii)

Actually, my perceptions of marginality date from earlier in my life. As are many other feminist academics of my acquaintance, I am from a working-class background (my father was a truck-driver and my mother a part-time department store cashier). I was the first member of my family to go to college. Graduate school was not even part of our awareness. The elementary school system that I attended could be characterized as 'inner city' even then. And I was a bookish 'ugly duckling' who was beloved by my teachers, but ignored by my peers.

Moreover, I was raised a cultural Jew in a completely non-Jewish part of Brooklyn (this was quite a feat at a time when Brooklyn was predominantly Jewish). My ethnicity further alienated me from the culture of my mostly Catholic peers, but did not give me easy access to Jewish peers because of geographic distance. After junior high school I went to an elite (albeit public) girls' high school in Manhattan (Hunter College High School) where admission was based on a competitive exam. There, however, I was a working-class girl from Brooklyn with a somewhat inadequate education dealing with upper-middle-class girls from Manhattan (the high school was then located in the upper East side and used by affluent parents as an alternative to private school if their daughters could pass the admission exam). I felt quite marginal in this environment as well.

My experiences up to this time had led me to believe that the meritocracy works. I performed very well academically at Brooklyn College so I had no reason to believe that I could not do as well in a PhD program. In some ways my marginalization had sheltered me from the sexism of the 1950s. Since there was no one in my family with whom to compare myself in terms of class identity, I ignored gender constraints as well. As Naomi Weisstein (1977) – a classmate in graduate school – has eloquently related, Harvard was quite an awakening in this regard.

Professional socialization in graduate school
As I wrote in the earlier brief biography, I was the only woman in my year of graduate school in the experimental psychology program.[2] There had been two women accepted the year before – one also from Brooklyn College. Unfortunately, Irma married and became pregnant during her first year and left the program. Throughout my first year as a graduate student, faculty kept asking me if I was going to get pregnant too. I guess all of us 'girls from Brooklyn' looked alike.

I have since learned from male classmates that they perceived the years of graduate school as dehumanizing too, but at the time, they didn't confide this. The style at Harvard was 'academic macho' which meant pretending that one neither studied nor worried and passed exams through innate brilliance. The male faculty (of course, there wasn't a single female to be found) took on the most promising (and arrogant) male graduate students as apprentices. However, they did not want female apprentices (see Laws, 1975, for a discussion of tokenism in the academic world). In my second year of graduate school, they did not offer me the usual research assistantships that my surviving male classmates received. Instead, they found me a teaching assistantship at the Massachusetts Institute of Technology (MIT) where a graduate program in psychology was being started and they did not have enough graduate students of their own to teach undergraduate sections.

The faculty and graduate students at MIT were very supportive and I eventually found my PhD thesis advisor there. So, one could say that Harvard had done me a favor. However, I was forced to commute between institutions for my stipend and was tracked, unlike the males, into teaching rather than research. The male graduate students, on the other hand, learned to write grant proposals, to conduct research, and to give professional presentations.

I think my experience was fairly typical for women during this time. Naomi Weisstein (1977) writes about not being allowed to use equipment for her research because she might break it. Indeed, she might have; the men broke it all the time. Most of the women who were enrolled during the six years I was in graduate school did not complete the program and have disappeared from the profession. The only one who is still active in the field prefers not to talk about her years at Harvard because she finds it too painful.

The faculty at Harvard did not seem to feel that training women for their doctorates involved any responsibility for them afterwards, although they usually succeeded in finding positions for my male peers. As I found out accidentally later on, letters of recommendation could contain potential bombshells. For example, one faculty member from whom I had received As wrote that I was argumentative (I **was** outspoken in his seminars) and another stated that I was 'ambitious' (I was, but 'highly motivated' might have been less loaded). These letters resulted in a 'stress interview' for a postdoctoral position at Yale Medical School where I was asked whether I got along with other women (which seems ironic now) instead of what kind of research I was interested in. I must have given the 'right answers' because I did get the position.

Of course, I was left to find my own faculty position after receiving my PhD (at that time, informal channels or 'the old boy network' were used to help place the men). The field was still expanding then so teaching positions were not hard to find. Positions at elite research institutions (comparable to those that almost all my male classmates obtained) were not available for women in experimental psychology. The percentage of women in this subdiscipline at the time was less than 10 percent. Most of the women could be found in teaching institutions or as research associates at large universities where their husbands were employed. I found myself a position in one of the former type of institution – Hofstra University.

Times of turmoil – the late 1960s and early 1970s

The later years of the 1960s and the early 1970s were times of political turmoil. It was much easier to get involved in the inner city in New Haven than in Cambridge. During the year I spent as a post-doctoral fellow at the Yale Medical School (1964–5) I worked with the New Haven chapter of the Congress of Racial Equality (CORE) and on anti-Vietnam War activities. I remained a social activist after I married and my husband and I helped to organize the Eugene McCarthy presidential campaign on Long Island.

My political views were not particularly popular at Hofstra where I was one of the first two young women hired by the psychology department. My personal style was also rather 'hippie' at the time. For example, I had long straight hair down to my waist (I did wear it up for classes). One of the senior women in the department was incensed by my style which she felt would lead the students not to respect me. She requested that I cut my hair before she would let me teach graduate courses. I was still politically naive and somewhat arrogant (I thought my professional credentials were more import-ant than my appearance) so I laughed, told the story to others, and did not cut my hair. I also did not get tenure.

I would not suggest that there was a direct connection between hairstyle and tenure. However, this anecdote is indicative of the dilemmas encountered by at least one young female faculty member during a period when the 'rules' were changing. There were a lot of double binds around. For example, as a female faculty member I was expected to be nurturant towards students. This was especially important during the Vietnam War when a male student could be drafted if his grade point average fell too low. But I also wished to maintain acceptable standards. Evidently, my standards were too high for the institution at the time. One of the rationales eventually used to deny me tenure was that my student evaluations indicated I was 'liked only by the good students'.

Another dilemma during my early years as an assistant professor involved pregnancy, childbirth, and childcare. I thought I could combine both a career and children – rare among earlier genera-tions of women academics (who were sometimes penalized pro-fessionally if they even married; cf. Scarborough and Furumoto, 1987). I tried to time my pregnancies to coincide with academic vacations. Unfortunately, I miscalculated on my first pregnancy and was informed that insurance regulations would not permit me to teach at the institution during late pregnancy. My graduate seminar met at my home for a few weeks – much to the displeasure of higher authorities.

No one during my graduate training had ever pointed out to me how difficult it would be to maintain a career in physiological psychology and have any semblance of a normal lifestyle. The fact that animals had to be fed every day or that brain operations could not be interrupted for family emergencies was not seen as relevant when the researchers were male. The practical problems that I encountered trying to do such research combined with the increasing irrelevance I found in studies of the caudate nucleus in rats (on which I had done my PhD dissertation) moved me to reconsider my research goals.

Here again, my lack of professional socialization and my marginality may have proved to be an advantage. I was not in contact with a network of professional peers who could serve as research collaborators, supports for grant preparation, or sources of conference invitations. I was, therefore, unaware of how problematic it would be to change fields of research even from one subdiscipline of psychology to another.

This change came about gradually through a research collaboration between the other young woman in the department, Beth Raymond, and myself. Beth had been trained as an experimental psychologist with a specialty in verbal learning and memory. She also had enormous expertise in statistics. Like me, she was beginning to find her research dry and irrelevant. We discussed research questions that interested us and, not surprisingly, given the social turmoil of the time, found we had a mutual interest in person perception. We began to ask questions in this area without tying them to any particular theoretical framework (Raymond and Unger, 1972; Unger and Raymond, 1974; Unger, Raymond and Levine, 1974). Our first studies involved the effects of deviance in attire and were later extended to race and sex as cues for helping others.

During this time I also became involved in developing curricular materials for a course in the psychology of women. Two texts had been published in the area (Bardwick, 1971; Sherman, 1971), but I found one too subjective and stereotypic and the other had a dry academic style that made it difficult to entice students. I had, by then, met Florence Denmark and found that she shared my concerns about the developing field and the textbooks which were currently available. We began to work on our own book – a combination of text and reader (Unger and Denmark, 1975). During this period (1972), I moved to Montclair State University where I have remained.

When I interviewed at Montclair I was much more aware of potential political problems in decisions about promotion and tenure than I had been six years previously. During the hiring interview I announced that I was in the process of shifting fields from physiological to social psychology and that I was interested in developing a course on the psychology of women for the institution. There was much ignorance about the area, but not too much hostility, and I was hired. Some of the questions asked were amusing and, in hindsight, predictable. They included: 'Don't we cover the area in human sexuality?' 'Will we have a comparable class in the psychology of men?' 'Is there enough material for such a course?' And, 'Who will teach this course if you do not?' The answer to the latter question was a chorus from all the other women in the room. Obviously, Montclair was a much more comfortable academic environment for me than Hofstra had been.

An informal history of feminist psychology

While I was beginning my career and having children (two daughters, one born in 1968 and one in 1970), other women were entering psychology and also encountering sexism both on a personal and a professional level. Leonore Tiefer (1991) has written a history of the founding of the Association for Women in Psychology (AWP) which details the climate of the times. Book titles were unabashedly sexist and heterosexist, positions were advertised for men only, and if women were interviewed for positions, they were routinely asked about their marital and childbearing plans.

AWP began from informal conversations at meetings of graduate students and younger academic women who, like myself, had been influenced by popular feminism (the National Organization of Women – NOW – was founded in 1966). It was an enormous relief to share experiences with other women who were having difficulty getting positions, were underemployed, and, somewhat later, were encountering difficulties obtaining tenure. We also shared stories about the difficulties of finding mentors, juggling roles, sexual harassment, and the alienation we felt from being in a virtually all-male environment.

Many warm relationships were developed during this period although we rarely got together more than once or twice a year. Because of the omnipresent sexism and the difficulties of maintaining multiple roles, many women did not attend professional conferences because they did not see any value in them. I had been encouraged to continue to do so by Florence Denmark who was already active in the Eastern Psychological Association by the early

1970s. Despite difficulties with childcare arrangements, I became and have remained a regular conference attendee.

This cadre of conference attendees were the foremothers of AWP. My more vivid memories of this period, however, were not of official meetings and proclamations, but some of the more informal actions that we took. For example, after we heard Nancy Henley's early piece on the politics of touch (1973), some of us agreed to touch the males at the convention first and see what happened. There were a lot of rumbles of consternation about the 'uppity' women who put their hands on a male shoulder or arm or who insisted on initiating a handshake, but we had learned that Nancy was right. We also helped integrate the 'men only' bar at the Queen Elizabeth Hotel in Montreal to protest our exclusion. Even those of us who did not drink insisted on doing their socializing there.

We also had long emotional conversations about current problems and future plans. Our friendships transcended geography and subdisciplinary affiliation. They served as the nucleus for more formal networks as women in psychology became increasingly politically organized.

The history and politics of convention presentation
Recently, I examined the programs for APA conventions from 1965 through 1974 (the year after Division 35 was founded) to see if the extent of women's contributions to these meetings confirmed my memories about the scarcity of women. The numbers I found indicated the reliability of my memories. In 1965, for example, twelve women chaired symposia or delivered invited addresses at APA. Presumably, somewhat more women appeared in symposia or gave papers, but these figures are minuscule when one considers that over 1700 participants were listed in the program. Only two presentations were on the psychology of women – a symposium chaired by Jessie Bernard on low-income family patterns and one presentation on need achievement in women. This convention, however, also included a symposium entitled 'Effect of maternal behavior on cognitive development and impulsivity'.

In 1966 there were two symposia on the psychology of women, none in 1967, and two again in 1968. The number of convention presentations were growing during this period, but only fourteen women chaired symposia or made invited presentations in 1966, seventeen did so in 1967, and twenty-three in 1968. Nineteen women appeared in featured positions in the 1969 APA program, but this program contained the first harbinger of change – a symposium chaired by Joann Evans Gardner with what must be the longest title in APA history: 'What can the behavioral sciences do to modify the world so that women who want to participate meaningfully are not regarded as and are not in fact deviant?'

The symposium included presentations by two men: Donald Broverman on 'Sex role stereotypes and clinical judgments of mental health' and Paul Rosenkrantz on 'The effects of maternal employment on the perception of sex roles'. Both of these papers were also published soon afterwards and contributed to the early literature on prejudice discussed in Chapter 2 of this volume. An additional paper was presented on 'Continuing education: The responsibility of the behavioral sciences' and the discussant was Wilma Scott Heide, a president of NOW.

The APA convention in 1970 was strikingly different in terms of the presence of feminism in its program. Eleven symposia were presented which included titles such as: 'Women psychologists: psychologists? militants?'; 'A monkey on the psychologists' back: the evolution of women'; 'The fall and rise of feminism'; and 'Social psychology and women's liberation'. Familiar names began to appear on the program such as Martha Mednick, Sandra Tangri, Matina Horner (all of whom knew each other at the University of Michigan), Judith Long Laws and Naomi Weisstein (who were involved in feminist activist politics in Chicago), and Nancy Henley – another founding member of AWP. A few early activists whose names appeared frequently on APA programs during this period – Joan Joesting and Miriam Kieffer (recently deceased) disappeared from organized psychology soon afterwards. Others such as Joan Saks Berman (a clinical psychologist who was also part of the Chicago group) never joined APA. Joan has, however, attended every AWP conference, maintains a network of diverse connections, and has been an important source for some of the early history of the field.

The surge of feminism could not have been predicted from earlier APA programs. In fact, the women who had been active in the earlier APA conventions were not the women who sponsored these feminist symposia. Instead, feminist activity within APA was provoked by AWP whose behind-the-scenes activities during this period have been recounted by Leonore Tiefer (1991).

Most of these programs were sponsored by Division 9 of APA (also known as the Society for the Psychological Study of Social Issues, SPSSI) although several other APA divisions had a greater percentage of women members. There was no connection between the proportion of women members or, even, women's contributions to the programs of particular divisions, and feminist programming. For example, although Divisions 12 and 16 (Clinical and School Psychology) had fifty-four female symposia chairs or invited speakers during the years from 1965 to 1973, they sponsored only four symposia on the psychology of women. In contrast, SPSSI had forty female chairs or speakers, but sponsored twenty feminist symposia during these years.

SPSSI's support in this area was due to the organizational involvement of AWP activists such as Joann Gardner (who was a member of SPSSI's executive committee during this period) as well as more mainstream feminists. The latter group were part of APA's Ad Hoc Task Force on the Status of Women which was responsible for the formation of Division 35. This task force was chaired by Martha Mednick and included Helen Astin, Tina Cummings, and Miriam Kieffer among its members (Women's Program Office, 1993).

By 1971 the task force was co-sponsoring APA symposia such as one entitled 'Clinical psychology and theories of feminine personality' chaired by Helen Astin. In 1971 there were eight symposia on the psychology of women, seventeen in 1972, and fourteen in 1973. By 1974, of course, Division 35 had been formed and its programs were an official part of APA. The division sponsored eleven symposia in its first year.

What does this history tell us? Programs on the psychology of women did not 'ignite spontaneously' under the influence of the burgeoning feminist movement. Organizational activism, both inside and outside APA, was necessary for networks to develop, programmatic themes to coalesce, sympathetic divisions to be identified, and symposia to be proposed. These things are not easily done in ignorance. The women who were involved in the early feminist programs had also been involved in other APA programs over time (their involvement can be documented in programs from 1965 through 1970 – not always on topics related to women, but almost always with some social issues theme). Once the new division was formed, however, new names began to appear in these programs.

The origins of Division 35

By 1970 the Association for Women in Psychology had begun its practice of having business meetings on the day before the APA convention began. These meetings were interminable affairs since we followed the feminist model of permitting everyone to speak until consensus was achieved. There were neither formal votes nor formal officers. Because the group was relatively small and well acquainted, this collective model of organization worked quite well for a few years (for a more formal history of the organization see Tiefer, 1991).

At the same time that AWP was in its formative stage, other organizations of women within psychology began to take shape.

The first of these was the Committee for Women in Psychology (CWP) which was formed to deal with sexism within APA (partly because of pressure from AWP). Unlike AWP, it was formed to work from within rather than outside the organization. As one might expect, CWP was initially less radical and activist than AWP. It was comprised of more established academic women as well. The differences between the two groups in both age and status were to prove problematic during the early 1970s.

CWP decided that an important step in legitimizing women in psychology would be to create a division of APA on the psychology of women. Accordingly, they engaged in a petition campaign within the APA membership and acquired enough signatures and commitments to induce the APA Council of Representatives to accept the division (Mednick and Urbanski, 1991).

The goals of the division, as first stated, were not particularly activist in nature:

> To promote the research and study of women, including both biological and socio-cultural determinants of behavior. To encourage the integration of this information about women with the current psychological knowledge and beliefs in order to apply the gained knowledge to the society and its institutions. (Excerpted from Article 1.2, Division 35 By-Laws)

Instead, the organizers stressed the scientific value of scholarship on women. Of course, this was partly a strategy to obtain legitimacy from the male establishment, but it also reflected the professional commitments of many of the senior women who organized the campaign.

Most, if not all, of these women were unaware of the existence of AWP – a group comprised of graduate students, new PhDs, and clinicians who had no academic affiliation. AWP was, in turn, not involved in the efforts of CWP in organizing a division on the psychology of women because most of its members were either not members of APA, uninterested in, or hostile to the formal professional organization. It was with some surprise, therefore, that members of AWP discovered upon reading their program for APA '73 that a meeting to elect officers for Division 35 (the psychology of women) would be held at the end of the convention.

AWP's all-day meeting at the beginning of the convention in Montreal was quite tumultuous. Although I do not remember exactly who said what, some members were completely against any involvement in psychology's organized structure. They saw such involvement as a 'sell-out' of radical feminist principles and procedures. Others objected to the name of the division. They preferred terms such as 'psychology for women' or 'feminist psychology'. Still others argued that since the division was already in existence, we could not ignore it. Those of us who could change our travel plans agreed to attend the organizational meeting and attempt to shape the newborn division in feminist directions.

The senior women who had worked so hard to establish the division were unaware of these events. The cadre of 'radical feminists' (as we were seen by them) was mostly unknown to them and had, as yet, few professional credentials. On the other hand, the members of AWP recognized the senior women, but were unaware of any activities on their part on behalf of women other than the formation of the division. There was a great deal of mistrust on both sides which emerged openly when a slate of officers for the next two years was presented by the organizing group. At this point, Joann Gardner (whose political skills derived from her involvement with the national board of NOW) demanded a five-minute caucus.

Those of us from AWP were in a quandary. We clearly out-numbered the division's original organizers and could, therefore, elect anyone we wished to any office. We felt, however, that the group had worked very hard, had accomplished an important breakthrough, and deserved positions of leadership. We decided on a compromise solution of sorts. We agreed to run AWP candidates for all the positions on the slate that were filled by women who were not present at the meeting. Thus, Florence Denmark (one of the few senior women who was part of AWP) became Division 35's first program chair, Annette Brodsky became a pro-tem representative to APA Council, Barbara Wallston became elections chair, and I became the first membership chair. Amusingly, we later found out that this 'hostile takeover' could have been prevented. Most of these positions were supposed to be appointed rather than elected.

The women from CWP who had organized the division retained the positions of president-elect, secretary-treasurer, representative to APA Council pro-tem, etc. Thus, the first executive committee also included Elizabeth Douvan and Helen Astin (first and second presidents of the division), Martha Mednick (its fourth president), Nancy Anderson, Tina Cummings, and Lorraine Eyde (the latter three women were from the Washington, DC area and were more involved in organizational activities involving women's rights than scholarship in the area). Although we AWP-ers saw ourselves as willing to compromise and to earn our way by doing jobs that required a great deal of work with little prestige, the original organizers were not pleased. They did not know who we were professionally and distrusted our political 'radicalism'.

The first few executive committee meetings of Division 35 were decidedly cool. Martha Mednick, a peacemaker who came to straddle both factions, was sometimes distrusted by both. Fierce arguments erupted over such issues as whether executive committee meetings were open or closed. Helen Astin, who was president during one such battle, tells of asking Georgia Babladelis (the first editor of the *Psychology of Women Quarterly*), in Greek, whether a particularly combatative non-member should be allowed to remain. Some years later when things had apparently calmed down, Martha Mednick recorded a series of oral histories of these events from the viewpoint of individuals on both sides of the controversy. The project aroused so much residual emotion that the tapes were sequestered not to be heard for many years (unfortunately, these tapes appear to have been lost).

In spite of this contentious beginning, the division quickly became a force within APA. I processed over 350 membership applications during my year as membership chair. Virginia O'Leary, a later membership chair, and I analyzed the nature of this early membership (Unger, O'Leary and Fabian, 1977). It was, as it remains, 93 percent female. During the 1970s, a majority of the membership held academic positions, although this has changed (as has APA) in the direction of a larger percentage of clinicians in private practice. The membership came from virtually every subdiscipline of psychology (primarily from clinical and counseling psychology with a surprisingly small 8 percent from social psychology). Of course, no one was trained in the psychology of women. We had the joys and the challenge of helping to develop the field.

Some of us, even from initially 'opposing sides', became close. We shared a great deal about our personal lives – divorce, illnesses, career disappointments and so on. I remember, in particular, one all-night 'encounter-like session' at an executive committee meeting in Colorado that was energized by Carolyn Sherif and included Barbara Wallston, Lucia Gilbert, Michele Wittig, and Arnie Kahn as well as others who did not quite stay up all night. The emotional support was more important to me than much of the official business which could become quite bureaucratic at times.

Feminist organizations in psychology as they are now
This kind of emotional rapport has disappeared to an extent. Some of the newer members have complained about their feelings of isolation and lack of personal contact with senior women. Various attempts at formal mentorship arrangements have not been successful. This appears to be a problem of having a large membership as well as a sense of legitimacy that we lacked at the beginning. It also

suggests that even a feminist ideology is not always sufficient to deal with the structural problems of a large organization.

Although both AWP and Division 35 have grown in recent years, the two organizations have evolved somewhat different identities. Some tensions between them remain. AWP has continued to be an 'outsider' organization with an activist stance and no formal association with APA (although it holds business meetings at the annual conventions and maintains a suite of rooms at a convention hotel for informal programming). The annual AWP party is considered an excellent place to meet feminists from a variety of areas and their book exhibit assembles recent feminist books from all the professional presses. Their annual distinguished publication awards are eagerly sought accolades.

Because of its informal structure (there are still no elected officers and the organization is run by an 'implementation collective'), AWP appeals to younger women and to those who are not so enmeshed in academic pursuits. It has a large proportion of members who are clinical psychologists either in private practice or in public service settings. Over the years, it has also had a much larger number of 'out' lesbians in its leadership than has Division 35. Tensions sometimes surface between the two 'official' feminist groups because of differences in focus, legitimacy, and sexual orientation. However, the organizations cooperate on the costs of the convention suite and on a number of student prizes.

In the past, the leadership in the two organizations overlapped considerably more than it does today and a number of women have worn both hats quite comfortably (for example, all of the initial insurgents from AWP on Division 35's first executive committee eventually became presidents of the division). The groups seem to have diverged more in recent years and AWP conferences (held independently of APA in the spring) have become overwhelmingly clinical in focus. Relatively few senior feminist academics attend unless they are specifically invited to give presentations (AWP is aware of this problem and has recently taken steps to make those primarily concerned with empirical research feel more welcome).

The growth and increased legitimacy of Division 35 has had some negative consequences as well as the obvious positive ones. Events are no longer small and cozy and many newer members feel quite alienated. Some of the passion has also disappeared. The close supportive relationships (which, for me as well as others, was one of the major rewards for involvement) have dwindled too. I know of no recent examples of cooperation similar to one some years ago where four well-known women got together and discussed what they each knew about the women's studies chairship for which they were all leading candidates. As the rewards for feminist scholarship have increased with the legitimacy of the field, competition has also increased.

Strains also exist within Division 35 that parallel those found in APA as a whole. A majority of Division 35's membership identifies with clinical and counseling issues, but the leadership of the division, as well as of its journal, is dominated by women with academic affiliations. In part, this is due to the fact that these women have more time to become involved in organizational matters than those whose primary income derives from private practice. The latter group, however, tends to feel somewhat disenfranchised and points to the fact that only three presidents of Division 35 have been in clinical practice, although several others have been academic clinicians (see Appendix).

Until recently, both AWP and Division 35 could rightfully be termed racist organizations. I remember only one early member of AWP who was African-American – Kitch Childs, an outgoing, outspoken lesbian clinician. Carolyn Payton, former director of the Peace Corps, was somewhat involved in Division 35, but never held formal office, partly because, as a matter of principle, she refused to run for a 'minority' seat for APA Council and was not elected to a 'regular' position.

Both groups have made enormous efforts to be more inclusive and these have been facilitated by the fact that an increasing number of ethnic minority women have entered psychology in recent years. The division has had its first African-American president, Pamela Reid, and several Black women have served as representatives to the APA Council, as program chairs, membership chair, etc. Their involvement has gone far beyond tokenism. Both organizations have had less success in drawing in and retaining Latina[3] and Asian-American psychologists and there are still very few Native-American women in the field.

Men have been largely missing from both organizations since their inception, although there have been a few notable exceptions. Richard Roistacher (who took the first class in the psychology of women at the University of Michigan with Judith Bardwick) was one of the founding activists in AWP and its first corresponding secretary. Allen Gross and Arnold Kahn were active early members. The latter two once raised our consciousness about our own homophobia by dancing together at an AWP dance. Allen Gross has left psychology, but Arnie Kahn has remained committed to feminist causes for more than twenty years and is still the only man to have served as an elected officer in Division 35 (he was secretary-treasurer).

Involvement with feminist organizations confers more 'deviance' on men than women because those in the mainstream discipline cannot attribute it to 'self-interest'. Publications in feminist journals appear to be less problematic and a number of men have served on the editorial boards of *Sex Roles* and the *Psychology of Women Quarterly* as well as published in them.

Another group that is largely missing from the organizations today are younger women who identify themselves as feminist psychologists. Some feminists have argued that this is due to our own success – younger women feel feminism has succeeded and does not need their contribution. Others have argued that feminism was a generational phenomenon. Thus, the feminists of the 1970s became radicalized by racial inequality and opposition to the Vietnam War and simply transferred their militancy to their own struggle for equality. Younger women, growing up in the 1980s (the so-called Reagan years) are more individualistic and less concerned with social justice. It is not clear how we can reach them. My desire to reach this audience is one of the reasons I have written this book. It is also one of the reasons I have authored a number of textbooks (in 1975, 1979, and 1992–6), although texts do not have high prestige value in the academic world.

Feminist scholarship in the 1970s and beyond

Although I plan to discuss specific aspects of feminist scholarship in later chapters in this book, some discussion here may be helpful for understanding the circumstances in which the psychology of women began and grew. The first paper that I know of in the area was Naomi Weisstein's pioneering work which was first published in 1968. Recently, a celebration of its twenty-fifth anniversary was published in the international journal *Feminism & Psychology*. In it, Weisstein (1993) gives some details about the circumstances that led to the paper.

The paper (like Naomi) was not typical of much of the subsequent work in the psychology of women. It was a radical, polemical piece that foreshadowed later feminist theoretical concerns with social constructionism. It appears to have had more impact on feminists outside psychology than within it. The psychology of women (even today) remains more empirical and less theoretical than feminist scholarship in most other disciplines. The strong positivist, empiricist orientation of psychology has had a great influence on our study of women and gender. Many of the women in the field had internalized its norms and, even when we began to reject them, it was difficult to find publication outlets for work that was 'deviant' in both method and content.

It is not surprising, therefore, that my first work in the area was both empirical and atheoretical. Since there were no journals that focused on women or gender, these publications appeared in journals such as *The International Journal of Group Tensions* and the *Journal of Social Psychology*. As it became increasingly easy to present papers in the area after the formation of Division 35, I gave a number of papers at APA that were never published. Some of these were submitted to professional journals, but were rejected. The rationales for rejection are, in retrospect, curious as well as sexist. For example, one paper that I did with a colleague at Hofstra, Diane Krooth, on fear of success among housewives, was rejected because the topic was too 'narrow'. None of the journal editors ever questioned whether studies of 49 percent of the human race were also narrow.

Nancy Datan, who was interested in the sociology of knowledge, had planned to edit a volume of rejected early work by feminist psychologists with commentary on the rejection criteria. Because of her premature death, this project never happened. I do not know how many papers she could have obtained. I suspect that many feminist psychologists accepted the decisions of the reviewers, buried or burned their manuscripts, and went on to do more 'acceptable' work. Those who were unable to do so found it difficult to remain in the academic world. Many names that appeared on early AWP and Division 35 programs are unfamiliar to today's feminist psychologists.

Publications in the 1970s, as is still true today, were the coinage for tenure and promotion. It was no accident that a number of the featured speakers at an early research conference sponsored by AWP had either just been denied tenure or were battling for it (Unger, 1982; see Reading 1, p. 63). Scholarship about women and gender suffered from a number of forms of illegitimacy. It was conducted by a low status group, focused on a devalued group, and stressed theories and methods that were antithetical to a field aspiring to be as scientific as possible. Thus, even when papers were published, they were not valued as highly as more mainstream publications.

I avoided some of these problems at Montclair because it was a public institution which focused on teacher education (similar to many polytechnic institutions in the UK). At this time, the institution did not stress research. Personnel advisory committees (responsible for tenure and promotion) were, nevertheless, delighted by any evidence of scholarly productivity. I did not, however, become a faculty member at Montclair because I thought the institution would be more tolerant of divergent scholarship. I did so because I was part of a dual-career couple with two small children and I could hold the position and still live conveniently near my home.

It turns out, on hindsight, that institutions like Montclair were, in general, more supportive of feminist psychology than many more elite institutions. For example, if one looks at the institutional location of the first ten presidents of Division 35 (see Appendix, p. 211, one finds four from large state universities (Michigan, UCLA, Alabama, and Penn State), two from public universities in New York City (Hunter College and the City University of New York Graduate Center), three from colleges which began as institutions for the education of teachers (Montclair, California State at Northridge, and George Peabody), and only one from a private institution – Howard University (a traditionally Black university). The institutional affiliation of subsequent presidents has been similar. To date, no president of Division 35 has been located at what might be termed an elite private college or research university.

Courses in the psychology of women developed initially in public institutions and have proliferated there. According to a recent market survey by McGraw-Hill, most of the courses in the area can be found in mid- and lower level institutions. In general, women's studies have come late (if at all) to the more elite institutions.

I was startled by the extent of this lag in scholarship when a few years ago I was invited to give a talk to the graduate students in psychology and philosophy at Harvard. Excited by the idea of finally talking at my alma mater, I prepared what I perceived to be a cutting-edge talk about the current state of feminist psychology. I have rarely so misjudged my audience – which looked confused from about my third sentence. I found out later that there were no courses on the psychology of women or gender available to them and they would have been better served if I had given them my introductory lecture to the course.

Although the journals could not be found in the Harvard library when I gave my talk in 1990, research in the area of women and gender has proliferated since the inception of *Sex Roles* in 1975 and the *Psychology of Women Quarterly* in 1977. The international journal *Feminism & Psychology* was founded in 1991 to give priority to specifically feminist work. Mainstream journals in the USA also pay more attention to sex and gender issues now. For most feminist psychologists, however, there still appear to be two tracks for publication – feminist and mainstream. And psychologists who publish on women and/or gender in mainstream journals are much less likely to cite feminist publications than feminists are to cite mainstream contributions (see Fine and Gordon, 1989).

Traditional scholarship in psychology remains primarily empirical in focus. Thus, young scholars who are interested in feminist issues and academic careers find themselves required to do quantitative empirical work. In comparison to other areas of feminist scholarship, the psychology of women lacks connection to postmodern and poststructuralist theory. It is judged harshly by feminist theorists for its devotion to numerical data. Since the psychology of women is also devalued within psychology (ironically, because of its connection with ideology and theory), feminist psychologists often find themselves in a double bind. 'Good' psychological research can only be done at the expense of 'good' feminist scholarship. This intellectual division is problematic for both groups of scholars.

What my feminism means for me

It is important to me to be both a scholar and an activist. This was not always true. I cannot say that I was a feminist from the earliest point of my professional life. Unlike my classmate in graduate school, Naomi Weisstein, 'it took me a lot longer to identify the fundamental sexism of psychology and in academia as a whole' (Unger, 1993b, p. 211). Until graduate school the meritocratic system seemed to have worked for me. I blamed my growing sense of alienation from psychology on my own inadequacies as a person and as a researcher.

I became a feminist through writing my first textbook with Florence Denmark. In part, this was because she introduced me to the world of organized psychology (which I had thought was irrelevant). Mostly, though, I became a feminist as I read more and more sources needed to write the text. I recognized that my own experiences of injustice were shared by others and were grounded in structural processes rather than personal inadequacies.

The book was driven by passion. We wanted to demonstrate that psychological research could both illuminate the way sexual inequality was produced and maintained and to show that such inequality had no basis in fact. We still believed in the power of science to effect social change.

I have always regarded the writing of textbooks as a political act. When I coauthored the first text *Woman: Dependent or Independent Variable?* (Unger and Denmark, 1975), formal resources were much less available than they are today. We rummaged through all sorts of places 'outside' psychology such as nursing journals, linguistic tracts, and the popular media for source materials. We wanted to move psychology beyond its narrow concern with laboratory research. But we also wished to use such research to legitimize the study of women. This ambivalence is still present today. Feminists continue to wrestle with the need to legitimize the scholarly base for women and gender within traditional psychology while, at the same time, deconstructing that tradition.

Our book was long and hard-covered, as was my second text, *Female and Male* (1979a); the third, *Women and Gender: A Feminist Psychology* (coauthored with Mary Crawford and first published in 1992) was just long. Although both aspects of these books have been criticized for reducing accessibility, they were the result of conscious choice. I wanted to establish a respectable database similar to those in more traditional areas such as developmental or social psychology. The need for legitimacy also led me to seek highly reputable publishers for the latter two textbooks (Harper & Row and McGraw-Hill).

Many people reading this introduction are probably amused by the notion that I continue to view myself as an 'outsider'. Partly this is a consequence of my early history, but it is also due to some deeply held epistemological convictions that I believe are shared by other social activists. I have found that many influential feminists have a contradictory view of themselves and the world (Unger, 1984-1985). They recognize that authority is not synonymous with truth, that people are not always rational, and that chance is important in human affairs. On the other hand, they also possess a deep conviction that their actions can change reality. This contradictory view is what gives them the wisdom to understand social injustices and the energy to challenge them.

I believe that the ability to maintain such contradictions may be promoted by identification with one or another form of marginality. Some of the women I have most admired as feminist psychologists have either spoken of or written about their marginality. Clara Mayo considered herself marginal – perhaps because of her early experiences as a refugee child from Austria (LaFrance, 1990). Nancy Datan (1980) wrote movingly of her experiences as a brilliant working-class Jewish college student whose mother was concerned only with her marital prospects (I had much the same experiences. When I was accepted to Harvard, my mother worried that I would never be able to 'find a man who would be good enough for me' and lamented her never-to-be-born grandchildren). Barbara Strudler Wallston suffered for many years with a chronic physical ailment.

I am not sure from where Carolyn Sherif's sense of marginality came (cf. Unger and Kahn, 1998). It may have been due to a long marriage to one of the founding icons of social psychology and her need to combine professional and familial roles with little recognition of the former from her husband's colleagues (see Sherif,

1976). It was Carolyn who nurtured the concept of social construction for me and for feminist psychology as a whole (cf. Sherif, 1979, 1982). Carolyn also trumpeted the need for continued feminist commitment to social change. But it was also Carolyn who told me that social change took a long time.

I am somewhat less impatient these days than I was when I was younger. I believe I am also somewhat more tolerant than some of my feminist friends and colleagues. I am not, for example, comfortable in labeling the feminist scholarship of others as 'good' or 'bad' simply on ideological grounds. I am really more interested in knowing what it is supposed to 'do'. Theory and research separated from social activism is not what I had in mind when I became a feminist (Unger, 1995a).

There has been some discussion of reflexivity in the psychology of women, but few examples of it. I have edited several journal issues and one book in which I have attempted to designate work that I think is important to the field (cf. Unger and Serbin, 1986; Unger, 1989a; Unger and Sanchez-Hucles, 1993). This book represents another form of denotation. It is an attempt to demonstrate that just as we cannot separate the subject from the object of research, we cannot separate the person, the profession, her work, and her politics. In this book I am attempting to light up my little corner in order to help illuminate the whole.

Notes

1 This is the official name of the field in the United States, although it has always been considered problematic. See my comments in this chapter on the founding of Division 35 (Psychology of Women) of the American Psychological Association as well as those by Wilkinson (1996).

2 Harvard University, in common with other elite universities in the United States, was slow to award women doctorates (cf. Furumoto, 1979) and both Naomi Weisstein and I enrolled at Radcliffe College (then the undergraduate women's college) although all of our courses were with our male classmates. Harvard did not award degrees to women until 1964 and my master's degree is from Radcliffe. Harvard and Yale continue to have the lowest percentage of tenured women faculty of any major university (11 and 12 percent, respectively).

3 The division elected its first Latina president, Melba Vasquez, in 1997.

2

Feminism and empiricism in psychology

The political becomes professional

The use of empirical studies of prejudice and discrimination
Political activism preceded scholarly research on women for me as
well as for others. When I first started to do research in the area I
was interested in demonstrating that discrimination against women
could be empirically verified. I saw this research as a form of
political action. I wanted to use the methodology of psychology to
demonstrate both that prejudice and discrimination against women
existed and that these attitudes and behaviors had no basis in fact. I
still had faith that 'good science' could find the 'truths' that would
free us all. Of course, this belief has been seen as hopelessly naive
and positivistic by some feminist critics today. However, for me,
experimentation represents one form of rhetorical argument against
prevailing standards (Unger, 1996).

Others in the second wave of scholarship on the psychology of
women also began with attempts to demonstrate the extent of
discrimination against women. Although we were fueled by feminist
critiques of sexism within academia and in society as a whole, most
of us did not, at first, extend this critique to psychology as a
discipline. Instead, we used traditional psychological methodology
either to look at sexism within psychology and academia in general
or to look at the processes of sex discrimination on an interpersonal
level. Only a few, such as Naomi Weisstein (discussed in Chapter 1),
attacked the methods and theories of psychology. Our studies did,
however, deviate from traditional scholarship in at least one major
way. None of them could be characterized as disinterested.

The first empirical study I ever conducted in social psychology
was neither about women nor gender. It was, however, provoked by
personal and political concerns about prejudice and discrimination.
The 1960s were the peak years of 'hippiness' in the USA. Shortly
after I was married in 1966, my husband and I went to the theater
with my new in-laws, to see an off-Broadway production in the East
Village – a part of New York City that had then and continues to
have a bohemian cast. Since it was a beautiful summer day, hordes
of people in colorful attire and interesting hairstyles were sitting on
the steps of their houses, walking about, and generally 'doing their

thing'. When we met at the theater, my father-in-law said, 'Those hippies – they all look like they have venereal disease.' I thought he knew about some physical stigma of which I was unaware and asked him how he knew. He replied, 'I can just tell.'

My late father-in-law was not an uneducated or ignorant person. He had a master's degree and taught in the New York City school system. His remarks were made at a time when Abie Hoffman (a radical social activist) had just declared that 'hippies are the new niggers'. Rather than get into an argument with my father-in-law, however, I decided to find out how widespread was prejudice against hippies and how it compared to racial prejudice. I thought if I could show him how unrealistic his stereotypes were, he would change them. This was the impetus for our first study which we eventually entitled 'The apparel oft proclaims the man: cooperation with deviant and conventional youths' (Raymond and Unger, 1972).

Of course, we did not tell this story in the introduction to this paper. Instead we stated:

> The present study represents an attempt to establish social deviance as an experimental variable. The major objectives of the study were (a) to find out whether the general public reacts differentially towards individuals who appear to be members of the hippie and black nationalist subgroups as compared to their black and white conventional counterparts, (b) to determine whether the degree of ostensive similarity between the requester and the respondent is related to the degree of cooperation obtained, (c) to measure these reactions in a nonreactive social situation so that the subjects would not be influenced by the demand characteristics of the laboratory experiment. (Raymond and Unger, 1972, p. 75)

This introduction fulfilled the requirements for psychological publication at that time. We made no mention of any personal interest in the outcome of the study and, indeed, divorced ourselves completely from it. The study was written in the prescribed language of distance and objectivity. As feminist philosophers of science noted (Payer, 1977), this kind of depersonalized language established the discipline, rather than its practitioners, as the source of authority and made truth claims difficult to challenge. Purportedly, we were only trying to find out the 'facts.' We went on to describe the methodology of the study:

> The studies were conducted in naturalistic settings (various supermarkets) where different subsets of the general population could be sampled. The task chosen involved an apparently casual request so that the subjects would be unaware that they were taking part in an experiment. For the present purposes, a hippie or black nationalist was defined only in terms of differences from the norm in hair style and attire. These are cues which should lead the observer to infer that the individual belongs to a deviant

subculture, whether black or white. Specifically, it is hypothesized that individuals dressed in deviant attire, regardless of race, will receive less cooperation than their conventional counterparts. Cooperation was operationally defined as the willingness of subjects to comply with a request for change. Furthermore, Brown (1) has indicated that hippies and black nationalists see similarities between their groups; however, it is questionable whether the general public considers the two groups similar in deviance and differentiates them from their black and white conventional counterparts in the same way. (Raymond and Unger, 1972, pp. 75–76)

Although the study did have some characteristics that were not common in social psychology at the time (it was not conducted in a laboratory and the populations studied varied in terms of sex, race, and age), much of the methodology of scientific experimentation was retained. We manipulated our 'subjects' without their awareness and, of course, without their consent. And we defended our procedures as operationally defined (without specifying, of course, that we were the people who had constructed the definitions). We used the passive voice as much as possible to divorce ourselves from the process. We also devised a theoretical justification for the study involving more formal theories about prejudice and discrimination than our own.

This methodology exemplified 'good science'. We would not have been able to publish the study without using it, nor would we have been able to publish the study if we had acknowledged its subjective origins. I am more uncomfortable about defending our use of experimental deception even to this mild degree, although it is still common in many areas of social psychology. When such studies become public (as ours did when the Long Island newspapers publicized the results), they can lead people to be mistrustful of even apparently innocuous requests.

This kind of deception is usually justified in terms of the value of the findings that could not otherwise be obtained. In a summary of our conclusions, we noted that:

Experiment I demonstrated that white subjects were less likely to comply with the requests of both black and white deviants than with the requests of their conventional counterparts. Experiment II demonstrated that black subjects cooperated with the white deviant to the same extent as the white subjects did; however, they cooperated more with the black deviant. Experiment III showed that persons over 30 were less cooperative with deviants than those under 30. The results were explained in terms of Rokeach's theory of belief incongruity. (Raymond and Unger, 1972, pp. 81–82)

In other words, we were able to demonstrate (using conventional methods and accepted technical standards) that prejudice and discrimination existed based solely on external criteria (both race and attire) and that the meaning of these cues varied in different communities. These results foreshadowed later work by myself and others indicating that the bases for such negative judgments were external to the target individual and not, therefore, 'his or her fault'. They represented my first (but, certainly not my last) attempt to use the formal procedures of experimental psychology to make a socially activist argument. I believe this use of research by feminist empiricists within psychology has been misunderstood and under-valued by feminist critics outside the profession.

Contextualization within the experimental paradigm

Our second study involved women as well as men as targets of prejudice. Unfortunately, I cannot claim that this was primarily the result of a desire to be more inclusive in terms of gender. We were actually more interested in testing two hypotheses that had emerged from our first study. We wanted to find out if discrimination occurred in contexts that were less overtly threatening (the first study involved the exchange of money in outdoor shopping malls) and we wanted to find out if deviance produced the same results when a woman rather than a man served as a cue for behavior. We assumed that if fear was motivating the lack of cooperation, women would be less frightening no matter how they were dressed.

We contrived two naturalistic situations that differed from the original study in terms of their potential danger. In one, differentially attired women and men who appeared to be purchasing a few items at a supermarket requested permission to 'go ahead in line'. In the other, male or female drivers (in cars with either 'hippie' bumper stickers or undecorated cars) delayed at a red light. Again, we compared responses to members of a normative population with the responses toward members of a socially deviant group – hippies. The results were mixed and we titled the paper that derived from this research 'Are women discriminated against? Sometimes!'.

We found that hippies were uniformly discriminated against in both situations. Regardless of sex, they were less likely to be permitted to go ahead in line and honked at more quickly than conventional individuals. Women were, however, favored in the first situation and treated more negatively in the second.

We analyzed the difference between the two situations in terms of power and dependency:

> In the first experiment, the female's behavior fit the stereotype of the 'poor damsel in distress.' In this situation, the female, especially if conventionally dressed, has indicated that she has no power, but that rather all power is in the hands of the other individual. In the second

experiment, however, the female possesses some degree of social power by virtue of her ability to frustrate another individual. Although the car may have stalled, it is not obvious that she is in a dependency relationship with the driver behind her. In fact, she has placed herself in at least a position of equality with that driver.

The differential effect of social deviance and sex on the two tasks provides interesting information about this hypothesized power relationship. Social deviance uniformly produces discrimination in both situations. Moreover, it reduces cooperation toward women in all experimental conditions. It is possible that choice of deviant clothing and personal style reflects a challenge to social power that lacks any real power to back it up. (Unger, Raymond and Levine, 1974, p. 79)

We concluded:

It is hypothesized that females will be treated as members of a minority group when they aspire to equal power or status with men. They will receive decreased cooperation from both men and women under these circumstances. Membership in other minority groups (e.g., social deviants) will further decrease cooperation even in tasks in which they are favored as dependent individuals. (Unger, Raymond and Levine, 1974, p. 80)

This study differed from those found within mainstream social psychology in a number of ways. First, the theoretical rationale we offered for the study was derived from sociology rather than psychology:

Beginning with Helen Hacker's (1951) well-known article, there have been a number of attempts to extend the definition of minority group to women. Obviously such a definition cannot be defended statistically since women make up more than fifty per cent of the population. Therefore, attempts have centered about the role characteristics of members of minority groups – in particular, the fact of discrimination and the awareness of such discrimination. Women, because of their high social visibility and ascribed social and intellectual inferiority, have sometimes been compared to blacks by Women's Lib "activists." (Unger, Raymond and Levine, 1974, p. 71)

Analyses based on power and status were not likely to be found in psychology journals of that time. We, however, wanted legitimacy in terms of psychological conventions. The discerning reader will notice, therefore, that we continued (as in the earlier study) to write in the passive voice in an effort to make the findings 'more objective'. We also carefully distanced ourselves from political feminism both by the use of the passive voice and quotation marks around the word 'activists'.

Studies had to be presented in this manner in order to be published by mainstream journals (the only ones that existed at this time). We were able, however, to introduce context into the experimental paradigm. Although we did not yet have the theoretical language for the distinction, we were aware that roles and contexts were defining characteristics in the treatment of women.

The study also illustrates early attempts within empirical psychology to compare women and other oppressed groups. These comparisons led me to stress the importance of status and power in later work. The theoretical justification for concerns about power continued to be borrowed from sociology (cf. Hacker, 1951). As I will discuss in Chapters 3 and 6, power remains a problematic area for psychologists.

This study was presented as part of a panel at the American Psychological Association meeting in Honolulu in 1972 which was organized by Florence Denmark and myself. It was subsequently published in 1974 in *The International Journal of Group Tensions* as part of a special issue on women edited by Florence Denmark. The beginning of her overview of the issue made her political views clear: 'There is a pervasive climate of discrimination against women in our society' (Denmark, 1974, p. 3).

The panel and journal issue included papers on the personality characteristics associated with prejudice against women (one by Philip Goldberg and another by Thomas Miller), as well as on the sex composition of groups in which women did or did not discriminate against other women (by Ruana Starer and Florence Denmark). It also included contributions from some early members of AWP, including an article coauthored by Miriam Kieffer entitled 'Women who discriminate against other women: the process of denial'. Her study compared the comments of those women who opposed a questionnaire about the status of women in psychology to those who favored it. In another article, Rona Fields summarized findings about women in psychology in the early 1970s and Helen Hacker contributed an update on her classic paper twenty years later.

Despite the importance of many of the contributions, none of these studies have ever received much attention and have been ignored by feminist historians as well. The journal's obscurity may explain this neglect and I wonder how many other early feminist papers and articles have also disappeared for similar reasons.

Early studies on sexism

As could be seen from the literature review in this article, we were certainly not the only researchers beginning to look at what is now known as sexism in interpersonal behavior. For example, Philip Goldberg (1968) conducted an early study in the area showing that women were more likely to evaluate essays purportedly written by women more poorly than identical essays purportedly written by men. Kay Deaux (1971) had (unbeknownst to us at the time) conducted a very similar study to ours on horn honking and men and women drivers.

The only major difference between the two studies was the measure used. Since Deaux's study was conducted in the mid-West, she was able to use the incidence of horn honking as a measure of discrimination against women drivers. In the New York City area everyone is honked at. Therefore, we used the latency of the first horn honk as our measure of discriminatory behavior.

All of these studies were atheoretical in nature. They were designed to show that discrimination against women existed in a variety of circumstances – in minor as well as major arenas. They formed a counterpoint to studies of discrimination at an institutional level such as that by Helen Astin (1969) on the woman doctorate in America. Funded by the Russell Sage Foundation and using 'real' rather than analogue data, she was able to document discrimination against women in academia. She found that even when women had academic qualifications equivalent to those of men and had contributed equally to their disciplines in terms of scholarly publications, they were promoted more slowly and received fewer rewards.

Linda Fidell (1970) provided a dramatic example of such discrimination within psychology in a study that probably could not be replicated in today's more suspicious times. She sent department 'chairmen' (used advisedly in terms of the time period) a collection of resumés of junior faculty with the justification that she was trying to find out what criteria determined whether or not they would be hired and the rank and salary that would be offered them. The chairs received different versions of the same resumés – with male or female names attached. She found that men were more likely to be hired than women with the same qualifications and offered higher ranks with less qualifications. Her study was considered important enough to be published in the *American Psychologist*, the journal of record of the American Psychological Association.

This study was an empirical verification of what those of us in the job market during this period already knew. It was, however, the kind of evidence that psychologists were more willing to listen to and accept. It provides another example of empiricism used as an argument for social action.

Early textbooks and their contents

The first two texts on the psychology of women were published at about the time this research was taking place, in 1971. They were extremely important because they gave a scholarly foundation to courses on the psychology of women that were being developed. I believe it is worth examining these books in some detail because they were quite different from texts that appeared somewhat later. The differences were partly due to the training and interests of their authors (both clinical/personality psychologists) and partly due to what materials were available. But they also reflected the state of the art of the psychology of women at its inception.

The chapters in Judith Bardwick's book emphasized psycho-analytic theory; sexuality and the female body (with particular emphasis on psychosomatic dysfunctions involving the reproductive system); and differences between male and female brains. It also included chapters on identification, self-esteem, achievement, and changes in motives and roles during different life stages. One chapter was entitled 'Dependence, passivity, and aggression'.

This rather brief book (218 pages) illustrated the intrapsychic bias of psychology. This bias is retained even within the psychology of women today and contributes to its conservatism relative to feminist scholarship in other disciplines (Kahn and Yoder, 1989). The book also assumed the existence of major sex differences in personality and behavior and stressed the negative correlates of female reproductive phenomena such as menstruation, pregnancy, and menopause.

Bardwick was, at best, ambivalent about feminism. Consider, for example, these quotes from her book:

> Feminism is not and actually never has been a widespread movement among American women, and the goals and values held by most women are gratified primarily in the traditional feminine activities. Given the extent of the preference in the culture for masculine activities, one must ask why this is so, why so few women are motivated to perform professionally. Most women may never have developed a strong achievement motivation as children and adolescents, they may fear failure because they fear competition and the implications of public failure, and they may fear that success will make them less feminine. (Bardwick, 1971, p. 145)

These comments clearly blame the victim – giving little consideration to external barriers, although Bardwick did acknowledge restrictions on women due to lack of institutionalized childcare arrangements.

In the paragraph following the one above, it is clear that the psychology of women of the time applied only to white, middle-class, heterosexual girls and women.

> We are rather glib in assuming that girls are second-class citizens; until a girl marries and has the responsibility of home and children she is more

likely to be pampered. Indeed, if she has been successful as a female, she is courted. In these affluent times I think there are very few privileges that middle-class girls are cheated of in comparison with their brothers. (Bardwick, 1971, p. 145)

Later in the book, Bardwick asserted:

I have tried to stay out of the feminist fight in these pages, partly because I think the data fall where they fall and partly because I personally don't think that work is the route to all good things for all women, just as I don't feel that a total immersion into Kinder, Kirche, and Küche, barefoot in the summer and pregnant in the winter, is ego-enhancing for all women. But I think the inclusion of a more passionate position might be enlightening. (Bardwick, 1971, p. 195)

She then went on to quote extensively from Sandra and Daryl Bem's (1970) article 'Training the woman to know her place'. This piece was one of the most important early works by feminist psychologists and Bardwick was correct in labeling it passionate (while, at the same time, distancing herself as an impartial scholar). However, she further commented that 'the Bems make Betty Friedan look like an apologist' (pp. 197–198) and followed the Bem and Bem segment with an extensive excerpt from a *Minneapolis Star* article in which the author interviewed eight well-educated young women to see if they were 'afflicted with the Friedan Syndrome'.

With this kind of bias it is not surprising that the Bardwick text drew heavily from clinical source materials. There were 183 journal articles referenced in the book. Twenty-two of them were from the psychiatric literature, nine from psychoanalytic journals, seven from other clinical/counseling journals, and thirty-seven were from medical journals. In contrast, only fifteen references were from social psychology journals with an additional four from sociology. Little of the emerging work on sexism was discussed. For example, there were no references to Weisstein's important paper, nor any mention of sex-role stereotypes. Neither the word 'discrimination' nor the word 'prejudice' appeared in her subject index.

Julia Sherman's book was published the same year, but received less attention because its academic publisher, C.C. Thomas, did not promote it as much as Harper & Row highlighted Bardwick's text. Its list of chapters also indicated a preoccupation with biological and psychodynamic issues. These included chapters on biological and psychological sex differences, several chapters on female development with an emphasis on Freudian theory, as well as chapters focusing on particular life stages such as adolescence, pregnancy, and motherhood.

This text had, however, a more feminist flavor than did Bardwick's. For example, although Sherman extensively discussed reproductive events and their relationship to women's psyches, she also acknowledged the important role of societal values and socialization on women's behavior. The book was also more inclusive. An examination of the subject index shows four page references to black women, four on homosexuality, and nineteen on social class (there were 246 pages in the book). Although 'feminism' was not a category in her subject index, Sherman's commitment to egalitarianism is evidenced by five page references to 'equality' and five to the 'double standard'. Although neither Weisstein nor Bem and Bem were included, research by early feminist scholars such as Pauline Bart and Cynthia Epstein (both sociologists), Helen Astin and Inge Broverman and her colleagues was cited.

An examination of the journals used as resources indicated even more reliance on medical sources than Bardwick (142 of the 473 journal articles cited). There were also 48 references to psychiatric journals, 37 to journals in clinical psychology, and 18 to psychoanalytic journals. However, there were also 40 references to articles from the social psychological literature and an additional 30 articles from sociological journals. The difference between 10 percent of such articles cited in Bardwick versus 15 percent in Sherman may not appear substantial. Given, however, the state of research in the field, finding 70 articles about the social context of women and sexism represented quite an achievement.

The entrance of social psychology

The psychology of gender prejudice
It is interesting that many of the early researchers and scholars in the psychology of women were clinical, personality, or counseling psychologists. Even some of the early research on sexism – which was social psychological in terms of both method and content – was conducted by clinical psychologists. I remember being quite surprised to discover that Philip Goldberg was a clinical psychologist as were most of the researchers involved in the early studies on sex-role stereotypes such as Inge Broverman and her colleagues.

A major exception to this trend was the publication in 1972 of a special issue of the *Journal of Social Issues* (SPSSI's official journal) entitled 'New perspectives on women'. This collection was edited by Martha Mednick and Sandra Tangri. It was an extraordinarily useful resource which provided powerful scholarly material for the new courses on the psychology of women. Many of the articles were reprinted in the 1970s and early 1980s, but may not be as familiar to the new generation of feminist psychologists today as they are to those of us whom they energized when we were that younger generation.

The issue focused on the theme of achievement. Achievement was an early major focus in the psychology of women as high-achieving feminists tried to figure out why women were not as successful as men. Both Mednick and Tangri were also affiliated with the University of Michigan, whose psychology department included a number of researchers doing work in achievement. The 'Michigan connection' was clear in the contributors to the journal which included Matina Horner's classic work on 'fear of success' (which had been her doctoral dissertation at the University of Michigan) and other articles by faculty members and graduate students associated with this university.

The issue also included an important article summarizing their work on sex-role stereotypes by Inge Broverman and her associates as well as a paper on personality by Rae Carlson – one of the earliest psychologists to critique psychology for its differential treatment of women and men (Carlson and Carlson, 1961). In keeping with the interdisciplinary nature of the journal, Mednick and Tangri also included an article on female German playwrights and an article enigmatically entitled 'The emancipation of man' by Olaf Palme, the prime minister of Sweden.

Despite its theme of achievement, the issue focused more on internal variables such as attitudes and motives than on external barriers to success. The psychology of women seems to have begun to turn inward at this point. Having demonstrated that prejudice and discrimination against women were pervasive, researchers began to ask questions that were generated by more disciplinary concerns such as: What are the characteristics of people who stereotype? Do sex-role stereotypes have any basis in fact? Do stereotypes influence behavior?

In other words, researchers in the psychology of women began to move away from exploring the cues for prejudice to the examination of the psychology of prejudice. This was a move from behavior to attitudes. It helped make the psychology of women more legitimate within the discipline, but at some cost to activist research. For example, behavior can be changed by rules and laws whereas attitudes require much more long-term solutions such as changes in familial socialization or educational strategies. Internal or intrapsychic explanations for social inequalities are very popular with society as a whole as well as within the discipline. Nevertheless, they continue to be seen as problematic by more activist feminists in the field. As Martha Mednick (1989, p. 1122) has pointed out: 'The focus on personal change diverts scholarship and action away from questions that could be directed toward an understanding of the social foundations of power alignments and inequity.'

I do not think that this change in focus was primarily due to a need for respectability, although the need to publish surely played a role in what questions we asked. Part of the reason why my own research changed focus at this time was because demonstrations of the existence of societal stereotypes had become 'too easy'. In a textbook that I wrote in 1979, I subtitled the chapter on stereotypes: 'Proving the obvious: from womb to tomb' (Unger, 1979a).

Part of the reason for the change, however, is the insidious influence of the intrapsychic bias on psychology as a discipline. Many of us have been socialized to believe that we are not doing psychological research unless we can 'explain' what is going on within people's heads. The need for this kind of explanation eventually led to the 'cognitive revolution' of the 1980s with its view of prejudice as a form of 'normal' information processing.

Of course, research on prejudice and discrimination continued. For example, Nancy Henley's pioneering work on the politics of interpersonal touch was published in 1973 and inspired a large number of studies on nonverbal behavior. Some more mainstream social psychologists, including Kay Deaux (Deaux and Lewis, 1984; Deaux, Kite and Lewis, 1985) have worked extensively on applying social cognitive theory to perceptions about women and men.

The content of sexual stereotypes

Research on stereotypes illustrates both the strengths and weaknesses of attempts to analyze attitudes about the sexes. The first research in this area (in the second wave of feminist scholarship) was conducted by a group centered around Clark University in Worcester, Massachusetts. This group has always presented difficulties in citation because, in an effort to maintain egalitarianism, they kept changing the order of authors in various publications. They began their studies on sex-role stereotypes early (Rosenkrantz et al., 1968; Broverman et al., 1970; Broverman et al., 1972) and found that sex-role stereotypes were more ubiquitous and extensive than any of us had supposed. They documented the existence of stereotypes in college students, in their parents, and in mental health practitioners. They found that sex-role stereotypes had changed little from the last time anyone had looked for them (cf. Kirkpatrick, 1936; McKee and Sheriffs, 1957).

Their work provoked a great deal of additional research in an area which had been rather quiescent until then. For example, I began to explore the question of the accuracy of sex-role stereotypes with a colleague at Montclair (Unger and Siiter, 1974). We used a technique (ranking) that did not require our subjects (college students) to dichotomize traits as 'male' or 'female' as the Broverman studies had. Instead, male and female college students were asked to rank a group of eighteen values in terms of either their importance to themselves, to others of their sex, or to members of the opposite sex. We found that the mean rank order of values attributed to self by females and males was very similar – their correlation was 0.91.

The order of same sex attributions also closely matched the rank order generated by each sex for themselves (0.94 for females and 0.81 for males). But the pattern for opposite sex ranking was startlingly different.

When individuals were asked to rank order the values perceived as important to the opposite sex, a different picture emerged. The correlation between the opposite-sex rankings of males and females was .34, which did not differ significantly from zero. In other words, there was little or no relationship between the rank order of values as perceived for members of the opposite sex by males and females. . . . Each sex tended to misperceive the values of the opposite sex, despite the fact that self-ranking of values by both sexes was much the same. (Unger and Siiter, 1974, p. 3)

Their misperceptions were related to gender stereotypes.

Males ranked the following values as higher for females than females ranked them for males: loving, honest, cheerful, forgiving, clean, and helpful. These are values stereotyped as female in our society. In the other four of the ten significantly different value rankings, females ranked the following values as higher for males than males ranked them for females: independent, ambitious, intellectual, and logical. These are values stereotyped as male in our society. Thus, the differences in opposite-sex rankings seem to portray the female as being less concerned about achievement and more concerned about nurturance and inter-personal behavior than the male. Again, if one assumes that the self-ranking of values are the truthful, veridical picture of a person's values, then it appears that perceptions about values of the opposite sex may be more a reflection of popular notions about "proper" male and female roles than they are a reflection of reality. (Unger and Siiter, 1974, pp. 3–4)

We noted that our study focused more on the similarities between the sexes than on the differences between them and concluded:

Since the self-values held by the two sexes on campus were almost identical, the provocative question is, on what basis do males and females make their judgments about the values of members of the opposite sex? It appears that very few "grains of truth" need to be present for stereotyping to take place. (Unger and Siiter, 1974, p. 4)

As our title indicated, we found that 'a grain of truth' had very little weight in determining what men and women believed about each other's values.

Although we presented this study at a professional conference and I subsequently reprinted it in a monograph on sex-role stereotypes (Unger, 1975), the study was never published in a professional journal. This was partly due to the fact that there were still no feminist journals and partly the result of an ethical decision about which I am still ambivalent. The mainstream journal to which we submitted the paper sent it to an expert (and feminist reviewer) who knew we had done the study and declined to review it. This action left the paper to be reviewed by less sympathetic and knowledgeable psychologists and the editor at the time decided not to contest their split decision.

I did not resubmit the paper to other mainstream journals (as I would today) for a variety of reasons. There were few journals for which the material would have been seen as relevant and we could expect reactions similar to those we had received from the first. As I mentioned in Chapter 1, I was also not in a 'publish or perish' situation at Montclair so I did not feel pressured to get the paper published at any cost. Finally, the paper had been presented and the data were in print. I had an answer to my question about whether sex-role stereotypes were accurate which I could offer to others. Publication was simply not that meaningful to me under these conditions.

Ron Siiter and I did, however, continue to do research in this area for some time (Siiter and Unger, 1975). Before the area became popular, we explored ethnic differences in sex-role stereotypes. We found differences between ethnic groups in terms of the extent to which each group stereotyped and also misperceptions between the sexes within each ethnic group studied – German-American, Italian-American, Jewish-American, and African-American. 'For all four ethnic groups studied, the extent of perceived dissimilarity between the sexes was much greater than the actual differences between them' (Siiter and Unger, 1975, p. 26 of ms). We concluded: 'The men and women of various ethnic groups are surprisingly alike. They are most alike in terms of beliefs in their own differences' (p. 27 of ms).

Current studies of stereotypes have shown depressingly little change over time (Ruble, 1983). The area has been largely abandoned once again by feminists, partly because of methodological problems and partly because researchers have been unable to show what personality characteristics or negative attitudes toward other groups correlate with gender stereotypes. Recent research on stereotypes has primarily been conducted by cognitive psychologists who view the phenomenon as an aspect of normal information processing. These researchers have begun to demonstrate that individuals who hold negative attitudes about women create different subtypes of women (for example, feminist rather than housewife) and react more negatively to the term than do more egalitarian men (cf. Haddock and Zanna, 1994). However, these researchers are more individualistic and apolitical in their focus and would not be likely to make statements such as:

> Sexism approaches being a culturally fixed and almost universal attitude . . . it would seem that final explanations of the phenomenon are not profitably to be looked for at the level of individual psychology. Indeed, neither explanation nor solution is likely located there, although the price of sexism is paid for person by person. (Goldberg, 1974, p. 62)

The cues for stereotyping

Philip Goldberg continued to devise creative techniques for looking at sexism. He was the first investigator to demonstrate prejudice against feminists (Goldberg, Gottesdiener and Abramson, 1975). He asked students to sort photographs which had previously been evaluated for attractiveness into 'feminist' and 'nonfeminist' categories. Less attractive women were more likely to be perceived as feminists even though, in actuality, feminists did not differ from nonfeminists in their physical appearance. This study received much attention and many replications including one by me and my students (Unger, Hilderbrand and Madar, 1982).

Because of his premature death, Goldberg did not receive the plaudits from feminists that he deserved for his pioneering work. He was also a rather shy man who did not travel much. I met him only once when I gave a colloquium at his institution, Connecticut College. He was, however, a superlative and supportive colleague. For example, he gave me the photos from his original study so that we could perform a controlled replication of his study.

Our first studies led to an interest in physical appearance that continues today. As a feminist, I have sometimes been challenged to defend this research area. I did so in a book chapter summarizing my work entitled 'Personal appearance and social control' (Unger, 1985b).

> Since feminists have been well aware of the pernicious effect that the stress on personal appearance has had on women, it might appear strange to assert that physical attractiveness has become an important variable in the study of women. There are several reasons for feminist interest in this variable. First, it is clear that physical attractiveness is in the "eye of the

beholder." No objective standards for evaluation appear to exist. Moreover, perceptions of physical attractiveness are socially labile – standards vary widely among cultures and within the same culture over time. Thus, physical attractiveness represents a pure example of a stimulus effect, an effect which operates by way of differential perceptions, cognitions, and attributions produced by variations in that stimulus. To the extent that such perceptions are found to be similar between individuals, we may think of such effects as social variables and they are frequently studied under the term "stereotype."

Physical attractiveness may serve as a model for a more important social variable – the sex of the stimulus person. Perceptions are based on the external properties of the person and differentiation between persons is maintained by relatively unconscious social norms about how individuals with such characteristics do and should behave. There is a great deal of social consensus involving these expectations. (Unger, 1985b, p. 142)

This chapter was much more overtly feminist than my previous work. It was not written for a mainstream psychological journal, but for a collection of presentations from the first International Interdisciplinary Congress on Women which was held in Israel in December 1981. It illustrates another aspect of empiricism used as argument against the status quo. In it, I attempted to use my own and other's data to elucidate some of the more subtle forms of sexism as a means of social control:

Since attractiveness attributions operate in both directions – what is beautiful is good, but what is good is also beautiful – presumptions involving attractiveness may also serve as a social control mechanism to keep women out of gender inappropriate occupations and political activities. Attractiveness stereotyping is a particularly subtle form of social control; although it appears to be universal, it is rarely explicitly recognized or discussed. (Unger, 1985b, p. 148)

These words were, of course, written before Naomi Wolf's bestselling book *The Beauty Myth* put discussions of the meaning of women's appearance into the popular media. They were also written before evolutionary psychologists seized upon women's attractiveness as a mechanism for sexual selection (cf. Buss, 1989).

Nevertheless, I would stand by the conclusions of this paper which stress attractiveness bias as a 'minor form' of violence against women:

Attractiveness stereotyping is a subtle form of violence against women – keeping them in their place without giving them anything to react against. It is an especially pernicious form of social control because the definition of attractiveness comes from the outside – it begins with the eye of the beholder. The victim can do little to alter her position on the subjective scale of beauty, has fewer alternative sources of societal esteem than do men, and may even be blamed for her vanity and self-concern. When the attractiveness evaluations of others are incorporated, the victim's behaviors serve to validate perceptions about her and maintain the stereotype. It is these subtle nonconscious mechanisms that may prove the most resistant to change. (Unger, 1985b, p. 148)

More recently we have found that attractiveness stereotypes have the potential to affect both sexes negatively because their impact occurs at the earliest instant of perception (Locher et al., 1993). Our conclusions were expressed in 'correct' psychological jargon, but our feminist convictions were made clear in our last paragraph:

Results of the present research suggest that perceptions of differential attractiveness occurs effortlessly or automatically with the initial encoding of sensory data, and that physical attractiveness implicates gender stereotype memory frames at the perceptual end of the social information processing spectrum. The finding that neither occupational status of the target nor observer's sex influenced subjects' perception of attractiveness in Experiment 1 indicates that automatic processing of attractiveness cues may be relatively resistant to top-down influences. This conclusion is also supported by the fact that no important differences in evaluative judgments based upon physical attractiveness was observed between subjects given a single glance at targets and those whose search strategies were influenced by gender stereotypes.

These findings support Deaux and Lewis' (1984) contention that once "information about physical appearance is provided people seem to rely heavily on it to make inferences about other aspects of the person" (p. 1003). If physical attractiveness is detected automatically as is indicated by the present findings, and if it is the most important determinant in judgments about gender as suggested by Deaux and Lewis (1984) and Spence and Sawin (1985), then it is essential that the source of the gender attractiveness linkage resulting in stereotypic evaluative judgments be sought at the early stages of information processing.

It was once thought that it was possible to distinguish between sex as a stimulus variable and gender as a social categorization system (Unger, 1979c). The present findings suggest that sex and gender are inextricably confounded at a very basic level of perception. The descriptive and prescriptive functions of stereotypes seem to be present once the stimulus information necessary to evoke a stereotype is apprehended. It may be impossible to separate perception and evaluation. This finding has important implications for the idea that the sexes can be "separate but equal." (Locher et al., 1993, pp. 741–742)

As I write this, the paper has been out for a few years. We have received a large number of reprint requests, especially from people outside the USA. I believe this response indicates that an experimental 'argument' may reach people who would not look at an overtly feminist one.

Some conclusions

As I have indicated in this chapter, feminist empiricist work within psychology puts researchers into a double bind. In order to do this kind of research we must, in some sense, 'sell out' to methodologies that we criticize in other contexts (see Chapter 4). What is dangerous about such activity is the risk that we will incorporate the belief that these methodologies are the only way to understand 'reality' or even come to believe there is a single reality. Such beliefs produce researchers who write and talk only to others within the discipline. This behavior may be good for their careers, but it is certainly not good for feminist scholarship.

On the other hand, experimental research, when it is carefully constructed and clearly presented, can provide evidential support for law suits and changes in institutional policies. As I found out during my year in Israel (certainly not a feminist country), 'data' in the form of numbers may persuade people who are unwilling to listen to feminist 'polemics'. Susan Fiske and her colleagues (Fiske et al., 1991) have demonstrated that experimental research on stereotypes can even influence the US Supreme Court. With their help, the American Psychological Association filed an *amicus curiae* brief which was cited by the Court in its ruling supporting a case involving employment discrimination.

Ironically, feminist empiricists within psychology may have been more successful in persuading mainstream psychologists to take sex and gender seriously than they have been in reducing the suspect nature of quantitative methodology for many women's studies scholars. Part of the problem is that neither the replicability nor the usefulness of research have ever been particularly compelling questions for the humanities at any time and have been made more problematic by postmodern critiques which argue that there is no such thing as objectivity or 'truth'. This dilemma may be resolved by regarding all truth claims as forms of argument. Thus, any methodology may be used as a tool by feminists as well as by others. Although Audre Lorde (1984) has suggested that 'the master's tools cannot dismantle the master's house', it is pretty hard to tear down that house with one's bare hands (Unger, 1996).

Feminist empiricist work within psychology appears to be emerging from a period of quiescence as postmodern arguments have begun to lose some of their force. A number of researchers, including myself, now claim the label (cf. Shields and Crowley, 1996). A task force on experimental psychology has recently emerged in the Association for Women in Psychology – an organization whose annual meetings have sometimes stressed spiritual and/or body work over databased presentations. It is probably too soon to predict what directions such research will take, but it will surely be applied to women's issues such as sexual violence. Feminist empiricists will have certainly accomplished our goal if future readers of this chapter will be unclear on what the fuss was all about.

3

Power, status, deviance, stigma: the problem is always power

Some historical background

The first wave of feminism in the USA ended when women obtained the right to vote after World War I. At that time, women believed that their votes would eventually destroy power differentials between the sexes. The second wave of feminists recognized that little had changed in nearly fifty years. This group of activists was more aware of the social and economic bases of inequality than the previous generation had been.

Despite the fact that feminism is almost synonymous with changes in power dynamics, many of the psychologists who became interested in gender issues in the early 1970s managed to ignore the central role of power. This neglect is less surprising when one realizes that power remains a problematic area for psychology in general. The study of power and related concepts such as status, influence, and control has waxed and waned throughout the twentieth century (Griscom, 1992).

Important social psychologists such as Dorwin Cartwright (1959) and Carolyn Sherif (1982) had called for renewed attention to power in their presidential addresses to the Society for the Psychological Study of Social Issues (SPSSI) and Division 35 respectively. Nevertheless, power continued to be ignored, especially by US psychologists. There is a variety of explanations for this neglect of power – ranging from methodological to theoretical to metaphysical in nature. I considered some of them in an article I wrote for the fiftieth anniversary issue of the *Journal of Social Issues*, SPSSI's official journal (Unger, 1986a).

The article was part of a celebration of the surprising longevity of a socially activist organization within psychology. I happened to be the only person interested in history who was serving on SPSSI's executive committee at the time the issue was being planned. I volunteered to help edit the issue, but realized that I could not do so alone. I therefore brought in Benjamin Harris as a coeditor. Harris is/was a radical revisionist historian of psychology and to balance his position, the SPSSI leadership decided to add Ross Stagner as a third editor of the issue. Stagner had been one of the founding members of SPSSI fifty years before.

The issue became a compromise between ceremonial and revisionist history. Historians wrote the articles and SPSSI leaders who had been involved in the actual events commented upon them. Since I had been interested in how psychology as a discipline dealt with issues of power, I decided to write a paper on this theme rather than on the rather dismal history of women within organizational psychology (cf. Capshew and Lazlo, 1986).

I attempted to make several arguments simultaneously. Like others who wrote articles for the issue, I wanted to remind readers of some of the more radical aspects of SPSSI's history. I was especially anxious to remind them that the distinction between 'pure' and 'applied' research was not as important in the past as it seems to be today. I wanted to show the uses to which history could be put to help explain the patterns of current research in social issues. Finally, I wanted to examine one strand of that research – on power – to show how some areas are neglected and some questions are not asked.

Since this article was primarily about SPSSI rather than Division 35, it is not reprinted in its entirety here. What is relevant for this chapter are the results of my examination of *Psychological Abstracts* for articles using various terms related to power at five years intervals between 1967 and 1982:

> These results show a preference for research on perceptions of power rather than on behaviors using power. Very few of the abstracts sampled involved studies of people who act in real-world political or social arenas. In fact, the only such study found within the sample was one of Latin American student leaders, published in Spanish by a female investigator.
>
> Many of the studies appeared to be focusing on powerlessness rather than power. Much of the work had been conducted on relatively powerless populations such as children and college sophomores, the chronically mentally and physically ill, and the institutionalized aged. Cartwright's (1959) assertions about the use of safe populations for the examination of power are also supported by a survey of those few papers abstracted under the term **dominance** (the term was dropped somewhere between 1967 and 1972). Most of the studies indexed under that term involved social relationships within rat colonies; and one paper dealt with the evolution of hornlike organs. (Unger, 1986a, pp. 218–219)

I also found that researchers from nondominant groups within psychology's hierarchy (Europeans and women) were more likely to study status and power whereas male psychologists in the USA seemed more interested in interpersonal influence and locus of control. Relatively marginalized individuals may recognize more easily than members of dominant groups that the equation of influence with power is only possible when one strips situations of their historical and social context:

> Once social scientists begin to look at power relationships within the context of the normative social structure rather than within the laboratory, a number of paradoxes in our current definitions of power begin to emerge. What kind of power, if any, is exerted in behaviors described by the term "helpless power"? What is the relationship between the perceived and actual control of circumstances? How do we resolve the contradictions between positions of prestige and those of real power? Such paradoxes are particularly likely to emerge when attention is focused on the actions of women (or of other nondominant groups). (Unger, 1986a, p. 220)

Psychologists' neglect of power also impedes their ability to deal with social problems:

> It is important for psychologists to recognize that individuals do not solve social problems by themselves. They need social support, as well as access to and the ability to use resources. The availability of support and resources depends upon factors not always under the individual's control. Power, as well as social knowledge, is integral to the solution of important social problems. Consideration of the differential distribution of power among different segments of the population at different times may help to explain why social problems are rarely solved. They are either temporarily resolved or made to disappear by the selective use of history. (Unger, 1986a, p. 225)

I concluded this article with a discussion of the value of an historical and sociology of knowledge perspective for psychology.

This paper was not, however, one of my more successful attempts at psychological critique. If citation is any indication of its impact, it has rarely been cited. There are several explanations for its invisibility. It may be the historical nature of the particular issue in which it appeared. As part of their lack of concern with contextual issues, psychologists in the USA seem to be particularly reluctant to pay attention to history except that of a ceremonial nature. Or it may have been the 'wrong' paper for the 'wrong audience'. Until recently, members of SPSSI have not been any more interested in issues involving 'real power' than members of any other academic interest group.

Power and nonverbal behaviors

Most of the women who have looked at power recently would label themselves as feminists. Power was introduced into feminist psychological vocabulary early through the work of Nancy Henley. Henley came to the study of the nonverbal communication of power by way of her interest in psycholinguistics. She recognized that the differential use of nonverbal gestures was akin to the unequal use of 'polite' and 'familiar' forms of grammatical address in many languages and to the use of titles versus first names in our own and other societies. Her first study of sex, race, and class differences in 'touch privilege' (Henley, 1973) had been her PhD dissertation at Johns Hopkins University. As I mentioned in Chapter 1, her earlier presentations of this work had excited many of us and we even 'tried it out'. Her subsequent book *Body Politics: Power, Sex, and Nonverbal Communication* (Henley, 1977) was a witty, readable, and powerful survey of how we tend to confuse power differences with sex differences.

Henley's work has been more explicitly feminist than that of most other psychologists – even those who have been affiliated with the psychology of women from its very beginning. It is impossible to determine whether her acute awareness of how microprocesses reflect and maintain socio-structural sexism is a cause or an effect of her cross-disciplinary work with feminist political scientists such as Jo Freeman (Henley and Freeman, 1975) and sociologists like Barrie Thorne (Thorne and Henley, 1975). Her analysis of the power of nonconscious behaviors is both eloquent and succinct:

> Social interaction is the battlefield on which the daily war between the sexes is fought. It is here that women are constantly reminded of what their "place" is and here that they are put back in their place, should they venture out. Thus, social interaction serves as the locus of the most common means of social control employed against women. By being continually reminded of their inferior status in their interactions with others, and continually compelled to acknowledge that status in their own patterns of behavior, women may internalize society's definition of them as inferior so thoroughly that they are often unaware of what their status is. Inferiority becomes habitual, and the inferior place assumes the familiarity – and even desirability – of home. (Henley and Freeman, 1975, p. 391)

Henley's work quickly stimulated a number of articles and books on nonverbal sex differences including several of my own (cf. Frieze and Ramsay, 1976; Unger, 1976, 1978a; Weitz, 1976; LaFrance and Mayo, 1978). Later, she collaborated on the topic with Clara Mayo (Mayo and Henley, 1981). This book extended the work on gender and nonverbal communication to areas such as leadership cues, visual behavior and dominance, and the correlates of conversational assertiveness. Unfortunately, the book did not receive the broad attention it deserved because its publisher, Springer-Verlag, appears to be committed to small press runs and little publicity about its offerings.

In the introduction, Mayo and Henley pointed out some of the reasons why the study of nonverbal behaviors is so important to psychologists interested in women and gender. Their first and most important point is that nonverbal behaviors are outside one's awareness. An individual who seeks to change these behaviors must make the unconscious conscious. Of course, this makes nonverbal behaviors very difficult to change.

Mayo and Henley stressed the relationship between gender-linked nonverbal behaviors and the relative powerlessness of women and girls. Findings that women are better at identifying nonverbal cues than men may also be explained by power differentials. Finally, Mayo and Henley pointed out that the use of 'masculine' nonverbal behaviors by women can lead to social sanctions.

Curiously, this book had little to say about race and class differences in nonverbal behaviors, despite the fact that Henley's earlier work clearly made the connection between race, class, and gender (she has, however, recently published work on language and ethnicity; cf. Henley, 1995). The articles in this book were also more theoretically and methodologically 'psychological' than Henley's own research. Her interdisciplinary work analyzed the systematic nature of power and dominance much more overtly than work within psychology usually does. As Joan Griscom commented: 'Her studies of interpersonal nonverbal communication indicate that large-scale social control is both exerted in small interactions and internalized within individuals. Her work shows that the institutional and the interpersonal, the external and the internal, are inseparable' (Griscom, 1992, p. 400).

Sex differences as power differences

Henley and her collaborators stressed the societal dynamics that produce group and individual differences in power. US psychologists, including myself, were not yet ready to cope with society except through the person as an intermediary. Instead, we focused on questions about how power differences were perceived and communicated.

The most important early work in this area was by Paula Johnson (1974, 1976). It, too, began as a doctoral dissertation. She used a theoretical framework based upon French and Raven's (1959) typology of sources of social power; for example, expert, legitimate, referential, and informational. She added one source – helpless power – that had not been included in the original typology. She found that when both male and female college students did not know the sex of the power user, they inferred that users of expert and legitimate power were male and that users of helpless power were female.

Johnson also found a 'grain of truth' in these beliefs. When given the opportunity to choose power strategies, males never chose helpless power, whereas females were much less likely to choose expert or legitimate statements than males. These choices are more a matter of power than sex. For example, current research shows that, cross-culturally, the choice of indirect power strategies is one of last resort and is a reflection of a person's status rather than his or her sex (Steil and Hillman, 1993).

I considered Johnson's findings about the nature of social sanctions more interesting than those about sex-related differences. Although users of 'male' power were seen as more powerful and competent than users of 'female' power, women who used forms of 'male' power were penalized. They were seen as colder and more aggressive than comparable males, but were not seen as more competent than men. Other researchers during this period found similar results. For example, Hagen and Kahn (1975) found that both women and men were more likely to exclude a competent woman from their group than a competent man, whereas they were more likely to include an incompetent woman than an incompetent man. The men appeared to like competent women only when they did not have to interact with them. Similarly, only feminist women were found to prefer a 'masculine' competent woman to a 'feminine' one (Spence, Helmreich and Stapp, 1975).[1]

Despite these early studies, the role of peer sanctions in producing sex-related differences in behaviors related to power has remained relatively unexplored. There is even less work on how such patterns develop in children. I did an early literature review in this area which indicated that, similar to the situation for adults, boys possess more ascribed status than girls and are, behaviorally, the more powerful sex (Unger, 1976). In this article I reviewed the empirical literature on children's perceptions of power in their friends and their siblings in terms of both psychometric and behavioral measures; on the classroom as a social system; and on what I termed the 'unexamined effect of physical power on social power'. I concluded:

> Although physical size is at least as obvious an ascriptive characteristic as the gender ascription to which it is highly correlated, almost no note of this variable has been made in the extensive literature on sex differences. Is it because it is socially unacceptable to admit that the use of force is more a "norm" in interpersonal behavior than psychologists would like to believe? Is physical size so "obvious" a variable that it has no psychological "value"? Or, do we prefer the illusion of sex differences to the possible reality of power differences? (Unger, 1976, p. 7)

However, I also warned about a simple equation of sex and power using some of Elizabeth Janeway's (1974) observations in this area which I believe warrant repeating yet again.

> Janeway (1974) points out: "As always, the world belongs to the power-ful, and though, almost universally, the powerful are male, we can't reverse that statement. Males are not almost universally powerful" (p. 187). She suggests a new phrase: "The weak are the second sex." It is this equation of weakness and femininity, Janeway believes which underlies a great deal of masculine reaction to a redefinition of women's role. A step up for women may be seen by men in reverse, as a step down to an inferior level, women's level. The division of the world by sex instead of power creates an alliance of both weak and powerful males by means of anatomy. The existence of such an alliance could explain why social scientists are so reluctant to admit to a confusion of gender and status. (Unger, 1976, p. 7)

Some of these comments foreshadowed the current debate about ethnicity and identity politics (see Chapter 5). I argued then (as now) that it is important for feminist psychologists to study vari-ables other than sex (Unger, 1992, 1995a). 'Psychologists need to study characteristics other than gender – such as race and age – which also convey information about ascriptive status to see if they produce similar role inequities' (Unger, 1976, p. 7).

The major difference between adults and children in terms of gender-differentiated aspects of power was that boys appeared to be more overt in their dominance behaviors than men. But the litera-ture suggested a continuity of asymmetrical power relationships between the sexes from childhood through the college years. At the time, I believed that men did not have to use direct aggression to maintain their power since women had internalized their secondary status by the time they reached late adolescence. Like most psycho-logists of the time, I was not aware of the extent of the violence directed against women which effectively silenced them.

I was, however, aware of the aggression directed against little girls by their male peers because I had two young daughters at the time. At ages six and eight, they were just the 'right' age to be the target of much verbal teasing and occasional physical 'horseplay'. (I have never regarded the loss of a knitted hat on a cold winter day as innocuous.) Since my daughters were, like myself, small for their age and not willing to behave submissively, they were probably teased more than their more acquiescent friends. As their mother, I could do little. As an academic, I could research their plight to find out how common it was. To my surprise, I now know that even some of the pejorative 'regional' terms used exclusively to label girls (such as having 'cooties')[2] in New Jersey could also be collected in

Michigan schools (Thorne, 1986). Sociologists have been better than psychologists at documenting the sexism in children's collective culture.

What is seen and what is neglected

With hindsight, it is interesting to look for other areas that have been neglected by feminist psychologists. I have already mentioned our neglect of domestic violence, but other areas were also overlooked. In 1975, for example, the first and only fully funded national conference on the psychology of women (sponsored by the National Science Foundation and the National Institute of Mental Health) was held. Many of the papers presented at the conference were eventually published in a volume edited by Julia Sherman and Florence Denmark (1978) entitled *The Psychology of Women: Future Directions of Research*. The areas covered in this anthology included a keynote address on androgyny (Sandra Bem); two chapters on female development (Jeanne Block and Nancy Russo); a chapter on the social psychology of female sexuality by Pepper Schwartz (a sociologist); the psychological aspects of menstruation, childbirth, and menopause (Mary Parlee); and several chapters on various aspects of work and achievement by Helen Astin, Judy Laws, and Janice Gump – an African-American graduate student at the University of Michigan at the time of this conference. Irene Frieze and her students contributed a chapter on attributions about success and failure; Florence Denmark and Sandra Tangri collaborated on a chapter on affiliation, achievement and power; and Ravenna Helson offered an innovative chapter on creativity in women. My chapter was entitled 'The politics of gender'.

Although I touched on it in my paper, none of the presentations focused on violence against women. There was no paper on motherhood (except as one of a number of reproductive events) and none on mental health issues. The themes stressed in the conference represented the state of the art in the psychology of women at that time. It was mainly an academic discipline where researchers concentrated on topics that were important to themselves. Thus, there were five presentations on work and achievement in contrast to part of one presentation on affiliation and none on motherhood.

My chapter was closely related to the developmental paper that I described earlier in this chapter (in fact, although the dates of publication are reversed, the 'adult' paper was written first). Its abstract describes the ambitious amount of material I attempted to cover:

This chapter makes the case for the position that much of the behavioral differences between males and females is due to status and power differences rather than sex differences. It is suggested that male gender, in itself, carries with it stimulus value connoting high status and power which is relatively independent of characteristics considered to be appropriately masculine or feminine. Treatment of the gender with low ascribed status (i.e., females) parallels the treatment of other low status individuals under all conditions examined. Three aspects of the psychological and sociological literature are reviewed in detail with reference to the hypothesis that sex differences can more parsimoniously be viewed as power differences: nonverbal measures of dominance and submissiveness; husband-wife power relationships; and gender differences in small group behavior. Review of the literature in these areas tends to support the hypothesis.

Other points raised by this review suggest that performance differences do not easily eliminate sex-related differences in ascribed status due to differential perceptions of competent performance on the basis of gender. Assertion of competence and power by a female is likely to define her as a deviant and make her liable to social sanctions. Gender/status identity is institutionalized by our society. It is also suggested that the covert role of physical force and differential size and strength between the sexes may have been underestimated as a source of behavioral differences between them. Lastly, the scientific and social function of reevaluating data in an area such as power, status, and gender is briefly considered. (Unger, 1978a, p. 463)

This paper clearly borrowed from the work of Nancy Henley and her associates. Its review of nonverbal sex-related differences was similar to others done at about the same time (cf. Frieze and Ramsey, 1976). I believe the more original contribution (and a theme to which I return every few years) involves the question of why disconfirming behavior does not change gender stereotypic perceptions. I also focused on institutionalized sexism – a subject which continues to be neglected by psychologists.

I borrowed heavily from sociological theory and research for arguments connecting ascribed status, social structures, and interpersonal sexism. I was very excited about these connections which were, at that time, new to most psychologists. However, one of the other participants, who was more familiar with sociological theory, was amused by my naivety (and, by extension, the naivety of most of feminist psychology).

There are certainly holes in feminist research agendas today, just as there were in 1975. The researcher's personal context appears to play an important role in determining what questions are central to her. For example, I became interested in the use of peer sanctions on children when my own children were the recipients of such constraints. Feminist psychologists are also less interested in work issues today as it becomes clear that economic equality (even if it can be made to exist) does not guarantee social equality between the sexes.

Today, aging has become a more popular topic for research as the researchers themselves have grown older. Nancy Datan (1986) made this point very clearly in writing about how her own life stage influenced the kinds of questions she asked about the impact of menopause on women. She made it even more dramatically in her last paper where she discussed the sexist assumptions involving breast prostheses and breast cancer (Datan, 1989). This autobiographical aspect of our research is often ignored because of the dictates of 'scientific' writing. Feminists in other disciplines are more liberated (cf. Reinharz, 1992).

An apparent digression: organizational power and networks

The establishment of Division 35 as a part of APA helped to give legitimacy to scholarship on the psychology of women. A fully funded invitational conference on future developments in the area, held in Madison, Wisconsin in April 1975, could not have occurred without such legitimization. This conference illustrates how power works at an organizational level. It was organized by Florence Denmark and Julia Sherman with the important support of Nancy Russo who was working in the central office of the American Psychological Association at the time.

This was the first such conference to which I had been invited and I was very excited about it. It brought together young aspiring feminist psychologists and some of the most senior women in the field. A list of the participants reads like a 'Who's Who' in the psychology of women today. Besides the people mentioned earlier, senior commentators included Jessie Bernard, Mavis Hetherington, Martha Mednick, Julia Sherman, and Janet Spence. A few junior scholars who later contributed much to the discipline also served as commentators. They included Kitch Childs, Wendy McKenna, and Karen Paige. A few men who had done good work in the field such as Joseph Pleck and Robert Brannon were also invited. Two of the participants were African-American and several were lesbian, although I am not sure whether they were 'out' at the time.

Since I was not privy to the decisions about what topics should be covered, nor about who was to be invited to present a paper at the conference, I feel free to look at the pattern of participation to illustrate the power of professional networking. (There may be some inaccuracy in this analysis because I do not know who was invited but was unable to attend, nor how this differential participation may have influenced the topics chosen.) The 'Michigan connection' I discussed previously was certainly present (Robert Brannon, Janice Gump, Karen Paige, and Sandra Tangri had all received PhDs from that university). But there was also a New York City cluster, as well as a California one. Organizational networks were also important. Helen Astin, Florence Denmark, and Martha Mednick were the second, third, and fourth presidents of Division 35 and Judy Laws, Sandra Tangri, Bob Brannon, and I had all been early contributors to AWP.

Networking was particularly valuable for those of us who were junior at the time. It gave us an opportunity to meet senior women and learn from them. But not all our efforts to acquire professional socialization were successful. One of the junior participants kept trying to find out from the more senior women how they dealt with the sexism in psychology. Many of the senior women were, however, still denying that such sexism existed or if they admitted that it did, saw it as an individual matter that could be overcome by hard work. One of them told me that if we insisted on doing work in an 'illegitimate' area, we should expect to pay a price in our careers. She was not hostile about the issue, just matter of fact. We were all in the same place for several days, but we were not always speaking the same language.

This conference illustrates some of the benefits and costs of professional networks. The more junior participants did not have the clout to obtain funding from prestigious governmental agencies. We were given an opportunity to interact with senior women and with each other. But it is not clear why some of us were perceived to merit inclusion and others were not, although most of the people invited were already regular participants at APA conventions. It is easy to defend the selection criteria as the participants included four future presidents of Division 35 and seven future recipients of its Carolyn Wood Sherif award. However, such accolades, like much else in psychology and in life, are the result of complex interactions. It is difficult to determine how much we contributed because we were at this conference. Others who were equally worthy and who also made significant contributions later were not able to take advantage of this opportunity.

Fellow status, women, and APA

Although it appears that Division 35 was somewhat nepotistic in its early decision-making, the organization was and remains more inclusive than most large, formal structures of its nature. Rewards of any kind are, by definition, exclusionary. There has always been much argument within Division 35 about such rewards. For example, Virginia O'Leary (the second membership chair of the division) and I once wrote a position paper attempting to change the honorific within APA from 'fellow' to 'distinguished member' in order to make it less sexist. Such a change (and 'member' also has its male connotations) would not, of course, eliminate the selective aspect of the citation. For this reason, some women who merit this status have consistently refused to be considered for it. The prevailing view within Division 35 has been to keep 'fellow status' – conferred upon individuals by APA for 'unusual or outstanding contribution or performance in the field of psychology'. The consensus has been that it may have some value for career advancement and that we should not deny feminist scholars any opportunity for recognition.

At one point during its more 'radical' days, SPSSI did not nominate APA fellows, but now does so for reasons similar to those of Division 35. However, fellow status is not easy to attain for someone, no matter how good their scholarship, who is not connected to a professional network. Candidates must be nominated by a division within APA and have letters of recommendation from at least three people who are already fellows. When I was nominated in 1978, I knew well only one current fellow, Florence Denmark. However, Carolyn Sherif, who was then fellow chair for Division 35, offered to write a letter for me and to find a third person to do so (Martha Mednick). I was flattered by the composition of the group (three women I greatly admired) and would have been satisfied even if the application had not been positively acted upon by APA.

Division 35 has attempted to retain the cooperative spirit shown in the story I have just recounted. Fellow chairs continue to help nominees find people to recommend them (this is particularly difficult for candidates from small, non-elite, or isolated institutions where no one else may be an APA fellow). It is easier now that there are many more women who are fellows of APA than there were twenty years ago.

Nevertheless, sexism within the profession continues. The percentage of women who are fellows of APA (20.2 percent) remains much lower than the percentage of women who are members of the organization (41.8 percent). Data collected by the Women's Program Office of APA (1993) indicate that, during the last ten years, if a woman is nominated to fellow status by a division she has an equal chance of being elected as her male counterpart. However, fewer women in APA are members of divisions and divisions are less likely to identify and nominate qualified women. Every year since 1979, the proportion of women nominated has been lower than the proportion of APA's women members.

Power and organizational change

Political change may be viewed in terms of both organizational influence and intellectual impact on psychology as a whole. Women have held more positions of leadership within APA since 1972, but it is also clear that their position is not all that secure. Data on the female presidents of APA are most illuminating in this regard. Although there were two early women presidents (Mary Calkins in 1905 and Margaret Washburn in 1921) the next woman to be elected was Ann Anastasi who became president in 1972 (Hogan and Sexton, 1991). Although neither Anastasi nor Leona Tyler (president in 1973) could be characterized as feminists, they were elected during a period when the second wave of feminism was cresting. The later three women presidents (Florence Denmark in 1980; Janet Spence in 1984; and Bonnie Strickland in 1987) had a more feminist identity. However, although a number of women have run for this office since 1987, only one, Dorothy Cantor, has been elected.

Women's involvement in other leadership positions within APA (such as major committees and journal editorships) has also not been commensurate with their numbers within the organization (Women's Program Office, 1993). Increased involvement has been a consistent goal of the Committee for Women in Psychology, but Division 35 seems to be less interested in this issue in recent years and AWP has never concerned itself with political power within APA.

When I was active in APA politics (during my term as Division 35's representative to APA Council in 1976–9), the women's caucus[3] had more 'clout' than it does now. At that time we were part of a social issues coalition that acted as a counterweight between the competing factions of experimentalists/academicians and clinicians/practitioners. Since these blocs have split and each faction now has its own organization, social issues concerns have declined in importance for both. I do not feel particularly comfortable at either the annual conference of the American Psychological Society (where I find the papers too positivist and socially irrelevant) or APA (where I find too many papers about the problems of private practice).

Increasingly, all groups within psychology seem to be creating their own spaces with narrowly defined boundaries. In addition to AWP's annual conference (which began before this trend), SPSSI has begun to sponsor research conferences, and many other smaller 'private' conferences are also available. Communication about such activities has been facilitated by the growing use of electronic mail and women's discussion groups on the Internet. The crowded national conferences are alienating, but I miss the seredipitous encounters they also made possible. For example, I first met a prominent male contributor to the psychology of women when I 'caught' him perusing the author index of my textbook at an APA book exhibit.

The case for and against networks

Professional networks can be extremely important to women – especially those from relatively low status or isolated institutions. However, networks can limit involvement as well as facilitate it for those individuals who are in them. Several years ago I analyzed the leadership of SPSSI in terms of institutional and scholarly affiliation as well as sex, ethnicity, and other demographic variables (Unger, 1986b). In my conclusion to this paper, I noted that:

> What do all of these statistics tell us about SPSSI and its leadership? They suggest that charges of "inbreeding" were probably more correct in the past than they are today. On the other hand, they indicate that SPSSI has been less committed to diversification in the racial and ethnic characteristics of its leaders than its commitment to social activism would suggest. It is also not clear why the organization remained unaware of the leadership potential of its large percentage of women members until 1972. And although the sex composition of the leadership has become more consonant with that of its membership, these data suggest that racial and ethnic integration have a long way to go. (Unger, 1986b, p. 86)

I also called for attention to the limiting nature of networks as well as their advantages and for creative ways to foster diversity within them: 'At a time when the profession of psychology has become larger, more complex, and more impersonal than in the past, institutions such as SPSSI have the responsibility of developing alternative structures that increase the diversity of its leadership' (Unger, 1986b, p. 87).

Some formal and informal networking appears to be essential to bring members of disenfranchised groups into a system. For example, special efforts have been made by various presidents of Division 35 to bring ethnic minority women into its organizational structure. A section on Black women's concerns has been in existence since 1984. Many of the women leaders within this group have moved into more general leadership positions. Martha Mednick has been especially active in supporting African-American women. She has taught at Howard University for many years and has published collaborately with a number of her students. She has been instrumental in developing a 'Howard University connection' similar to the 'Michigan connection' discussed earlier. For example, Pamela Reid (the first and, thus far, only African-American president of Division 35) attended Howard as an undergraduate.

While ethnic diversity is increasing, disciplinary diversity may be decreasing in Division 35 in a way similar to the decline found in SPSSI. Many of the founding leaders of Division 35 were committed feminists whose major scholarly field was not the psychology of women. However, individuals such as Nancy Anderson, Laurie Eyde, and Tena Cummings who had been on the first executive committee, were quickly replaced by women for whom the psychology of women was a major scholarly focus. The division may have become a little less politically activist because of these changes. Certainly, more dramatic actions have been carried out by AWP than by Division 35. One example of such an action occurred during an AWP research conference in the mid-1970s at which everyone was invited to bring, read, and then shred their 'favorite' piece of sexist psychology.

Advocacy and scholarship: How compatible are they?

The issue of the compatibility of activism and scholarship has always intrigued me, probably because I have been involved in both throughout my academic career (see Reading 1 at the end of this chapter). I have found my organizational and scholarly activities to be mutually supportive. Political activism helped me to find collaborators and sympathetic colleagues. Such activities have also suggested ideas for scholarly research. Conversely, my scholarship helped to make me known to others and lent legitimacy to my political agendas.

The more problematic issue for me has been the degree to which activist and/or feminist research is considered to be legitimate scholarship. I wrote an article about these concerns for a special issue of the *Psychology of Women Quarterly* on teaching the psychology of women (Unger, 1982). This article recapitulated questions I had asked as early as 1973 and extended them. I considered three potential sources of illegitimacy: women as scientists and/or knowledge producers, women as a content area, and feminism as a theoretical framework. I used a systemic analysis based on a sociology of knowledge framework and concluded that professional legitimacy was largely a matter of power. In contrast, to a more individualistic, 'psychological' analysis, I suggested that legitimacy is a property largely conferred by others and would be more easily influenced by collective rather than personal actions.

Reflections on personal and social change

US psychologists have been reluctant to define power in structural rather than personal terms in contrast to some European psychologists (cf. Apfelbaum, 1979). Feminist psychologists' neglect of the structural bases of power has made them more reluctant to use terms such as 'dominance' or 'patriarchy' than feminists outside the discipline. Our neglect of the external realities of power has also left feminist psychology with a number of unresolved dilemmas.

One such dilemma is the relationship between personal and social change. This dilemma pervades all aspects of the discipline – from the practices of individual clinical therapists, through pedagogical issues, to the operation of large-scale organizations. Clinicians have long been aware that insight does not always produce personal change. Social psychologists also recognize that the connection between personal and social change is unclear even in directionality.

Carolyn Sherif devoted most of her scholarly life to the issue of social change. Her book *Orientation in Social Psychology* (1976) was a personalized account of scholarship that was published well before such autobiographic narratives were fashionable. It was not a huge success in terms of sales, but had an enormous impact on those of us who were attempting to combine activism and scholarship. It is instructive that both Carolyn and Muzafer Sherif derived from the Lewinian tradition of social psychology in which the dividing lines between research and application were virtually nonexistent.

Carolyn Sherif had been isolated from US social psychology for some years when Division 35 was born (cf. Unger and Kahn, 1998). She actually had to rejoin APA to become a member of the Division. She rapidly became an integral part of its leadership and a major source of support and encouragement to younger members who were still trying to find their niche in both theory and research. She paid a great deal of attention to many of us, read our work carefully, and criticized it, warmly and gently, but firmly. She had the knack of pointing out flaws while still making people feel good about themselves.

I consider myself very lucky because Carolyn was the president of Division 35 in 1979–80, the year before I became president. I had the benefit, therefore, of her experience and counsel in learning how to do the job. I, and others, have saved many of her letters. She is one of the few people whom I have met about whom I would use the description 'wise'.

Carolyn was helpful to me not only in organizational matters, but also in coming to terms with the major intra-disciplinary shift that I made from physiological to social psychology. I had an 'identity crisis' during this period, trying to figure out what I should call myself. The psychology of women had not been in existence long enough to make identification with it meaningful to others and there was no such thing as feminist psychology at the time. Carolyn felt that being a self-taught social psychologist was an acceptable label. I look back on this crisis with some bemusement now because I have to remind people of my original disciplinary roots. We all find it very funny that my doctoral dissertation was entitled 'The effect of spatial and temporal alternation procedures on rats with caudate nucleus lesions'.

Living with contradictions

Because I have lived with so many contradictions in my personal and professional life, I have never found the idea of contradiction as problematic as many psychologists. I made this concept the central theme of the first Carolyn Wood Sherif memorial address which I gave at the APA convention in Los Angeles in 1985. Although I rewrote some of these ideas for a subsequent book chapter (Unger, 1988b), I prefer to reprint the original talk in its entirety for the first time here (see Reading 2 at the end of this chapter). I consider the opportunity to give the first address in her honor (this is an ongoing activity of Division 35) one of the most personally meaningful (as well as frightening) experiences of my professional life (made even more difficult by the presence of Muzafer Sherif and several of their daughters). I know that other later recipients who knew and admired Carolyn have felt the same way.

In my talk I explored the concept of the double bind as a nexus of personal and structural forces. I argued that our inability to differentiate between definitions of ourselves that are generated by others and our own self-definitions is a major source of both self-doubt and social paralysis. I also argued that women, and other low status individuals, lack the power to name themselves. When self-definitions and those of more powerful others are contradictory, as they often are, any behavior may be liable to social sanctions. Since perceptions about lack of control over one's life are self-destructive, it may be necessary for a woman's mental health to ignore the contradictions and accept the sanctions as personally deserved. Thus, I argued that only collective changes in consciousness can foster social change. This paper was the first time I discussed the social construction of reality using that term, and could as easily be placed in Chapter 5 where I will discuss the personal and societal construction of meaning. However, I believe its emphasis on how the 'same' environment can affect women and men unequally justifies its inclusion in a chapter on power. Elucidation of the psychological mechanisms through which dominant groups maintain their hegemony is an area to which feminist social psychologists have much to contribute. I believe Carolyn Sherif would have contributed significantly to this area if she had not died at such a relatively early age.

Some current developments in the area

Feminists recognize the interactive nature of the person and her social context. They also recognize that important aspects of the social context such as dominance cannot be easily reproduced in the laboratory. Although the laboratory experiment has been attacked by feminist psychologists for many years (see Chapter 4), only recently have feminist researchers begun to offer some viable alternatives. These include comparisons between historical cohorts (Stewart and Healy, 1989; Apfelbaum, 1993) and between culturally diverse populations (Landrine, 1995).

Once psychologists involve themselves in situations where 'real' power differences exist, they find that their definitions of psychology also change (cf. Fine, 1983; Lykes, 1989). It is clear that what terms we use for 'power' determines how we look at it. For example, looking at sources of power as within the self can mask the extent and violence of many women's oppression (cf. Kitzinger, 1991; Reid, 1993).

There appears to be a resurgent interest in problematizing power among feminist psychologists. For example, an entire issue of the *Psychology of Women Quarterly* on women and power was published in 1992 edited by Arnold Kahn and Jan Yoder. However, most of the papers in this issue analyzed power at an interpersonal rather than at a structural level. This is, of course, an improvement over intrapsychic conceptions of power and control that appear to do little but increase the number of self-help books written for women (Crawford, 1989).

Ignoring the importance of power differentials in women's and men's lives has resulted in a psychology of gender that stresses 'sex differences' (cf. Mednick, 1989). This theoretical position is very comfortable for those who prefer a conservative status quo. Studies documenting differences between women and men (for example, fear of success, women's ways of knowing, and more recently, conversational misunderstanding) have received great attention from the media. Interactive and systemic theories of power have, in contrast, received little attention and are seen as polemics rather than respectable scientific research.

A number of feminist scholars have recently attacked the individualistic focus of even feminist psychology as a force for conservatism (Kahn and Yoder, 1989; Weisstein, 1993). However, such concerns appear to be more salient for the leaders in the field than for most of its practitioners. Although several presidential addresses to Division 35 have focused on power (Sherif, 1982; Reid, 1993), change in research priorities has been slow. Today, it is mostly those who are interested in ethnic, racial, and sexual diversity who are overt in their discussion of dominance and subordination. In my more pessimistic moments I would argue that this resurgent interest in power – fueled by its particular historical circumstances – will, like earlier waves of interest, soon disappear.

Notes

1 Contemporary research indicates that little has changed in this area. For example, Linda Carli (1990) has found that women's use of passive influence strategies are more effective with men in mixed-sex groups. Women, however, are more influenced by assertive women. This, of course, produces another double bind for women since many social situations involve both sexes and it is difficult to figure out how a woman can be passive and assertive at the same time.

2 Mythical sources of pollution possessed only by girls which can be 'caught' by boys who have close contact with them. Cooties may be a synonym for 'head lice', but this connection is not made explicit by the children who use the term.

3 The women's caucus was originally a group composed of any woman member of the APA legislature who chose to affiliate with it. As the group acquired political influence, however, it attracted non-feminist women and some men which has diffused its activist agenda.

Reading 1

Advocacy versus scholarship revisited: issues in the psychology of women (Unger, 1982)

The psychology of women has suffered from an identity crisis from the time it came into existence as a self-defined sub-division of psychology. I remember a heated discussion at the 1973 meeting of the Association for Women in Psychology about the appropriate title for the just-to-be-born Division 35. Most of us did not like the title then. Arguments about nomenclature have continued (Alpert, 1978; Mednick, 1976; Parlee, 1975; Vaughter, 1976). The "name" controversy reflects concern about the nature of the field as it is presently constructed. There is confusion about the apparently contradictory themes that coexist within it. Feminist researchers not only uncover information, but also make social judgments about the information they uncover. It is this socially activist component of the psychology of women which produces conflicts for those who have been socialized to believe that advocacy and scholarship are incompatible activities.

As the field was coming into existence in 1973, I organized a symposium for APA on issues inherent in teaching the psychology of women.[1] Most of the strains noted then are still relevant today. In the past nine years, however, we have learned a great deal about the forces which create these apparent paradoxes. This article is an attempt to examine the issue anew: to determine how much of the dilemma is due to the nature of the psychology of women itself and how much is a result of our interaction with the social institutions of academia and the structure of psychology as a scientific discipline.

An important distinction for this kind of analysis seems to be between women as researchers, teachers, and practitioners of psychology; women as a content area within psychology; and feminism as a theoretical perspective. Each of these components of the psychology of women appears to interact with psychology as a social institution in a distinct manner. Each of these components also interferes with professional recognition of the psychology of women as a legitimate area of scholarship. Feminist women who study women constitute a threat on a variety of levels. Although people in the field may or may not be feminists, may be women or men, and may or may not study women exclusively, our self-definitions are not the real issue here. How we are perceived as we impinge upon psychology as a whole is the basis for much of the paradox we perceive to exist within the field. The sources for resolution must be searched for in the interactions between women and social institutions. The limits of our power to control these interactions may predict the future of the field.

Psychology: in theory and practice

Assumptions in psychology

Most psychologists share a number of common assumptions which are rarely overtly discussed. As a researcher one is taught that science involves the objective pursuit of truth. (It is additionally implied that there is only one such truth available at any one time and that other disciplines do not have such clear access to that truth.) One is also taught that disciplines develop or advance (e.g., are built on an existing data base that determines which models and theories are to be accepted as valid). As a teacher one may subscribe to another set of myths. They include the idea that the pursuit of "truth" is as important to our students as it is to ourselves; that the classroom is a place for the exchange of information (unequal, to be sure, since the teacher possesses more information on the subject matter); that affective growth is largely irrelevant to the classroom experience; and that the acquisition of knowledge (defined as information that we, as experts, agree is important) can be monitored and rewarded by means of objective standards – tests and empirically based papers. As a professional one is taught that competence in the aforementioned activities will be rewarded by advancement; that the most meritorious advance fastest and become faculty at the most prestigious institutions; and that relationships with colleagues are based upon competence in the pursuit of knowledge. We are led to believe that both formal and informal judgments will be based on objective evaluation of our work rather than on other more personal characteristics.

Other views about the relationship between data, theory, and practice

All of these assumptions are probably somewhat incorrect! The issue of the objectivity of research has been scrutinized by feminist researchers and scholars from a variety of disciplines. Philosophers and historians of science have pointed out that what facts are regarded as scientifically valid depend on the institutionalized beliefs of the society in which the research is done (Payer, 1977). In the nineteenth century, for example, estrogen was dubbed the "female hormone" although the major source of supply was the urine of the stallion (Hall, 1977). In an extensive discussion of the influence of ideology on psychological theory, Stephanie Shields (1975a) has pointed out how the "facts" about sex differences in brain construction changed depending upon which theory about human neural function was current at the time.

Investigations which prove current theories incorrect do not necessarily change them. Carolyn Sherif (1979) cites a number of early findings by feminist researchers which contradicted the notion of women's impairment due to the menstrual cycle. She notes that when behavior could not be found to be deficient, researchers (mostly male, of course) switched to studies involving self-reports about the degree of impairment. It is only recently that feminist researchers have looked at performance again and found few if any effects due to the menstrual cycle (Golub, 1976; Rodin, 1976).

It may be instructive to look at the lack of relationship between the theory and practice of science in terms of the three ways in which the psychology of women appears to constitute a threat to established scholarship. Feminist theory challenges the status quo on several levels. First, it questions the definitions and assumptions about women disseminated by psychology. Second, it also questions the methods by which this information is generated. Finally, as its most revolutionary, feminist scholarship seeks to redefine the means by which data are examined and validated. Other revisionist theoretical perspectives have also encountered difficulty in gaining acceptance from established disciplines (Cole & Zuckerman, 1975). Systems are not likely to reward individuals for questioning the values of that system.

Feminist theory may be more vulnerable than other revisionist perspectives because of the nature of scholarship about women. Women have been a low priority as objects of investigation in many disciplines. In psychology this neglect has resulted in large gaps in our body of knowledge (Sherman & Denmark, 1978). Because of the dearth of information, psychological theorizing about women may be particularly vulnerable to the influence of popular stereotypes and hidden assumptions. It has been charged that scholarship has been particularly shipshod when women are the content area under investigation (Laws, 1979).

Since the study of women is regarded as a low prestige area, few eminent scholars of either sex have been interested in involving themselves in it. The study of women, therefore, has largely been conducted by younger scholars – primarily women. Women researchers are not new to psychology (Bernstein & Russo, 1974). They have, however, been largely excluded from the practice of science as it is institutionalized in our society (Caplow & McGee, 1961). Even when they investigate areas of interest to mainstream psychology, women never lose their class identity as females (Laws, 1975). Large numbers of female researchers threaten the comfortable club-like nature of scholarship as currently practiced. The threat is compounded when the problems they attempt to solve and the issues they examine are not those generated by male mentors.

The psychology of women and the profession of psychology

Issues of professional advancement
Hard work in traditional ways (e.g., publication in the "right" journals) is still seen as the way to get ahead in the academic world. Women faculty members appear to cherish the illusion of a meritocracy to a much smaller degree than do men (Ladd & Lipset, 1976). Their perceptions may be influenced by the fact that there is a much smaller relationship between productivity and rewards (promotion) for women than for men (O'Connell, Alpert, Richardson, Rotter, Ruble & Unger, 1978). Even women scholars who are highly esteemed professionals do not acquire the extrinsic marks of status accorded comparable men (Helson, 1978). There is considerable evidence that many sex inequities are due to informal social mechanisms rather than to formal procedures which can be dealt with by affirmative action committees (Rotter, 1978; Unger, 1978b).

While problems of professional advancement confront all female faculty members, there seems to be greater vulnerability for those involved in teaching and doing research in the psychology of women. At one of the recent Association for Women in Psychology midwinter conferences, three of the invited addresses were given by women who were encountering difficulty in obtaining tenure at prestigious institutions at that

time. All of these women ultimately received negative decisions. In at least some negative tenure decisions, activities in
the psychology of women or women's studies were cited as
interfering with "proper" professional work. Such activities
have been portrayed as trivial, irrelevant to more important
activities (in other areas of psychology), or as conflicting with
other activities required by the institution. Women receive
fewer "brownie" points for publishing on women or in journals on women. Although tenure is somewhat protective, a
number of cases of feminist women who are having difficulty
being promoted to full professor have been called to my
attention recently. Few jobs requiring expertise in the psychology of women are advertised in the *APA Monitor*. And,
even candidates for women's studies positions are expected to
have expertise in another area in addition to the psychology of
women.

Issues of professional legitimacy
These problems define an area which has not yet achieved
professional legitimacy. It is instructive to look at some of the
factors which may account for the lack of legitimacy of
the field. One factor which has been suggested is the content
of the field as indicated by its name. The content area may be
seen as too narrow in focus. When I first introduced a course
in the psychology of women at my institution in 1972, I
encountered a number of illustrative objections. "Will there be
a companion course in the psychology of men?" "The department already has a course in human sexuality!" and "Is there
enough material to support such a course?" It is difficult to
understand the basis for believing that a course which focuses
on about 52% of the human race (if it, indeed, focused only
upon women) is too narrow. Yet the breadth of courses on the
white rat or abnormal humans is rarely questioned at most
institutions.

   In fact, the psychology of women does not yet have a
unique content area. I recently investigated the textbooks
published in the psychology of women using a method developed by Daniel Perlman (1979) called "rear end analysis." The
measures involve looking up who is cited in author indices and
counting the number of pages in which each author is cited.
The most frequently cited individuals in these texts are persons
who are not necessarily defined as part of the field. In order of
number of pages, the researchers seen as most important by
psychology of women texts are: Eleanor Maccoby, Sigmund

Freud, Carol Jacklin, John Money, William Masters, Jerome
Kagan, Virginia Johnson, Judith Bardwick, Jessie Bernard,
Julia Sherman, Anka Ehrhardt, Inge Broverman, and Alfred
Kinsey (vagaries in the citation of second authors account for
the discrepancies between members of research teams). If one
combines research team members, it appears that those writing
about the psychology of women are most interested in sex
differences, the early origin of personality differences between
females and males, prenatal hormonal effects on sexual differentiation, male and female sexuality, and sex-role socialization. The area could more readily be labeled the psychology of
girls than the psychology of women!

The absence of a great deal of concern about societal practices in a supposedly feminist field is rather dismaying
(although there is some evidence of change in the most recently
published texts). Interestingly, instructors in the psychology of
women have been more careful to distinguish their courses
from those on sex differences than the authors of texts have
been. Russo (1982) reports that far more courses are taught in
the psychology of women than in the psychology of sex
differences or sex roles. It is important to distinguish between
these ways of analyzing material on sex and gender (Unger,
1979c), but the distinction is probably more one of process than
of content.

The consequences of illegitimacy – being ignored

The considerable attention paid to the origin of sex differences
in earlier texts in the psychology of women probably reflects
the reactive nature of a relatively new field. What is more
important here is the relative neglect of newer feminist analyses even within the field. Benign neglect of findings is even
more common in psychology as a whole. For example, the
1979 APA Master Lecture series was supposedly on sex and
gender, but largely concerned itself with developmental issues
and individual difference research. When the series was written
up in the *New York Times* science section, attention was paid
mostly to the purported hormonal predisposition of
masculinity and femininity.

It may be naive to assume that institutional ignorance about
the existence of the field is purely accidental. Ignoring
deviance is a preferred way of dealing with it for both individuals and social institutions (Unger, 1979a). Lack of attention requires little energy and does not risk arousing the
deviant to more aggressive action. Psychology, because of

the nature of its unstated assumptions, may be particularly resistant to broadening the scope of investigation (Parlee, 1979; Sherif, 1979). It is interesting to note that some of the ideas generated be feminist researchers have reached mainstream psychology,[2,3] but they are rarely attributed to sources within the field.

Lessons from the sociology of science

Distinguishing between feminism and newness
It is important to determine what aspects of the psychology of women contribute most to its lack of legitimacy. Is work in the psychology of women ignored or undercited because it is done by women, because it is about women, or because it stems from a new and revisionist theoretical perspective? Obviously, none of these characteristics can easily be separated from the others, but such an analysis can offer points for discussion when issues involving supposed conflicts between scholarship and advocacy inevitably arise.

The literature from the sociology of science suggests that it is feminist theory which is the most difficult for traditional scholarship to incorporate. New paradigms threaten the existing status hierarchies within disciplines and may require intellectual revolutions before they are recognized as valid points of view (Kuhn, 1970). Existing theories are not always altered in the face of discrepant evidence (Cole, 1975). Cole concludes that: (1) a theory is not rejected until a "better" one can take its place (better is operationally defined as one which provides more interesting puzzles for scientists to solve); (2) a function of theory is to provide puzzles for scientists; and (3) during periods of normal science, empirical studies that cast doubt on established theories are either ignored or misinterpreted. Cole also suggests that citations are often made to lend credibility to an author's work or that one function of theory is to legitimize the work of its user. In other words, theory exists to explain research rather than research being used to test theory.

These conclusions both predict and explain some of the problems that feminist theories are encountering within psychology. It explains why the information base in the psychology of women has exploded so rapidly – because its theoretical perspective provides many exciting new puzzles for women psychologists to explore. It also explains why the theoretical perspective makes many mainstream psychologists so uncomfortable: they are not yet ready to reject current theories nor to develop new research paradigms.

The dynamics of the institutionalization of new knowledge

The relative novelty of feminist theory is confounded by the fact that it is women who are doing the theorizing. Apparent theoretical breakthroughs are often made by individuals who have already gained considerable acclaim for other work within a field (Cole & Zuckerman, 1975). The work of established scholars is cited more than that of individuals who are less renowned (Merton, 1968). These findings are, of course, related to the point that people cite others to gain credibility for their own work. And, it is clear that women are less credible sources in science than are comparable men.

Women are at a disadvantage in terms of what is known about the dynamics of the institutionalization of new knowledge. In other newly emerging fields in which men predominate, the development of a different theoretical perspective is accompanied by a number of professional and organizational developments. Collateral as well as lineal networks are formed in which conferences are organized and attended, papers are read and criticized, and journals are edited and published (Cole & Zuckerman, 1975). It is possible to trace lines of descent in particular subfields showing the influence of mentor upon apprentice and of colleague on colleague.

Women in academia

Women are less frequently involved in the formal and informal social networks that support the development of new perspectives than are men. There are a number of reasons for this relative lack of involvement. First, women have not been welcome in most male-dominated professional organizations. They have received few professional rewards (e.g., editorships, offices, etc.) for involving themselves (Ruble, 1978; Tennov, 1975) and find themselves socially isolated. Second, women academics frequently have more teaching responsibilities than men and often teach at institutions where outside involvement and travel are not encouraged. Such institutions do not provide encouragement of extra-institutional interests in either female or male faculty. The stimulating atmosphere and contacts provided by research-oriented institutions account for a major amount of the variability between institutions in terms of scholarly productivity (Blau, 1975). Third, conference attendance may be seen as out-of-role for most women faculty, especially if they are married. Yet the knowledge exchanged and the contacts made at such conferences are fundamental in the development of new theoretical perspectives.

Since even academic women are socialized to believe that the acquisition of knowledge is a male domain, the fact that feminist theories have largely been constructed by women also acts to delay the legitimization of the field. Prominent women scholars are relatively rare and may have been socialized to believe that their sex is irrelevant to their professional inter-actions (Laws, 1975). Although femaleness may never be an irrelevant characteristic to others, such women may be reluct-ant to risk their legitimacy within psychology by identifying themselves with other women and women's issues. A study of the membership of Division 35 when the organization was just forming suggested that such social dynamics were operative at that time. The percentage of women fellows of APA who were charter members of Division 35 was lower than the percentage of women fellows of APA as a whole.[4] No such differences existed for Division 34 (population) which was formed at the same time.

Males also run the risk of losing professional credibility if they identify with feminist theory. The work of women does not lend stature to their own work. Although little work in the psychology of women has been cited in mainstream journals, it is noteworthy that far more citations appear for *Sex Roles* than for the *Psychology of Women Quarterly*. While this difference may partially reflect the relative age of the two journals, it also suggests that feminist studies are more acceptable when they are not labeled as sex specific. More men have been involved in the editorial process for *Sex Roles* than for the *Psychology of Women Quarterly* as well.

Legitimacy and power

It is relatively easy to delimit the factors which act to reduce the professional legitimacy of the psychology of women. It is more difficult to determine what we can and should do about them. First of all, it is important to distinguish between legitimacy and power. Many people interested in the psy-chology of women possess some degree of power – in terms of influencing students, some of our colleagues and, even to some degree, the rest of the field. Both the content and some of the ideas generated by the psychology of women continue to appear in mainstream journals although they are not frequently identified with it. The psychology of women appears to possess power without authority. Authority can be consensual; it can be conferred by historical precedent; or it may come from institutional fiat. Thus far, the field lacks all of these bases for authority. Others define us.

A reexamination of questions generated by the conflict between scholarship and advocacy may be revealing. Nine years ago, the questions I raised involved personal decisions. I believed that professional deviance could be dealt with by means of professionally responsible solutions. In retrospect, this belief may have been naive.

It is clearer today that issues of legitimacy and of the apparent conflict between scholarship and advocacy are inextricably entwined. Feminist scholarship is deviant scholarship in the sense that it questions the basic tenets of long-established fields. Deviance, however, is not a property inherent in certain forms of behavior, but a property conferred upon these behaviors by those who view them (Erikson, 1962). As long as we lack the legitimacy to define ourselves, those who identify with the psychology of women will exist on scholarly boundary lines. And, it is one function of those on such boundaries to provide information to others about the limits of permissable deviance (Erikson, 1966). The dilemmas created by being in such a position require collective rather than personal solutions.

While we must question whether it is desirable or even possible for feminist research to be incorporated into traditional disciplines, it is also important to remember that not all revisions of an acknowledged area become legitimized. Some unresolved questions in this area may be important for predicting the course of feminist scholarship. These questions are: (1) Does science always build on the existing data base? (2) How and why do changes from one theory to another take place? (3) How does the social organization of a field alter the degree of progress that appears to occur? (Cole, 1975)

It is important to find out how much control individuals and organizations can exert over the process of legitimization. To my knowledge there has been no research on the role that a self-conscious theoretical perspective can play in influencing its own acceptance.

There has also been little research on structures in which social deviance is a matter of choice and awareness. For example, how much impact do alternative structures have on disciplinary change? When we confer legitimacy upon each other, how much do our judgments influence the rest of the field? What is the political and personal difference between choosing to teach the psychology of women rather than that of sex differences or sex roles? And why, despite all the problems, do we continue to identify with the field?

Notes

1 Unger, R.K. Psychology of women: Advocacy vs. scholarship. Paper presented at the meeting of the American Psychological Association, Montreal, September 1973.
2 Gergen, K. Remarks on the crisis in social psychology. Paper presented at the meeting of the Society for Experimental Social Psychology, Princeton, November 1978.
3 Sampson, E. What would a "feminine" science be like? Paper presented at the meeting of the American Psychological Association, New York, September 1979.
4 McDevitt, M.A. An examination of the Queen Bee phenomenon in a professional population. Paper presented at the meeting of the Eastern Psychological Association, New York, April 1975.

Reading 2

First Carolyn Wood Sherif Memorial Address, American Psychological Association, Los Angeles, 26 August 1985

In *Orientation in Social Psychology* Carolyn Sherif stated: "Each of our lives may be more notable for its contradictions than for its consistency" (1976, p. 362). Psychology has always been more comfortable with consistency than with contradiction. Nevertheless, contradiction appears to hold many clues for understanding human behavior.

The theme I want to discuss is the various forms of contradiction to be found in the everyday lives of women and its relationship to social and personal change. I hope these ideas will serve a dual purpose. For social psychology, conceptualizing contradiction may further our understanding of how sociostructural factors are incorporated into our personal lives. For feminist psychology, it may reinforce the early message of the women's liberation movement – indeed, the personal remains political.

Both feminist psychology and the women's movement have long been concerned with the social origins of many inner conflicts experienced as personal. What I shall argue today is that the concept of contradiction is central to our understanding of the mechanisms by which social reality is translated into personal reality. First, I will discuss the conceptual background for a theory of contradiction with a particular emphasis on social constructionism. Next, I will discuss forms of negotiated understanding involving contradiction with a particular emphasis on social paradoxes and double binds. And, last, I will discuss the relationship between social and personal change and its implications for us as women and as psychologists.

A social constructionist framework

Many of us have had no difficulty accepting the idea that women are not born but made, but we have lacked a coherent theory and linguistic framework with which to discuss this insight. Psychologists have been slow to accept social constructionist views that have become popular in philosophy, anthropology, and sociology. Kenneth Gergen (1985) has ably summarized the assumptions and values of social constructionism for psychology. The points most relevant to the present discussion are:

1   Our experience of the world is dictated by the categories we possess to describe it.
2   The terms in which the world is understood are social artifacts – products of historically situated interchanges between people.
3   When they serve a social purpose, definitions can be sustained regardless of how well they actually describe reality. For example, the use of working women as a synonym for employed women effectively excludes domestic labor as work.

4   Forms of negotiated understanding are of critical significance in everyday life. Descriptions and explanations of
the world are themselves forms of social behavior. They
sustain and support certain patterns of behavior to the
exclusion of others.

Social constructionism challenges the concept of knowledge
as a mental representation of the "real world." Instead,
knowledge is defined as something people do together. Thus,
research on cognitive processes tells us less about an internal
cognitive world than about the nature of social discourse.
Reality is viewed as consensually defined. In terms of this
framework, there can be no "true" version of a situation.

Contradictions in the social reality about women

It has long been argued that women and men live in different
worlds (Bernard, 1981; Smith, 1979). However, it is the extent
to which the sexes share perceptions about their differences
that I find most compelling. Stereotypes about the nature of
the sexes have been documented from "womb to tomb"
(Unger, 1979a). Men and women agree about their own
differences to an astonishing degree.

A careful examination of the nature of stereotypes about
women reveals some interesting contradictions. Women are not
the target of stereotypes under all circumstances. They are most
apt to be the target of negative perceptions when they step
outside their normative roles. According to Ashmore (1985),
the most important dimensions by which female prototypes are
evaluated are working inside the home versus working outside
of it and respectable/not respectable (Ashmore, 1985). This
distinction between the domestic and public sphere does not
exist for prototypes of men, but has been noted by a number of
anthropologists as a basic distinction for women in many
societies besides our own (Rosaldo & Lamphere, 1974).

Goodness – in the sense of respectable/not respectable –
and normality – in the sense of prescribed roles and spheres of
action – appear to be unrelated to each other in perceptions
about women but not about men. It is only a short step from
viewing these properties in women as independent of each
other to viewing them as contradictory. Some of the earliest
modern studies in the psychology of women by Broverman
and her associates (Broverman et al., 1972) demonstrated that
femininity was seen as incompatible with autonomous

instrumental characteristics by both women and men. Horner (1972) also showed early that success in traditional male domains was seen as incompatible with normal womanhood. She noted that women are seen to be "desexed" by success, men by failure. Women may not be avoiding success as much as avoiding gender deviant behavior (Cherry & Deaux, 1978).

Social contradictions and double binds

As Carolyn Sherif has noted: "Both societies and people form cultural definitions about what can and cannot be changed and about who is and who is not responsible for their personal dissatisfactions" (1976, p. 369). I would like to argue today that our social system is so constructed as to make it difficult for women (and, perhaps, other low status role occupants) to determine what can and cannot be changed and exactly who is responsible for their psychological discomfort. This is demonstrated by the kind of social transactions in which women find themselves when they step outside of their "proper" domestic sphere.

The social transactions in which women are likely to find themselves involve one of several forms of the so-called double bind. There have been a number of different definitions of this phenomenon. The definition I would like to offer as most useful in this context has several components.

1   The individual is present in a situation in which her femaleness is defined as contradictory to other characteristics considered appropriate for that time or place. Contradictory definitions are more likely to appear, the further the woman moves from the domestic sphere. Under some circumstances her mere presence outside the home may evoke a set of socially mediated assumptions that betray the presence of usually invisible social controls. For example, sexual harassment on the job is seen by some as the price women pay for working outside their homes. Similarly, rape by a stranger within the home is usually punished more severely than a similar rape that takes place outside the home. It has been difficult, on the other hand, to convince public policymakers that rape can take place at home within the marital bond.

2   The woman's "out-of-place" property may be marked linguistically (as, for example, a woman doctor or a female executive). However, linguistic marking may not be present when the woman's out-of-place quality is due to some reproductive property that only women possess; menstruation or

pregnancy. In these cases nonverbal markers such as staring may be employed.

3   The woman's presence in the situation is "legitimate" in the formal sense (as her presence in a male urinal would not be), but produces discomfort in others. Discomfort is produced by the aforementioned discrepancies between characteristics expected from someone occupying her role and someone from her biological category. These judgments have the nature of implicit theories. They may not be attended to consciously by those involved in the situation and may be triggered as much by assumptions abut the relative status of women and men – at least in occupational contexts (Steffen & Eagly, 1985) – as by biological assumptions. The woman may not be aware of her property as a social stimulus because evaluations of the self and others appear to have a different base. For her, but not for others, biological status is largely irrelevant and it is her role-relevant characteristics that are seen as most important (Laws, 1975; Spence & Sawin, 1985).

4   The woman's behavior in the situation is seen as a matter of choice by herself as well as others. It is ironic that double binds occur only in contexts where a wide range of behavioral options seem to be available to women. Double binds do not appear to exist in traditional societies. They may be an artifact of rapid periods of social change and the changes in norms that accompany them.

This perception of choice in behavior may have important consequences for explanations of the situation by all of the participants in it. In terms of a theory of negotiated reality, explanations of causality constitute forms of social action. Explanations of situations may also influence the way we feel about them. Thus, recent studies by Smith and Ellsworth (1985) suggest that our feelings about events are influenced by the degree of control we perceive ourselves to have over them. For such fundamentally unpleasant states of emotion as sadness, fear, anger, frustration, and disgust, a situational control dimension was almost as important in defining what emotion was felt than all of the other dimensions studied combined.

5   One of the necessary features of a double bind is that any of the behaviors in which the woman engages may have both positive and negative consequences. This is due to several factors. First, it appears that so many prototypes of women exist and these possess such a variety of characteristics that a stereotype can be evoked which matches any possible behavior. It is difficult to find a characteristic that does not "fit" some

feature of "mother", "sex object", "pet", or "iron maiden" which have been described by some theorists as the four archetypal roles of women in western society (Wood & Conrad, 1983).

Second, as discussed previously, contradictory assumptions about women in the public sphere coexist so that behavior can be seen to be appropriate or inappropriate to some aspect of the coexisting mutually exclusive roles. Since any archetype may evoke some positive reinforcement (although it may be difficult for this audience to accept the idea of being rewarded for being a sex object or pet), no behavior in a double-bind situation can be perfectly adaptive. We have many clichés to describe this kind of situation: "From the frying pan into the fire" or the more familiar: "Damned if you do and damned if you don't."

This kind of analysis makes it clear that the dilemmas for women in these contexts involve situational causality more than personal flaws. Their behavior is a result of demands embedded in the social context. But because these demands are largely a result of implicit theories about women and their place and are shared by most participants in an interaction they become social reality. Acceptance of personal responsibility for problems posed by double binds is also enhanced by the relative isolation of women in the public sphere so that they have little opportunity to validate any other version of reality.

Group membership and social contradiction

It is important to stress that not all versions of reality have equal validity in our society. Members of groups with higher status have the power to control interpersonal transactions with individuals from groups with lower status than their own (Henley, 1977; Unger, 1978a). Thus, if there is disagreement about the construction of a particular reality, the males in the situation are likely to have the power to define that reality. Females in double-bind situations are at a double disadvantage. They are likely to possess lower status that the males in the situation because sex is itself a primary status variable (Unger, 1976, 1978a) and is also confounded with higher status roles in our society (Eagly & Wood, 1985). They are also likely to be a token minority in the public domains (Kanter, 1977) in which double binds are most likely to occur.

Of course, double binds are constructed for people other than women as a social class. In fact, much of the earlier work on double binds concentrated upon the role of paradoxical communication within the family in the production of schizophrenia as well as other somewhat less pathological patterns of behavior (Sluzki & Ransom, 1976). These familial situations have much in common with double binds found outside the home. They involve people in close habitual relationships in which one class of individuals (parents) have more power to interpret reality than another class (children).

It is somewhat less clear whether double binds operate regularly for members of other socially oppressed groups. Although blacks are clearly discriminated against in our society, it is difficult to determine whether they encounter double binds of the kind discussed here. Social contradiction may be less necessary for the control of racial minorities because they are already "marked" physically and do not necessarily cohabit constantly with the dominant group.

There is some indication of double binds regulating the behavior of adolescents of both sexes. Adolescence is a socially defined period in which it is unclear whether "child" or "adult" rules should be applied. Some of these rules – especially those regulating independence and autonomy – produce contradictory outcomes for the same behaviors. This kind of social regulation may help make adolescence the confusing period it is in our society.

Adolescents of both sexes and adult females share some properties as social stimuli. Both groups possess ambiguous social identities that present problems for those interacting with them. External appearance is seen as a more salient basis for judgments about them than it is for adult males. The focus on external appearance in adolescents may be enhanced by their rapidly changing physical appearance and the great amount of individual variation within a brief chronological period. Lack of correspondence between chronological age and level of physical maturation may make it difficult to decide whether child or adult behaviors are to be expected or rewarded in a particular individual. It is also of critical significance that both groups are in habitual relationships with individuals who have greater power to legitimate their reality than they do themselves.

Double binds and double standards

It is important to distinguish double binds from other contradictory social constructions that affect women as well as other socially oppressed groups. Marianne LaFrance (1985) has recently identified a number of social paradoxes involving women and mentoring. She asserts, for example, that to the extent that women receive the mentoring they need, they will be seen to need the mentoring they get. Also, the more mentoring is promoted for women, the more it affirms its importance for men. These paradoxes are produced because men and women in identical circumstances are not evaluated by the same criteria. Identical behaviors are attributed to different causes (Wallston & O'Leary, 1981). Success, in particular, is still measured in male terms.

The focus of such paradoxes, however, is outside of the situation – in the eye of the beholder – rather than in the perceptions of the participants. It may be argued that a true double bind does not exist unless all the participants – including the target individual – accept the strictures of the double bind as legitimate reality.

Some examples of double binds

It is too easy to find examples of double binds involving women in our society. Wood and Conrad (1983) have extensively analyzed double binds that enmesh the professional woman. Because of mutually incompatible definitions of professionalism and womanliness, it is impossible for a woman to fulfill both roles at the same time. A similar contradiction exists for physical attractiveness in women and their perceived ability to function in executive or managerial positions (Heilman & Saruwatari, 1979). Since (1) women are encouraged to be as attractive as possible, (2) attractiveness is highly confounded with femininity in our society, and (3) femininity is seen as incompatible with instrumental characteristics, it is easy to recognize the social construction of this particular double bind (Unger, 1985b).

The ubiquity of the double binds that women encounter is striking. Some binds, for example, appear to be tied more to the "unique" biological properties of women than to their perceived traits and roles. Lillian Rubin (1976) has discussed double binds that working-class wives encounter due to changing and contradictory definitions of female sexuality. They may be expected to engage in exotic sexual practices by their husbands who have incorporated recent data on female orgasm as a challenge to their virility. But, "letting themselves go" threatens these women's status as "good girls." There is little overt communication about this issue and little support from the males involved who are sending out ambiguous and ambivalent messages.

Pregnancy as a social stimulus rather than a biological event may also trigger a double bind. Pregnancy appears to signal a greater social need for female passivity that is communicated by staring as well as greater preference for passive behavior (Taylor & Langer, 1977). Nonassertive behavior is liked more even in a completely professional context. Thus, we found that students prefer a scientific experiment to be conducted by an apparently pregnant researcher who is passive whereas they prefer more directive behavior from her nonpregnant counterpart (Robinson & Unger, 1983).

Although the situations in which double binds occur appear to be diverse, a common pattern seems to emerge. They are most likely to occur when the woman's behavior is unexpected in terms of normative definitions of role and place. Double binds are more likely to occur in public than in private and when a relatively few people are involved in an interaction. Although other individuals in the interaction may be personally threatened by the woman's behavior (or, even, her presence), the greater threat may be to consensually defined social reality. The unpredictable character of the social transaction threatens usual explanations of causality – of the way things work.

Double binds are fundamentally uncomfortable situations for everyone involved. Their function, however, is to focus responsibility for the discomfort upon the individual who is the "intruder" in the situation. The target individual may accept personal responsibility for a number of reasons. First, a sense of control may be preferable to feeling at the mercy of external forces. Second, the individual is only exposed to one double bind at a time and may not recognize the pattern connecting apparently disparate events. And, last, since double binds are largely invisible, individuals may lack the means to identify them as a class of phenomena and a vocabulary with which to discuss them.

Responses to double binds

It has been argued (c.f., Wood & Conrad, 1983) that double binds cannot be said to exist if the bound individual does not act in such a way as to complete the interactive cycle. Confirmatory responses include accepting only one aspect of the contradictory definition. For example, a professional woman might take a nurturing or subsidiary role in a professional context. Or, she might identify completely as "one of the boys" even to the extent of devaluing the contributions of other women. Another confirmatory response involves attacking the perceptions or motives of other participants in the situation without recognizing the general social nature of the apparently personal dilemma. The individual may also withdraw from the situation which further isolates her from potential sources of validation of an alternative reality. Since all of these behaviors can be defined as fitting some female prototype, confirmatory behaviors tend to become self-fulfilling prophecies – further validating the definitions of those who dominate the interaction.

A more useful response to double binds is a renegotiation of the definitions involved. One such response consists of "reframing" – stepping away from the conventional perspective to offer a fresh definition of the terms involved. For the contradiction between professionalism and femininity, for example, feminists have offered the ideas that affective nurturant qualities are good for organizations and that competition and manipulation are both unprofessional and counterproductive for men and women alike. Individuals involved in double binds can also attempt to "redirect" the interaction; for example, refusing to discuss one's physical attributes in a professional context. Both of these tactics, however, assume that women are aware of the societal and situational nature of the double binds in which they are enmeshed and have more control over the negotiation of reality than they may actually possess.

Wood and Conrad (1983) have recommended transcending the situation by directly addressing the paradoxes and the social reality in which they are embedded. To do so, one must move away from the particulars of the situation to a more abstract, general view. This more abstract general view involves questioning philosophical and psychological verities that have formed Western reality for over 2000 years. In particular, we need to look at our tendency to reduce most concepts to dualisms (Jaggar, 1983). Social constructionism questions the reality/illusion dualism while feminist psychology questions our need to classify individuals into two genders (Kessler & McKenna, 1978). Paradoxically, the division of humans into two classes assumes the essential similarity of all humans. Dualism reduces complexity, but does not explain it.

Acceptance of contradiction and the reality of change

Does the acceptance of contradiction lead to personal and/or social change? The evidence is both positive and negative in this regard. On the negative side, people appear to be able to incorporate large amounts of contradictory information. Cognitive research shows that people tend to view behaviors consistent with stereotypic assumptions as dispositional or intrapsychic whereas they see behaviors that are inconsistent with their assumptions as situational in origin. Such nonconscious attributional processes may help to explain why stereotypes are so resistant to disconfirmatory evidence (Hamilton, 1979).

Stereotypes also appear to be resistant to the test of internal logic. For example, Spence and Helmreich (1978) have found that the degree of instrumental and affective characteristics that people perceive themselves to possess has no relationship to the extent to which they stereotype such characteristics as more or less appropriate to other males or females. In other words, people who see themselves as combining high levels of instrumentality and expressiveness are just as likely to sex-type others as those who show more gender-traditional self-ratings.

Part of the reason for this inconsistency appears to be the different information used in the evaluation of masculinity and femininity for oneself and others. Spence and Sawin (1985) found that people of both sexes use roles and traits to explain their own qualities, but focus more upon physical appearance when making the same judgments about others. This differential use of cues may also explain some of the confusion within a double bind. Participants are responding from "inside their own heads" and are unaware that they are using a different referent for defining important parts of reality.

People also seem to be able to ignore the possibility of negative consequences for themselves of biased realities directed against members of their own social category. Some recent data that we have collected may illustrate this point. Women greatly disagree with the statement that "At the present time, people are recognized for their achievements regardless of their race, sex, and social class." But, at the same time, they agree just as strongly that "At the present time, I am recognized for my achievements regardless of race, sex, and social class" (Unger & Sussman, 1986).

On the positive side, there is some evidence that women are beginning to reorganize their perceptual world. Recent studies

(Doherty & Baldwin, 1985) have indicated that women of all ages acquired a more external locus of control between the late 1960s and late 1970s. A similar change did not take place for men. Although some theorists have argued that external locus of control represents a deficiency in the understanding of the relationship between one's own behavior and its outcome, it can also be argued that external locus of control represents a realistic appraisal of environmental contingencies for groups with low power and status in our society (Furby, 1979). Thus, one can explain this change in women's belief patterns as a cultural shift. Women have become more aware of the external constraints on their ability to meet their goals in the labor force and in other settings.

An understanding of systemic and contextual factors has been linked with group identification and militancy in both blacks (Forward & Williams, 1970) and women (Sanger & Alker, 1972). It is important to distinguish between our explanations of control for ourselves and for the world in general. I have been recently conducting a series of studies on how people from various groups explain how the world works. Feminist psychologists and other socially activist academics believe more than others both that many structural factors are beyond the individual's control and also that individuals can change social systems (Unger, 1984–1985). Social activists appear to be able to maintain a contradictory cognitive schema that acknowledges both social injustice and the efficacy of individual efforts to change society. Such contradictory belief patterns may be particularly adaptive to a contradictory reality.

As noted earlier, beliefs about personal control and intentionality may be critical for the construction of alternative realities. Many attributional patterns are influenced by whether we believe behavior is under the control of the person or the situation. How we feel about a situation may also depend on how we answer certain fundamental questions about why it has occurred. Thus, our decisions about what we can or cannot change will be greatly altered by what we see as responsible for our personal dissatisfactions.

Unfortunately, our entire social system conspires to make it easy to personalize responsibility. For example, the English language has more than 15,000 trait adjectives but many fewer descriptors in terms of social roles (Ashmore, 1985). A discussion of individualistic bias in views of the self is beyond the scope of this paper, but a recent case study of change in the meaning and use of consciousness raising may be instructive. Rosenthal (1984) traces the ideology of consciousness raising from its beginning in radical feminism to the present day. Originally, consciousness raising was conceived as a short-term process for restructuring women's reality, understanding its political context, and mobilizing the anger needed to motivate women to change that reality. By the mid-1970s, however, consciousness raising had become a form of group therapy designed to effect personal change through shared understanding of the social circumstances of women.

This shift represents a complete reversal in the perceived source and, therefore, the remedy to women's oppression. As Rosenthal points out, the individualistic focus led to the conclusion that (1) personal circumstances and relationships are independent of the social environment and can be altered if the person is strong enough to do so and (2) failure to alter personal circumstances and relationships is a personal failure or the inability to overcome a deficient feminine socialization. In either case, the message is that political considerations are either unnecessary or futile.

Rosenthal suggests that part of the reason for the shift in consciousness raising from systemic to personal responsibility was due to a change in the kind of people who were being reached. As the feminist movement grew, consciousness raising was sought out and used by large numbers of women who were unfamiliar with or unwilling to accept a militant feminist message. As consciousness raising became more popular, however, it became less effective in creating even personal change. Paradoxically, the attempt to make consciousness raising more useful to women who found it difficult to accept its political rationale may have made it less useful to everyone.

The slowness with which people reconcile systemic responsibility and personal efficacy is disheartening. It may be necessary to accept that people must go through a developmental sequence of cognitive stages before they can transcend contradiction. Change is probably facilitated both by reference group identification as well as by changing one's circumstances. Thus, I have found that students who labeled themselves as feminist had more socially constructionist viewpoints than those who did not so define themselves (Unger, Draper and Pendergrass, 1986). Students who initially had more socially constructionist views about how the world works were also more likely to choose courses in women's studies than were students who had a more determinist view about the degree of

control people possess over reality. Both feminist and
nonfeminist students were changed further in a socially constructionist direction through exposure to the socially activist
content of women's studies courses. Feminists and nonfeminists changed to the same extent suggesting that an active
choice of one's circumstances may be essential for personal
change.

The uses of contradiction

As long as the terms that define the world are under the
control of a dominant ideology it will be easy for social
contradictions involving women to be ignored and personal
deficiencies to be emphasized. It is heartening that individuals
who identify themselves as feminists appear to be able to
incorporate contradictions into their personal epistemologies
(Unger, 1984–1985). However, social control through definition is evident in the negative connotations of the term
"feminist" even among many who agree with its postulates.
The *New York Times*, in fact, keeps telling us that we are in
the "post-feminist era" although I am not quite sure what this
means, especially from a newspaper that identifies two prominent former foreign policymakers, both of whom have earned
doctorates, as Dr. Kissinger and Mrs Kirkpatrick.

It is important to recognize that people can do anything and
to analyze the social programs that determine what they will or
will not do. One of the enormous contributions of the cognitive
revolution to psychology is the recognition that social control
often proceeds by way of the constraint of consciousness.
Definitions are simultaneously descriptions, prescriptions,
value judgments, and creators of reality. A language that can
seriously use such euphemisms as "benign neglect", "friendly
fire", or "moral majority" is obviously capable of incorporating
any contradiction.

The consequences of remaining unaware of the generic
function of contradiction in our society are both institutional
and personal. If we, as a collective unity, are unable to alter
the frame of discourse, we will either be coopted by mainstream psychology or remain isolated and illegitimate. If we,
as individuals, are unaware of how contradictions construct
and constrict our behaviors, we may come to accept one of a
large number of deficiency theories of female development.

Contradictory social messages are particularly destructive
because they make it difficult to locate the source of conflict.

Invalid problem definitions have been said to have a more pernicious effect upon the population studied than upon the progress of science (Caplan & Nelson, 1973). They can convince the target group of its own blameworthiness. The invisible use of power may facilitate the development of disorders such as learned helplessness, agoraphobia, and depression that are considered to be more characteristic of women than men. In another context, Jo Freeman (1975) has termed this process the tyranny of structurelessness.

We must transcend the intrapsychic vocabulary of psychology. But, we must not be caught in another dualism – the importance of the situation versus the person. The value of an analysis of double binds and other social paradoxes is that they illustrate the interactive nature of people and situations and support the view that change can emerge at any point in this dynamic whole.

The value of the study of paradox for philosophers is that it leads to questions about the nature of a system that can produce such a conceptual "trap." A more familiar analogy for psychology is the study of optical illusions which are perceptual paradoxes in the sense that identical physical stimuli produce several different sensory responses. The study of optical illusions produced the rich area of Gestalt psychology in which the organism and its environment are viewed as greater than the sum of their parts. In the terminology I have used today, multiple forms of consciousness may be seen as a normal response to some kinds of reality. The study of paradox can lead to a richer conceptualization of what must be known.

Paradoxes exist only because we accept the terms that constrain our thinking. Paradoxes alert us to a need to analyze the definitional process involved. However, the questions we raise and the methods we use to study them do not necessarily have to be framed in linear terms. It may be instructive to pose some still unanswered questions in terms of paradoxes. For example, if a person is seen in terms of one social category, is it impossible for him or her to be seen simultaneously in terms of other categories to which he or she is legitimately entitled? If a person is in the position to construct alternative realities that are accepted by others, is that person more likely to blame others for not having properly constructed their own reality? If a person is aware of alternative realities, is that person less influenced by the consensual reality defined by others?

Still other questions are raised by the relativistic nature of the social constructionist model. Does the acceptance of individual differences in the nature of reality imply that one cannot empirically study reality at all? Are there any standards for measuring the validity or reliability of particular views of the world? Do we have any criteria for determining whose model of the world is a better one? If reality depends only upon our frame of reference, why can't we substitute changes in consciousness for changes in social systems? Obviously, we need evaluative standards as well as scientific ones (Unger, 1983).

We also need to think about the kind of person who functions effectively in socially constructed reality. Does such an individual need a private and a public self, as Katherine Pope (1984–1985) has described in literary portraits of women by women? There are many dangers in such a psychically divided life. There are also many dangers in the unexamined living of a single reality. Perhaps, the ideal person for the model is one who can live in each reality as though it were the only one, but who knows that it is possible to stand outside all of them. The analysis of contradiction may be particularly helpful in this regard because it leads to the understanding of interpersonal transactions as forms of social fiction. However, we do not know under what conditions having alternative views of reality becomes useful in a particular reality. We will be busy with some of these problems for a long time. After all, paradoxes need paradoctors!

4

Feminist conversations about method and content

As soon as the Division of the Psychology of Women became an official part of the American Psychological Association (APA), critiques of psychology's method and content began to appear on the official programs at conferences. From the beginning, this critique had two distinct themes. One involved the analysis of sexist biases in traditional psychological methodology. The second examined the question of sex differences. Somewhat later, a third thread emerged which looked at the assumptions of psychology as a discipline which led to bias in both methods and question formulation and, thus, conclusions.

None of these areas were completely isolated from each other although, for the sake of clarity, they are discussed somewhat separately in this chapter. These areas were probably more distinct during the early stages of the field because most of us were engaged in challenging dominant paradigms. As the field has developed over the past twenty-five years, however, feminist assumptions have become less monolithic. The consequences of this sophistication have been a recognition of the interrelationships between areas of debate as well as more debates between feminist psychologists who hold different assumptions. The existence of such conflict may be viewed as problematic or as an opportunity for growth and the generation of new questions. Since I have learned never to expect closure, I find these debates exciting.

Charges of methodological bias

Concerns about methodological biases in psychology predated the existence of a formal field of the psychology of women. Rae Carlson (Carlson and Carlson, 1961) had, for example, raised early questions in the area in terms of the absence of women from personality research. These critiques were, however, scattered throughout the professional literature and generated little attention. Division 35's convention programs and, later, its journal became foci for such research and helped promote a critical mass of scholarship to which mainstream psychology was forced to attend.

I chaired a session entitled 'Sex difference or sex bias?' at the American Psychological Association in New Orleans in 1974 (the first year Division 35 had an official program at APA). It included presentations with titles such as 'Experimental design as a source of sex bias in social psychology' and 'Why researchers don't study women'. Both of these papers were later published and the article on bias in social psychology by Wendy McKenna and Suzanne Kessler (1977) was widely cited in later feminist critiques.

Division 35 provided a nucleus around which networks of individuals with similar interests began to form. These networks yielded participants for symposia who supported each other's work. For example, I organized and chaired two symposia for the Eastern Psychological Association in 1975 and 1977 entitled, respectively, 'Alternative methods for a feminist psychology' and 'Sex as a subject versus sex as a stimulus variable'. Similarly, Virginia O'Leary organized and chaired a symposium for the fifth annual research conference of AWP in 1978 entitled 'Feminist research: problems and prospects'. Many of the same people – primarily social psychologists – participated in these symposia.

Many of the papers in these symposia were eventually published in one form or another although not necessarily in journals. For example, Kathleen Grady's excellent and widely cited paper 'Androgyny reconsidered' (Grady, 1975) was published in a book of readings on the psychology of women edited by Juanita Williams (1979). Most of the 1978 symposium chaired by O'Leary became part of a special section of the *Psychology of Women Quarterly* that she edited in 1981. The paper contributed by Barbara Wallston to the symposium had developed into her presidential address to Division 35 (Wallston, 1981). This article continues to be cited because it ably addressed an issue that rarely concerns psychologists – how do we determine the questions about which we do research?

The titles of the papers in this special section are indicative of our fixation on methodology at that time. They included: 'Current methodological issues in paper-and-pencil measuring instruments' (Brannon, 1981); 'Sex bias in research design' (Grady, 1981); 'Appropriate control groups in feminist research' (Parlee, 1981); 'Sex as a social reality: field and laboratory research' (Unger, 1981).

My paper in this special section of *PWQ* anticipated my later interest in social construction (see Chapter 5). It addressed the question of why sex-related effects have a 'now you see them, now you don't' quality. I was particularly interested in the problem of unobtrusive methodology and the nature of gender-role demands. I had also begun to address the question of how our methodology predetermines our findings.

In this article I argued for a plurality of methodologies.

> The statement that results vary with the method used does not imply that any one method is better than any other. With respect to sex as a variable, there is no good reason to suggest that laboratory studies will produce more "real" or "better" effects than field studies (or vice versa for that matter). Exemplars of findings using various methodologies will be discussed. It is important to keep in mind that the inconsistency of sex-related effects does not occur at random.
>
> In general, it appears that sex of subject effects are found more frequently in field as opposed to laboratory studies. There are several alternative explanations for this phenomenon. Those who strongly support laboratory research might suggest that the numerous effects are due to lack of control in field research. Confounding variables such as differential attractiveness or status could account for many of the sex different effects found in the field. One might also suggest that the larger number of effects in the field is due to the lack of awareness of the participants that they are being observed. Sex-related effects are especially likely to be influenced by concern with societal norms or social desirability. It has also been suggested (Eagly, 1978) that the laboratory situation actually minimizes the extent to which sex roles operate by creating a "norm" of social objectivity. In the laboratory people are neither male nor female – they are subjects. It is likely that all of these factors operate at one time or another.
>
> Every methodology probably contributes its own source of bias. Thus, every methodology produces a different set of answers. It is necessary to identify the implications of each form for the analysis of the phenomena in which we are interested. The acceptance of such a multi-method approach requires that we accept that validity can take many forms. While sex-related effects found in the field are more likely to exist in other situations (external validity) we can be less sure that they are sex-related than when they are examined in the laboratory (internal validity). (Unger, 1981, pp. 646–647)

The paper that I had presented at the 1977 symposium at EPA entitled 'The rediscovery of gender' was considerably more sophisticated in its analysis of the relationship between assumptions and findings. It was very well received at the convention and many people urged me to publish it. There were, however, few places to publish theoretical papers, especially feminist ones. The major outlet was the *American Psychologist*, with a 95 percent rejection rate. Therefore, I submitted the paper there with little expectation that it would be accepted.

Surprisingly, the paper was not rejected outright. I received a rather sympathetic letter from an editor suggesting that although there were some good ideas in it, some reviewers had found it to be too 'polemical'. He suggested that I could 'tone the paper down somewhat and resubmit it'. I did so and it was published (Unger,

1979b) with a different title 'Toward a redefinition of sex and gender'. (See Reading 3 at the end of this chapter.)

Toward a redefinition

I re-examined the original paper recently to determine how much I had 'sold out' for this prestigious publication. I found I had eliminated a few of my best 'one-liners' such as the one in which I discussed the penis as a basis for sexual categorization. My comment: 'Like the "single black gene", a little bit of penis goes a long way' (p. 2 of Unger, 1977, unpublished ms) did not appear in the published paper.

I was able, however, to deconstruct some of the assumptions that underlie our terminology about sex and to introduce the word 'gender' into psychological discourse as a more neutral term. I was also able to raise some arguments about why studying sex 'differences' was not useful for psychology and to suggest that within-sex analyses and research on sex as a stimulus rather than a subject variable might be more worthwhile ways to proceed. Unfortunately, I did have to remove a final section entitled 'The scientific value of advocacy'. I am glad to be able to replace it here:

> My last point leads to a consideration of the scientific value of advocacy. Male and female psychologists alike would have remained unaware of the stimulus effects of sex if it had not been for the consciousness-raising effects of the new feminism. Sex as a stimulus variable is a pervasive aspect of our culture – so universal we do not even notice that it is there. Feminism led social scientists to pay new attention to sex as a variable and since the most obvious targets of sexism are women, women as researchers and women as the subject of research have been the most obvious result. Nevertheless, feminism, sexism, and the psychology of women are by no means identical.
>
> Feminism represents a wide spectrum of ideological beliefs about sex role equality, the place of women in society, change in societal structures relating to marriage, child-rearing, etc. Sexism implies a statement about the mistreatment of a particular group – females – because of their group membership. Those who study the psychology of women are usually concerned with the stimulus functions of sex. Gender may be defined as the responses learned as a function of these stimulus properties. Those who study gender may be male or female, they may use male or female subjects, and they may or may not be feminists. Being in possession of a political position does not mean that one cannot do objective research, particularly if one is aware of one's "bias." In fact, many issues relating to gender have been obscured by a covert "masculinist" bias in social science.
>
> A feminist position in research reflects a concern about the societal implications of one's work. It is not necessary to distort one's data –

sexist effects are widespread and easy to measure. In fact, the greatest difficulty in the area may be to get beyond the relatively obvious demonstrations of individual and societal sexism. Feminist psychology also implies a commitment to theoretical reorganization of the field to explore relationships relevant to both sexes which have been obscured by the limitation of research to just one. Sex, not the sexes, should be an object of study. And, as the field discovers gender, we may say as was supposedly said by an African politician discussing Livingstone's alleged discovery of Lake Nyasa: "That's funny, we knew it was there all along." (Unger, 1977, p. 14 of unpublished manuscript)

In retrospect, these comments do not appear to be particularly radical. However, claiming a feminist identity still makes one scientifically suspect and this twenty-year-old call for reorganization of the field does not, unfortunately, appear out of date either.

This paper was part of a torrent of criticism of traditional psychology that emerged in the late 1970s. Four presidential addresses to Division 35 in a row addressed similar methodological/conceptual issues (Wallston, 1981; Sherif, 1982; Unger, 1983; Wittig, 1985). Of course, they drew upon one another as well as upon other sources.

Ongoing dilemmas for feminist empiricists

The relationship between feminist and mainstream psychology

Our organizational alliances facilitated scholarly collaboration. For example, Barbara Wallston, Virginia O'Leary, and I had met through our activities within Division 35. We became friends and collaborators on a number of scholarly projects. We coedited two issues of a newsletter of the Society for the Advancement of Social Psychology on women, gender, and social psychology (in 1978 and 1979). This later became a book with the same name (O'Leary, Unger and Wallston, 1985), which was dedicated to Carolyn Sherif who had participated in the newsletter project, but died while the book was being written. One of our aims was to persuade mainstream social psychologists that the study of women and gender was a legitimate field of inquiry. Thus, we invited a number of contributors to write papers that made use of both traditional methodology and a feminist analysis.

We did not anticipate that virtually everyone we invited to participate would agree to do so. The book combined articles by people who were not part of our usual feminist network within psychology with articles by those who were. Authors discussed contextual aspects of sex-related differences in such traditional areas of social psychology as achievement motivation (Joseph Veroff); masculinity/

femininity (Janet Spence); aggression (Jacqueline Macaulay – a founder of AWP who was about to leave psychology for law); influenceability (Alice Eagly); and small group behavior (Kenneth Dion).

Less traditional chapters on theories of equity and justice and on women and men in love were written by Arnold Kahn and William Gaeddert and by Anne Peplau and Steve Gordon, respectively. Virginia O'Leary coauthored a chapter on sex-determined attributions and I collaborated on a chapter on sex-related effects in helping with Jane Piliavin. She supplied the more traditional social psychological material whereas I was more aware of the literature on women and gender. Although Piliavin had long been associated with 'mainstream' social psychology and I had had no formal training in the area, it was an extremely easy collaboration with surprisingly little disagreement about our conclusions. We both recognized that the social context made a difference in this area too.

Barbara Wallston and Kathy Grady (1985) integrated the scholarship about methodological bias in the book's opening chapter entitled 'Synthesizing the feminist critique'. If one uses citation as a criterion, this chapter had considerable impact upon thinking in social psychology. It is still cited even though most social psychologists tend to believe that anything written more than ten years ago is 'too old'.

At the same time, other feminists were producing guidelines for nonsexist research for the field as a whole (McHugh, Koeske and Frieze, 1986). These guidelines were largely the product of a task force that had been commissioned by Division 35. Another set of guidelines was produced by an APA task force somewhat later (Denmark et al., 1988). Still another reflection on methodological issues has been published recently (Rabinowitz and Sechzer, 1993).

All of this critique has had little impact on the way psychological research is done, although gender is now a 'respectable' area for social psychologists in the USA. There is even a lengthy chapter on gender in the most recent edition of the *Handbook of Social Psychology* (Deaux and LaFrance, 1998), but this chapter does not discuss many methodological innovations. It also contains few citations to the work of the social psychologists who contributed to our book.[1] It does, however, include several areas of research that concern feminist psychologists such as employment discrimination and sexual harassment, but without their emphasis on the need for social change.

Methodological critique within feminist psychology has changed over time. Some scholars are interested in the question of whether or not there is such a thing as a feminist method (Peplau and

Conrad, 1989). Others question whether it is possible to improve psychological methodology. They emphasize the inherent bias in every kind of methodology (Hare-Mustin and Marecek, 1988). Other feminist psychologists have moved away from traditional disciplinary concerns in order to respond to the postmodernist critique of any kind of quantitative methodology, its stress on subjectivity, and its disdain for our concerns about evaluation and validity. Yet others (Weisstein, 1993) ask whether postmodern relativism weakens the impetus for social change. It should be no surprise that students just beginning to study the psychology of women confess to deep confusion about their disciplinary allegiances and about what and whom to criticize.

Sex differences
The ongoing debate within the psychology of women about the issue of sex differences illustrates another of the subdiscipline's dilemmas. Differing feminist epistemologies determine which methods are valued and, thus, what evidence is accepted in this area. The current discussion of sex differences[2] was largely instigated by the publication of a book by Eleanor Maccoby and Carol Jacklin (1974) entitled *The Psychology of Sex Differences*. The title was a little misleading since it dealt largely with the psychological literature on sex differences in children. Nevertheless, the conclusions of this important book (considered a citation 'classic') have been frequently cited as well as misstated and misinterpreted.

Maccoby and Jacklin aimed to examine the question of whether the many sex differences purported to exist could actually be documented in the professional literature. They collected as many studies on various sex differences as they could find; classified them as to the behavior being measured; and noted how many significant differences between the sexes had been found and the directionality of such differences. This technique has become known as a narrative review.

As probably everyone who is interested in sex and gender already knows, they found that only four behavioral differences between females and males could be consistently documented. This conclusion was not, however, the same as saying that there were no other sex differences. It meant that if other sex-related differences existed, they were inconsistent and/or dependent on factors other than simply the subject's sex.

Researchers such as Jeanne Block (1976) immediately pointed out some of the problems in drawing conclusions about the non-existence of sex differences. She noted, for example, that the number of significant differences between the sexes increased as the age of the population studied rose from early infancy through adolescence. She also noted that the number of significant sex differences found increased as the size of the sample grew bigger. Her conclusion that a lot of sex differences are small in size is one that is still generally accepted today, although arguments continue about the importance of these differences (cf. Eagly, 1993).

Maccoby and Jacklin's study has become a fundamental part of US psychology. It is cited in virtually every introductory psychology textbook. Interestingly, however, it is the relatively small number of consistent sex differences that are highlighted in these texts rather than the much larger number of inconsistent findings. Sex differences are stressed rather than sex similarities (Unger, 1979b). Moreover, few of these texts go on to consider what factors might help to explain inconsistencies in these findings. In other words, few of them move from description to explanation.

The debate about the number and meaning of sex differences continues to rage today. The methodology used to determine whether such differences exist has become much more sophisticated (cf. Eagly, 1987 or Hyde and Linn, 1986 on meta-analysis). However, major unresolved conceptual questions remain. How big a difference is a meaningful one? How generalizable across contexts must the effect be in order to be considered a sex-related difference? Different positions on these two questions are characteristic of those feminist scholars who do or do not believe that 'real' sex differences exist.

Both the *American Psychologist* and *Feminism & Psychology* devoted special sections on sex differences in which a number of recognized experts argued a variety of positions on this issue. The *American Psychologist* discussions were initiated by Alice Eagly (1994, 1995), who argued that sex-related differences are less inconsistent and more important than most feminist psychologists believe them to be. Some of the same feminist psychologists (Hyde and Marecek) have taken issue with some aspects of her argument in both venues.

What I find more interesting, however, is the difference in the range of positions that anchor the articles in each publication. Thus, the *American Psychologist* special feature includes an article by David Buss (1995) which argues for an evolutionary basis for sex differences. The most socially constructionist argument in the issue is offered by Jeanne Marecek (1995).

In contrast, although the special feature in *Feminism & Psychology* includes articles which argue that feminists must reconsider their position on sex differences (Eagly, 1994; Halpern, 1994; Hyde, 1994), none of these papers argues a biologically determinist position. Instead, they argue that feminists must remain in this debate in order to have power over what is said. This feature is anchored in an article by Wendy Hollway (1994) entitled 'Beyond sex differences'. Hollway takes a postmodern position, arguing against dualisms and questioning the categories used for analysis. It is unlikely that such a paper would be published in the *American Psychologist*. Thus, only one extreme position in this debate is readily available to a US mainstream psychological audience.

These debates reveal a range of feminist positions. As Celia Kitzinger (1994) eloquently notes in her introduction to the special feature in *Feminism & Psychology*, this argument is about much more than methodology:

> The discussions here are, however, richer and more varied than might be suggested by this simplistic "pro" and "anti" dichotomy. The arguments of all the contributors are informed by their (explicit or implicit) theories about other key concerns of feminist psychology: the nature of women's oppression; the relevance of psychoanalytic, biological, and social explanations of, and challenges to, that oppression; the nature of science and the social constructionalist/essentialist debate; and the effects and implications of feminist intervention in social science research. Disagreement and agreement about many of these issues cuts across the "pro" and "anti" sex differences divide. (Kitzinger, 1994, p. 503)

As I have stated before, I do not believe the question of whether sex differences exist is a feminist question. However, I have, like many other feminist psychologists, written about the issue because it is difficult to ignore. My position at the moment (which could change) is that some behavioral differences between the sexes can be consistently measured, but I believe that these differences are small and very context bound. I define context in much broader terms than is usual in social psychology – in terms of cultural variables as well as the particular features of the social transaction. The title of an article 'Will the "real" sex difference please stand up?', which I wrote for *Feminism & Psychology* several years before the current debate, reflects these views (Unger, 1992).

These views were developed during a year of doing social psychological research in a very different culture – Israel. I had found in my research that although secular women had a different world view than secular men, there was no such difference in the world views of religious women and men. In fact, religious women's beliefs were more similar to those of secular men than secular women. Thus, groups of women could be as different from each other as groups of women were from men. These findings depended on what other variables were linked to sex. I used these data to argue that feminist researchers need to move beyond 'merely' examining sex.

The distinction between sex and gender

I am frequently given credit for introducing the distinction between sex and gender to psychology (Unger, 1979c). However, I do not consider citation prima facie evidence of importance or impact because my article on this topic is frequently cited for what I consider to be the 'wrong' reasons. Most people who cite it do so because of its attempt to introduce terminological clarity into the field. However, my efforts do not appear to have succeeded. Citations usually appear at the beginning of a book or article that then goes on to state that the author does not plan to use the distinction between sex and gender because it is not used consistently within the field. My arguments against sex difference research are usually ignored although I believe that these were the most important part of the paper.

I also do not believe that the distinction between sex and gender is either as clear or as useful today as it was when I wrote about it in 1979. At that time, I believed that terminological clarity could help us resolve conceptual confusion. As Kay Deaux (1993) has noted, however, what we call 'sex' and what we call 'gender' are based on implicit assumptions about causality. I now believe that our terminological confusions probably cannot be resolved until we come to grips with our nonconscious assumptions about sources of causality (see Chapter 5).

The difficulty of introducing disciplinary change was made very clear to me by an incident which provoked published comments by both Kay Deaux (1993) and Mary Crawford and me (Unger and Crawford, 1993). *Psychological Science*, a relatively new journal published by the American Psychological Society (a group that is primarily experimental in focus which has broken away from APA), decided to print an article about the distinctions between sex and gender by an author who has no credentials in the field (Gentile, 1993). I do not know why they made this decision to publish this article at this time, nor what led one of the consulting editors, Janet Spence, to seek comments on it. We agreed to write the commentary (as did Deaux) because we wanted to 'set the record straight'.

Despite the fact that there had been much discussion in the psychology of women about the distinction between sex and gender, Gentile cited only three references: the *Oxford English Dictionary*, an article by William Safire in the *New York Times*, and an article from the *Minnesota Daily*. This was masculine hegemony at its worst.

In our necessarily brief rejoinder, we tried to trace the history of the dialogue and feminist contributions to it. We also tried to show that this was an argument about causality rather than about terminology. Deaux made the point more wittily when she suggested in her title that Gentile's call for a five-fold distinction was a 'wrong number'. This may seem like a trivial incident, but it shows how feminist contributions to psychology can be ignored and erased. Feminist psychology was so invisible to the elite editors of this journal when they accepted Gentile's article that they were not aware of its poor scholarship, which ignored over twenty years of research published in refereed journals.

As I have stated repeatedly in this chapter and elsewhere, controversies about sex and gender are controversies over what is assumed to produce a particular sex- or gender-related behavior. Most often, such arguments have a covert 'nature–nurture' component. Our positions on biological and environmental or situational variables are usually covert because we have been taught to say that all behaviors are the result of a complex mixture of interactions. In practice, however, most psychologists lean toward either the biological or the environmental side of the equation. There is little contact between networks of individuals who hold differing assumptions.

Assumptions about biological versus environmental causality of sex and/or gender differences are also closely associated within psychology with beliefs about the degree of similarity or difference between the sexes. Not surprisingly, minimalists tend to stress current situational and contextual cues for behavior, whereas maximalists tend to stress either genetic or other biological factors or early differences in gender socialization. Minimalists also stress the degree that the sexes overlap, whereas maximalists see maleness and femaleness as more exclusive categories. Both positions can be found within the feminist psychologist community.

In the conclusion to their introductory chapter of their edited book *Making a Difference*, Rachel Hare-Mustin and Jeanne Marecek (1990) pointed out that both the maximalist and minimalist positions have major flaws. They attempted to transcend the terms of this debate. Borrowing heavily from postmodernist and deconstructionist theories about the construction of knowledge, they argued there is no one 'right' view of gender, but various views that lead to certain paradoxes:

> The meaning of gender as male–female difference presents us with paradoxes. Whether such representations of gender emphasize difference or minimize it, they are fraught with logical contradictions and hidden meanings. The representation of gender as male–female difference

obscures and marginalizes the inter-relatedness and commonalities of women and men. It also obscures institutional sexism and the extent of male authority. (Hare-Mustin and Marecek, 1990, pp. 53–54)

They also argued that focusing on gender similarities could have negative consequences as well. For example, this position ignores women's special needs in terms of child bearing and child rearing. Treating men and women as though they are equal is not always equitable. As a case in point, they cited the dire economic consequences for women of 'no fault' divorce.

When life experiences, training, and institutionalized sexism have produced major inequities between women and men, efforts to achieve formal equality may inadvertently make matters worse. Psychologists have come late to their recognition of the importance of the past and present societal context. Jo Freeman (1975), a political scientist, was an early proponent of the dangers produced by ignoring our past. I have often used her term 'the tyranny of structurelessness' to explain why 'identical' environments are not always the same for women and men. Apparent systemic equality will not produce the same outcomes if the individuals involved have had different socialization experiences prior to their contact with the social system (cf. Unger and Saundra, 1993). But marginalized individuals are often unaware of the impact of either past or current systems upon them.

Assumptions about sameness can have very negative consequences for women. For example, I was once refused tenure because of relatively low student evaluations. After I relocated to Montclair State I decided to take a look at biases in the teacher evaluation process. I examined 'real' faculty evaluations at Montclair which were coded so I did not know the names of the faculty members being evaluated. I found that although the average teaching evaluation was the same for both sexes, women faculty were penalized by students for having high standards, although such standards had no impact on the evaluations of men (Unger, 1979a). The instrument and the circumstances were apparently equivalent, but they did not allow for the sexism of students who seemed to punish women faculty for their demandingness and presumed lack of nurturant qualities.

This study illustrates the way in which quantitative methodology can be used to reveal subtle biases in apparently equal situations. The students' biases were a reflection of implicit assumptions of both women and men about the connection between sex and gender. Women faculty were penalized for traits and behaviors prescribed as undesirable in them which were seen as neutral for men in an equivalent role. In some ways the study foreshadowed some of my ideas about the social construction of gender – especially the idea that behaviors do not have meaning independent of their societal context.

Confounds between 'science' and politics

Questions about sex differences do not go away because they are tied to a number of covert political agendas. Some feminist psychologists such as Stephanie Shields (1975a, b) recognized early that sex difference research had never been politically neutral. Her papers, which were published in the *American Psychologist*, were both intelligent and passionate. They have, deservedly, been reprinted a number of times. I drew on them extensively for my own discussions of these issues. I still find it amazing that such sophisticated and conceptually rich papers were written when Shields was still a graduate student at Penn State. They were developed for a seminar with Carolyn Sherif who encouraged her to publish them.

Other scholars, both within and outside psychology, have documented the covert political agendas in sex difference research (cf. Rosenberg, 1982; Lewin, 1984). The paper that probably inspired most of us in this area was written by Carolyn Sherif (1979). It was read eagerly and cited extensively, despite the fact that it was published in a university press book (Sherman and Beck, 1979) that soon went out of print. Fortunately, it has been reprinted a number of times – most recently in *Feminism & Psychology* in 1998.

Sherif's article was rather long, but spiced by her incisive and witty writing style. She had the seniority and willingness to censure the field without the circumlocutions to which some of the rest of us resorted. At the very beginning of this article she stated, for example, that she had long ago been convinced that, 'the orthodox methods of studying and interpreting sex differences were capable of delivering only mischievous and misleading trivia' (p. 93). She explored such areas as hierarchy in psychology, 'objective' language as a disguise for ignorance or bias, and research as an interpersonal and cultural event. My favorite part of this article is her short course on how to perpetuate social myth:

> The lesson for those who want to perpetuate sex bias in psychological research is clear: Restrict the framework for study to a narrow span of time. Attend only to what you decide is important, ignoring as much else as possible. Label these important aspects in the language of "variables," both to sound objective and to mask your ignorance. Arrange the research situation as you choose. If you are biased, the situation will be. Record your selectively chosen data and discuss them as though dealing with eternal verities.

If anyone tries to refer to historical, cultural, or organizational circumstances outside of your own narrow framework, either (1) derogate such talk as referring to "soft" facts and "soft" disciplines which you see of being of little relevance to your carefully controlled variables and findings; or (2) suggest that everyone has different interests and yours happens to be in psychology, whatever its limitations, not in history, culture, etc. In either case, you will have removed the most effective and, ultimately, the only effective means by which your critic can expose your bias and show what you have done wrong. You will have put the critic in the position either of confining the discussion to your limited framework, or of going out to do another study to show that your research does not hold up – that it cannot be replicated or that it crumbles when another variable is introduced. (Sherif, 1979, pp. 107–108)

She pointed out that these procedures were exactly what happened over and over again in psychology, especially in areas where bias had been charged. She also gave examples of how hypotheses about sex differences change from behaviors to attitudes whenever behavioral research does not confirm psychologists' theories.

Carolyn Sherif had been a social psychologist for many years when she wrote this paper. Her husband, Muzafer Sherif (whom she married as a young graduate student) had been one of the founders of the field. By the time she wrote this paper, however, she was bitterly disappointed at the directions the field had taken. She felt that it had become a model-driven, laboratory science with little concern for or applicability to real-world problems. She did not believe that traditional social psychology would change (thus, she thought our book trying to reconcile social psychology with new views about gender was a waste of effort). She poured her energies into the emerging field of feminist psychology.

As the comments written for a recent reappraisal of 'Bias in psychology' (cf. Unger and Kahn, 1998) indicate, she had a great impact on a number of major contributors to the field. She certainly had a great influence on me. My presidential address for Division 35 was a response to her article on bias in psychology. In it, I tried to extend some of her ideas in terms of the relationship between methodology and models of reality (Unger, 1983). There seems to have been a direct, albeit unacknowledged, conceptual connection between Weisstein's (1968) influential early paper, Sherif's bias chapter, and my own article in this area. I find it interesting that Janis Bohan (1992) reprinted these three papers in that order in her book of readings on the historical development of feminist theory in psychology.

I was on sabbatical the year I wrote this paper. Since our children were ten and twelve at the time, I did not feel it was a good time either to uproot them or leave them for a visiting position somewhere else. So I compromised and accepted a visiting fellow position at the Center for the Study of Women and Gender at the Graduate Center of the City University of New York – an easy half hour bus ride from my home. Like most other positions of this sort it was unpaid, but did give me access to a desk, a good library, and several interesting people with whom to talk about my work. I spent much of this year doing library research and developing ideas for my address while, of course, working on organizational matters for the division.

I know now that many presidential addresses are ceremonial in nature (although this has not been true in Division 35). But I took the responsibility very seriously and wanted to say something that I believed to be important for the field. The talk was well received although, as usual, I tried to pack too many ideas into a relatively short speech. The published paper obtained several commendations, including a distinguished publication award from AWP (as had Sherif's bias chapter) and the label of the longest title in feminist psychology. (See Reading 4 at the end of this chapter.)

This paper (Unger, 1983) could be discussed in Chapter 5 since it concerned the relationship between our methods of inquiry and our assumptions about how the world works and how science should be conducted. Because I had time to do more varied reading than usual, the work was informed by scholarship from the sociology and philosophy of science. I include it here because I do not believe we can separate method from theory and that psychologists' attempts to do so have led us to ask overly simplistic questions. The psychology of women is not exempt from this practice. Our inability to avoid either 'sex differences' or 'sex versus gender' debates for very long is evidence of our complicity.

The social construction of gender

Jeanne Marecek and Rachel Hare-Mustin have been dedicated to changing the terms of the debate about difference. They organized a symposium entitled 'The future of difference' for the 1987 meeting of the American Psychological Association in New York City. This included presentations by Bernice Lott, Jill Morawski and myself, as well as the presentation by Hare-Mustin and Marecek that would become the *American Psychologist* article just discussed. These papers all became part of a book edited by Hare-Mustin and Marecek (1990). Parts of my chapter in this book are reproduced in Reading 5 at the end of this chapter.

In this chapter (Unger, 1990) I recapitulated some of the arguments against the study of sex differences that I had made more than ten years previously in my *American Psychologist* article. I noted that these criticisms still applied. I also recapitulated my discussion of the terminological and conceptual issues surrounding the terms sex and gender.

The more innovative parts of the chapter began with a discussion of the conceptual problems associated with meta-analysis (the method that has replaced narrative review as a way of examining sex differences). I also discussed the concept of 'doing gender' (a term borrowed from the work of West and Zimmerman, 1987) and attempted to translate its sociological framework into a language that I believed would be useful to psychologists.

I was particularly interested in showing how empirical research by traditional social psychologists could illuminate the social construction of gender. Thus, I discussed a number of laboratory studies that demonstrated the impact of the sex composition of the other people in one's environment and the potent effect on people's behavior of other people's beliefs about them (the so-called self-fulfilling prophecy). I argued that gender could be viewed as a 'verb' rather than a 'noun'. Accordingly, persons of either sex could be made to behave in a 'gendered' manner if expectations about them could be manipulated effectively. Most of such manipulations must, of course, be carried out when people are not face to face with each other. A person's sex is probably the single most salient characteristic he or she possesses and is not easily ignored. This argument is, of course, related to earlier feminist concerns with sex as a stimulus variable discussed earlier.

In this chapter I also discussed the way in which scholarship has created perniciously dichotomous views of gender by ignoring historical, cultural, and cross-ethnic analyses of the properties of women and men. In addition, I tried to show that the construction of reality was not a 'feminist plot' to destroy empirical psychology. I argued that constructionist processes could be found at many levels of psychology. As evidence, I drew upon some of Naomi Weisstein's innovative work on the construction of perceptual 'reality' (Weisstein, 1970; Wong and Weisstein, 1982). Finally, I called upon feminists to conduct a multitude of comparisons to combat what I saw as the dangers of a 'radical relativism' – one that destroys the evidential bases for meaningful socially activist research.

Despite my concerns about 'radical relativism', my position on this issue has been misunderstood. Like other social constructionists, I have been accused of trying to ignore reality. Perhaps the problem lies in my final paragraph:

I have always been struck by the large number of feminist articles and books that include in their titles references to mirrors, prisms, lenses, looking glasses, and so forth. At some level we have all been aware that reality is reflected in a variety of ways. The sexes will be as different or as similar as we want them to be. Knowledge exists only as the product of the questions asked. Multiple perspectives will produce multiple answers. One of our basic tasks is to make sure that the answers we get and use are not based on the values and self-interest of any single component of society – even ourselves. It is not meaningful to ask: What are the **true** differences? They are all a result of smoke and mirrors. (Unger, 1990, pp. 142–143)

Misunderstanding in this area may be due to an unstated hierarchy of methodology. Quantitative methodology is seen to produce more objective and 'real' data than more qualitative approaches. I argued that different methods produce different answers, but no 'answer' is better than any other. One of the most important things feminists contribute to psychology is the disruption of the idea that our answers at any one time justify a single institutionalized perspective.

Debates within feminist psychology

Feminist psychology has been in existence over twenty years and has become an integral part of the psychological community in the USA. Some of the differences within the feminist community are being aired more publicly now. These differences have probably been around since the field's inception, but we have been unwilling to discuss most of them because they were seen as divisive and dangerous to the field's claims to scholarly legitimacy.

I have never been very comfortable with the idea of wallpapering over our differences because I am rather blunt in my discussions with others (Nancy Datan once suggested that good feminists were the products of improper socialization and claimed she had the political acumen of a fire hydrant). I also do not believe that scholarship has to be monolithic in order to be legitimate. There is an analogy which is sometimes made about feminist scholarship that it can be seen as being like an 'onion', whereas mainstream scholarship has a more 'artichoke' view of knowledge. One must peel an artichoke to get to its core which is surrounded by prickly and useless thistles. On the other hand, every part of an onion is valuable in itself. For me, this analogy means being willing to consider all positions as potentially useful. For example, *Feminist Social Psychologies* edited by Sue Wilkinson (1996) illustrates the wide range of positions available within the field.

Probably because of this viewpoint, I am welcome in most camps within feminist psychology, but do not consider myself to be completely part of any one of them. What are some of these camps? Our arguments about the existence and importance of sex differences continue. It is important to remember a belief in sex differences is not the same as a belief in women's inferiority. Feminist psychologists who truly believe in working for women's equality are on both sides of this issue.

Clinical/experimental differences
There are also splits within feminist psychology between those who do empirical research and those who wish to apply feminist principles to therapeutic issues. Some clinical perspectives are more compatible with postmodernist theories about the situated self which are popular among feminist theorists in other fields. Both Rachel Hare-Mustin and Jeanne Marecek are clinical psychologists, in contrast to many others writing about sex-related differences who are usually social or developmental psychologists.

However, some clinicians' positions are not at all compatible with postmodern fluidity. Some take an essentialist and maximalist position on sex differences. They look to the work of Jean Baker Miller (1976) or Carol Gilligan (1982) who have stressed the differing psychological agendas of women and men. Neither Miller nor Gilligan was trained in empirical psychological methodology. The former is a psychiatrist and the latter's degree is in education. Both have remained rather isolated from organized feminist psychology in the USA. Miller's work is primarily theoretical in nature. However, Gilligan's findings on the different voices of women and men have been subject to a good deal of research scrutiny. Feminist empiricists are usually critical of her findings (cf. Crawford and Unger, 1990; Crawford, 1995). Differing views about what constitutes validity and proof probably account for a lack of acceptance of this work by empirical psychologists in contrast to its considerable acclaim by the feminist community as a whole.

Because of their focus on the individual's life story, clinicians often have a different view about what constitute psychological 'data' than do so-called empirical feminist psychologists. They do not feel they have to answer the question of whether a particular woman's life story is representative of any general phenomenon or law. But their focus on the particular rather than the generalizable has also allowed some of them to be more aware of culturally diverse women than most empirical feminist psychologists.

Sisterhood and evaluation

There are also differences among feminist psychologists about what constitutes 'good' feminist work. We continue to conceal the fact that we make value judgments because the existence of evaluative criteria is potentially the most divisive of all our differences. Making judgments also appears to stab at the heart of feminism – the idea that we are all 'sisters'.

I admit also to evading questions about evaluative criteria. However, those involved in any sort of gatekeeping function within the profession have had to make such judgments. We make judgments not only when we referee articles, but also when we decide who we will invite to participate in a symposium that we are organizing or a book or journal issue that we are editing. We also make decisions about those invitations we will accept and those we will decline.

An educated look at the participants of symposia or lists of contributors to edited books or journal issues can be quite illuminating. However, I am willing to make only myself the victim of this kind of scrutiny. Since 1985 I have been the editor or coeditor of two books (O'Leary, Unger and Wallston, 1985; Unger, 1989a) and two journal issues – a special issue on sex, gender, and social change for *Sex Roles* (with Lisa Serbin) in 1986 and a special issue on gender and culture for the *Psychology of Women Quarterly* (with Janis Sanchez-Hucles) in 1993. These collaborations have crossed intradisciplinary lines (O'Leary and Wallston are/were social psychologists, Serbin is a developmental psychologist, and Sanchez-Hucles is a clinical psychologist). Some of the same contributors appear surprisingly often. These contributors are often those I have met through my organizational activities.

To be fair, such network connections are neither totally inclusive nor totally exclusive. Some people whose work I most admire are not particularly prolific as writers, had nothing available on a particular theme when I requested something from them, or were simply too busy with other projects to oblige me when I asked. Conversely, the same explanations apply to my own responses to other people's professional requests.

Most feminist editors, including myself, also attempt to solicit manuscripts from people outside our professional networks by formally and informally advertising the project ahead of time. In practice, relatively few 'new' people respond to our solicitations. We frequently have to work long and hard to convince colleagues that our book or journal issue will make an important contribution to the field. I have discussed this problem with other editors who have had similar experiences. We find them difficult to explain because, supposedly, there are lots of young scholars out there who need publications. Unfortunately, this dearth of volunteers has produced something of an 'old girl network' within feminist psychology, despite our persistent efforts to keep this from happening. For example, the special features on sex differences in the two journals discussed earlier included three of the same contributors (out of five papers in one journal and six in the other) despite the fact that one journal is considered mainstream and the other feminist; and one journal is US based whereas the other is international in focus. There may be other reasons for this overlap. Nevertheless, readers are left with the impression of relatively few 'authorities' in this area.

It is not easy for me to state what criteria one could use to define work that seems exciting or important. I am more comfortable with denotative definitions – pointing to what I consider to be exemplary material. I admit to a fondness for theoretical originality or interesting hypotheses and questions, even if the research appears to be less methodologically tight than some empiricists would prefer. Much of the work in *Representations: Social Constructions of Gender* (Unger, 1989a) had these qualities. Although I had sole editorial control over the contents of this book and the series in *Imagination, Cognition, and Personality* from which it derived, I have sometimes had to argue with more 'data-bound' colleagues to insure that some manuscripts I have liked were published. In at least one case, a paper for which I argued received an AWP distinguished publication award and has been reprinted in a number of anthologies.

I have thought long and hard as to whether I wish to include the issue of 'quality control' in this book. It is bound to be controversial. However, if the psychology of women is to progress further, it must go beyond the 'add women and stir' framework found in many empirical studies. Simply examining populations of women in terms of otherwise standardized psychological paradigms is not enough. This is one of the distinctions between the psychology of women and feminist psychology that we have also managed to avoid discussing.

Dealing with differences among ourselves
Why are we so willing to conceal differences between us? Distinctions of any kind are problematic because, at the same time, they reveal our need to have our achievements recognized and threaten our need to affiliate with others like ourselves. Competition remains a particularly thorny issue for feminists to deal with (cf. Keller and Moglen, 1987). No matter how much we might deny it, I think few of us would be willing to publish our papers anonymously.

Differences between us also provoke the fear of backlash. This is not paranoid fantasy. The US media have frequently used disagreements among feminists to delegitimize feminist conclusions. Susan Faludi (1991) has provided many examples of this kind of media treatment in her book *Backlash*.

How can we deal with differences among us? By using contradictions, of course. While I think postmodernist and deconstructionist theories pose many problems for psychologists (cf. Burman, 1990; Weisstein, 1993), they do offer us a way to encompass differing views. They become problematic only when we equate 'discourse' with 'truth' and stop trying to use psychological methods (no matter how flawed) to document injustices and change social systems.

Is social activism dead?

A final controversy involves the degree of progress we have made and the extent of social activism still present in the field. This is very much a function of each person's particular standpoint. I believe, however, that neither Division 35 nor AWP have been as involved in social action recently as they were in the past. A number of early feminists besides myself have expressed their concern with this drift away from social action. Interestingly, different scholars have made contradictory attributions to account for its diminishment. Martha Mednick (1989) and Arnie Kahn and Jan Yoder (1989), for example, blame it on an overidentification with psychology's traditional concerns with individualism. In contrast, Naomi Weisstein (1993) believes our relative passivity is due to overimmersion in the relativism of postmodern theory.

Both of these positions are probably partially correct, but I believe an additional factor that encourages passivity is the sheer size of the enterprise and the number of women currently involved in feminist scholarship. It is virtually impossible for all of us to know each other as was true in the 'bad old days'. It is also difficult to convince oneself that one can change the system, especially if the system sometimes seems to have moved little in the past twenty-five years.

Of course, change is relative, but even little victories should be savored. The following story provides an excellent example of just how useful feminist scholarship can be. Dafna Izraeli, an Israeli sociologist, contributed an article on the invisibility of women in Israel's major ethnographic museum to the special issue on women and culture that I coedited (Izraeli, 1993). Her findings were publicized in the Israeli and US news media and have provoked an outcry about the treatment of women there. The museum has since added more material about women to its exhibits.

Although it may be easier to translate academic data into social action in a small country, it should be possible elsewhere as well. We need to broaden our criteria for publication in feminist books and journals to take into account the potential applicability of scholarship. The problem of 'Why are you asking this question?' needs to be extended beyond the introduction and literature review in our papers. Again, identification with a community of women may be helpful here since it helps us to recognize that the production of knowledge is not just for ourselves.

Notes

1   Alice Eagly and Janet Spence are notable exceptions probably because they continue to conduct laboratory-based quantitative research.
2   As historians have indicated, earlier discussions have occurred, see, for example, Russett, 1989; Shields, 1975a.

Reading 3

Toward a redefinition of sex and gender (Unger, 1979c)

Although the study of sex differences has been with us for many years, only recently has anyone paid serious attention to what is being studied. The question of what is being studied would be of only academic interest except for the political and social implications of the results of research in this area. Although researchers have usually had neither the interest nor the confidence to use sex as a major (or the only) variable (Grady, 1979), a body of findings has accumulated that relates sex tangentially to every conceivable phenomenon. Such sex differences are usually discussed briefly if they are found and are dismissed (often unnoted) if they are not. There is no parallel field of sex similarities integrating the numerous studies in which no difference between males and females has been found.

As with another organismic variable, race, it is by no means clear just what is meant by the term *sex*. Psychologists have tended to use the term interchangeably as both an independent and a dependent variable (Unger & Denmark, 1975). As the former, it is implied that sex is built into the organism by chromosomes, genes, and hormones. As the latter, it is assumed that sex is derived (except for physical structure) from the individual's postnatal experiences as defined by the socio-cultural matrix. Those who consider sex as a mainly biological variable tend to assume that psychological differences between males and females are the result of sex. Those who consider sex as a mostly social phenomenon tend to assume that the sex of males and females is a result of their different experience. It appears, therefore, that a reconsideration of terminology in this area would assist conceptualization here.

It is important to reconsider not only what is meant by the term *sex* but also what is meant by the term *sex differences*. If fewer and fewer sex differences can be unequivocally demonstrated, which seems to be the conclusion of an important book by Maccoby and Jacklin (1974), will the area cease to be an interesting one? This question relates to another that is equally difficult to answer: What is the relationship between the psychology of sex differences and the psychology of gender? Since there now exist a number of psychologists who stress that they study one or the other to the relative exclusion of the seemingly related field, this question, too, appears to be of more than academic interest.

A major problem in this area appears to be the too inclusive use of the term *sex*. In various contexts, *sex* can be used to describe the chromosomal composition of individuals, the reproductive apparatus and secondary characteristics that are usually associated with these chromosomal differences, the intrapsychic characteristics presumed to be possessed by males and females, and in the case of sex roles, any and all behaviors differentially expected for and appropriate to people on the basis of membership in these various sexual categories. It is the contention of this article that many issues can be resolved and more fruitful questions generated by reevaluating some of the ways that psychologists have defined the terms frequently used in this area.

Some definitions of terms

Sex as a subject variable
One of the reasons for the apparent confusion between the biological and social properties of sex is that psychology has

traditionally viewed sex in terms of individual differences. The most common methods of study were either self-reports of personality characteristics or preferred behaviors, or observations of subject differences in a variety of experimental contexts. Sex differences, however, often appear inconsistently. Some of the variables that affect whether or not subject sex differences are found include the size of the sample, the age of the subjects (Block, 1976), the social class and/or the culture of the subjects (Nadelman, 1974), and the sex of the experimenters (Holmes & Jorgenson, 1971). In fact, female experimenters have been found to be more likely to look for, or at least publish, a given sex difference than are males (McKenna & Kessler, 1977). A variable with this much variability would seem to be an unlikely candidate for one with much biological basis.

Sex as a stimulus variable
There appear to be two kinds of sex differences: one located within the individual and one existing within other persons with whom the individual interacts. The latter kind of sex difference may be termed a *stimulus sex difference* (Grady, 1979). In many of the areas in which hypothesized subject sex differences have not been substantiated by empirical research, stimulus sex differences have been found (O'Leary, 1977). In fact, men and women are especially alike in their beliefs about their own differences. To the extent that males and females share expectations regarding intrapsychic and behavioral differences between the sexes, the expression of such differences constitutes a sex similarity.

Gender
The term *gender* may be used to describe those nonphysiological components of sex that are culturally regarded as appropriate to males or to females. *Gender* may be used for those traits for which sex acts as a stimulus variable, independently of whether those traits have their origin within the subject or not. It refers to a social label by which we distinguish two groups of people. There is evidence that various components of gender-based categories are learned relatively independently of the biological information that underlies them. Thus, 2-year-olds can reliably sort photographs into male and female categories, but they are unable to sort their own pictures consistently in accordance with sex or to answer

correctly traditional direct questions about their sex classification (Thompson, 1975).

The use of the term *gender* serves to reduce assumed parallels between biological and psychological sex or at least to make explicit any assumptions of such parallels. *Gender* may be broadened to include both attributions made by others and assumptions and suppositions about one's own properties (gender identity). Societies prescribe particular characteristics for males and females on the basis of assigned sex (Vaughter, 1976). Indeed, such masculine or feminine qualities may even be assigned to inanimate objects on the basis of their designated sex (Tobach, 1971). Gender identity refers to those characteristics an individual develops and internalizes in response to the stimulus functions of biological sex. As such, gender identity may be a more important predictor of behavior than is biological sex. These distinctions have not been made, however, because psychologists have traditionally assumed a close correspondence between maleness and masculinity and femaleness and femininity. This assumption is now being questioned.

Physiologically, there is some suggestion that even the dichotomy between maleness and femaleness may not be as distinct as was once believed. For example, Money's extensive studies of humans with discrepancies among chromosomal, hormonal, and morphological indicators of sex suggest that the degree of correlation among such indicators may be lower than was previously suspected (Money & Ehrhardt, 1972). Despite the evidence of a large number of people with ambiguous sexual identities, investigators of psychosexual identification have been unwilling to tolerate the presence of more than two categories – male and female. This two-category system is most commonly based on the presence or absence of anything that can be defined as a penis. If a penis is present, most people categorize the individual as a male, even in the presence of such contradictory evidence as breasts or feminine hips (Kessler & McKenna, 1978).

The study of sex differences

Historical considerations
Despite evidence that biological sex is not an either–or category and the lack of clarity regarding biologists' definition

of sex, psychologists do believe that sex differences exist. Stephanie Shields (1975a) traced the history of the study of sex differences by psychologists from the mid-19th century and found that this field has never been completely free of social bias. Thus, we were told, apparent structural differences in the brains of females and males implied differences in their intelligence and temperament; hypothetically greater male variability in traits, which related to intellectuality and creativity, had implications for different educational and social structures; and assumptions about a "unique female nature" produced such psychological realities as the maternal instinct and female sexual passivity. As Shields noted, "When issues faded in importance, it was not because they were resolved but because they ceased to serve as viable scientific 'myths' in the changing social and scientific milieu" (p. 740).

Following her line of reasoning, it is plausible to suggest that issues involving sex differences cannot be resolved. Shields, for example, noted that when it was believed that the frontal lobe was the repository of the higher mental capacities, the male frontal lobes were seen as larger. When the parietal lobes came to be seen as more important, a bit of historical revisionism took place. Females were now seen as having equal or larger frontal lobes than males, but smaller parietal lobes. Widespread beliefs about sex differences in brain weight, brain contours, perceptual motor abilities, emotionality, and intelligence were prevalent during the 19th and early 20th century. Shields (1975b) pointed out that Leta Hollingworth and Helen Montague laboriously examined the hospital records of 2,000 neonates (1,000 of each sex) for birth weight and length in order to test the hypothesis of greater male variability. Other early feminist psychologists struggled to validate empirically beliefs about greater male variability in more psychological characteristics, such as intelligence or emotionality. Despite this amount of effort, few if any differences were found.

When an assumed sex difference is investigated and found to be nonexistent, the argument simply shifts to another ground. This leads to a question the understanding and answering of which is central to the whole area of sex and gender. What does finding a given sex difference in behaviour tell us? What are the mechanisms that produce such differences?

Maccoby and Jacklin (1974) provided an interesting point in this regard:

We invite the reader to imagine a situation in which all psychological researchers routinely divide their subjects into two groups at random, and perform their data analyses separately for the two halves of the sample. Whenever a difference in findings emerges between the two groups (and this would of course sometimes happen by chance even when no difference exists that would replicate with further samples), our imaginary researcher tests the difference for significance, and any significant differences are included in the published report of the study. If we are not told that the original subdivision has been made at random, we might misspend a great deal of time attempting to explain the differences. (pp. 3–4)

Their book attempts to determine whether assigning cases to groups by sex is any more meaningful for understanding behavior than assigning them at random. We should keep in mind, however, that selection of groups to study is not made at random. From the large number of subject or organismic variables by which humans could be grouped only a few such as sex or race are chosen.

Biological assumptions underlying research on sex differences

There is no denying that males and females may be different in some ways, just as tall people differ from short, fat people from thin, and even people with Type O blood from those with Type A. The major problem seems to be the use of sex differences as an explanatory rather than a descriptive term. The fact that sex differences are frequently used as an explanation rather than as a description suggests strong underlying (and unexamined) assumptions about the biological causality of sex differences. The source of these differences is still being sought in the central nervous system, and psychological theory in this area continues to suggest a direct hookup between the gonads and the brain. Aside from the fact that such simplistic assumptions are inappropriate given the inconsistent and variable nature of evidence about sex differences, such assumptions limit the range of research hypotheses investigated solely to the unidirectional subset implying causality only from biological to psychological phenomena.

Cerebral laterality: a new red herring?

The politicization of a research hypothesis

The area that most recently exemplifies the development and maintenance of ideas about the biological inevitability of differences between the sexes is that of cerebral dominance or laterality. Lateral dominance refers to the tendency for a person to favor one side of the body over the other in performing certain tasks. One of the most noted examples of lateral dominance is handedness. In right-handed people the left hemisphere of the brain is usually dominant. Studies of people with various kinds of brain damage also indicate that this half of the brain is usually dominant for verbal functions and that the right half of the brain is more important in tasks involving spatial configurations.

A variety of studies of brain-damaged people (Lansdell, 1962; McGlone & Kertesz, 1973) have suggested that females show fewer specific impairments following damage to either hemisphere than do males with a comparable degree of cerebral damage. This finding has led researchers to conjecture that as adults, at least, females appear to be less lateralized than males (Lake & Bryden, 1976). The hypothesis appears to contradict findings that girls are verbally fluent at an earlier age than boys and hence, more lateralized for verbal functions at an earlier age (Kimura, 1973). It is females' early advantage itself that is used by some researchers to explain their later degree of reduced laterality (Buffery & Gray, 1972). Somehow, the female brain specializes too early and is not able to "advance" further.

Sex differences in cerebral laterality are significant as an illustration of thinking that defines female biological processes as inferior. One could argue that the greater ability to recover from a stroke would define an area of female strength. Being lateralized, however, is in the process of being defined as good for people. The major basis for this contention appears to be evidence that children who have minimal brain dysfunction, dyslexia, or specific learning problems (however variously defined) are more likely to have ambiguous cerebral dominance than are those children who show no such impairments (Dimond, 1977). These children are also more likely than children in the general population to be left-handed, and left-handedness has been associated with less cerebral lateralization in some normal populations (Gilbert & Bakan, 1973). These hypotheses appear to represent a clear case of reasoning from effect to cause. In addition, they ignore those large numbers of left-handed individuals and even those with mixed dominance who appear to function effectively in the intellectual arena. These anomalous individuals, apparently unaware of the handicaps they have conquered, rarely come to the attention of the psychologist.

Differential laterality has also been used to explain sex differences in mathematical and spatial analytic skills. The kinship of sinistral and female in terms of brain function is all the more questionable because there is no evidence that left-handed individuals who show no evidence of neural impairment have any more difficulty in acquiring mathematical skills than do right-handed people about whom the same statement can be made. In a large-scale study of over 3,000 individuals from an unselected population, Kocel (1977) found no significant differences in any cognitive factor between right- and left-handed males or between right- and left-handed females. Variations in cerebral laterality appear to affect females and males in different ways that are too complex to be discussed in this context. Kocel noted that environmental factors may contribute to these effects:

> The fact that men and women and the right- and left-handed are usually easily differentiated, and that women and left-handers have often been discriminated against historically, raises important questions about the contribution of sociocultural factors to the relationships discovered. (p. 240)

The limitation of a research hypothesis

Biologically determinist hypotheses such as those involving cerebral laterality carry with them the assumption of relatively equal social environments. Such hypotheses reduce the probability that any researcher will examine the effect of environmental factors on behaviors that are defined as having a large biological component. Nevertheless, environmental characteristics may play a larger role than is usually assumed. A student of mine, Caroline Mossip,[1] examined spatial lateralization in girls and boys aged 3–11. Consistent with recent hypotheses about other forms of lateralization, girls showed lateralization at an earlier age than boys did. But boys' lateralization showed increasing development so that by the age of 9, their degree of lateralization surpassed that of girls. There was some suggestive evidence, however, that degree of lateralization was related to environmental factors, in particular, the kinds of toys that the children possessed. At every age, boys owned significantly more spatial toys (vehicles, sports equipment, construction sets, etc.) than girls did. Most interesting was the finding that the number of such toys owned was increasingly positively correlated with spatial lateralization in boys as they grew older. No such relationship was found in girls.

There are several interpretations possible from these data. Children's play preferences may reflect their development of laterality just as much as they may cause it. Girls may not have enough biological potential for spatial laterality to permit the environment to have an effect. However, we know that differential toy selection for boys and girls begins as early as the second year of life (Rheingold & Cook, 1975). Thus, we cannot assume that the psychosocial environment of females and males is an identical one in which purely biological effects can manifest themselves. Sharon Nash's (1975) studies which show that sex differences in spatial visualization in children are present only between boys and girls who prefer the sex role appropriate to their own sex also provide support for the position that social variables can affect supposedly biological ones.

Another major limitation of biologically determined hypotheses that I discuss only briefly here is their assumed irreversibility. It is strange that biological explanations are used to account for differences between males and females in verbal and mathematical skills, since most major differences between the sexes in these areas do not appear until adolescence and early adulthood (Maccoby & Jacklin, 1974). Any effects of differential maturation of the central nervous system would seem to have long disappeared by this time. For example, in discussing more major social differences between groups in early life – the cognitive development of normal South American Indian children who have been malnourished and isolated during the first few years of life – Jerome Kagan (1976) suggested that effects are reversible so that the group subjected to physiological insult reaches the cognitive level of American children by age 18. A number of studies (Hoffman & Maier, 1966; Witkin, 1967, cited by Parlee),[2] have indicated "improvements" in female problem solving and perceptual faculties in the direction of the male following short-term practice or instruction procedures. The evidence that sex differences do not usually decrease but increase with further socialization should suggest that biological explanations are masking more important (because they are more explanatory) social ones.

It is difficult to avoid confounding sex and gender. It is noteworthy, however, that one study of individuals with similar biological characteristics who were assigned different sexes at birth and raised in accordance with those assignments found differences based more on gender than on sex. Males suffering from testosterone insensitivity, who were therefore born with apparently female external genitalia, showed a typically feminine pattern of cognitive abilities on the Wechsler Intelligence Scale for Children when they were raised as girls (higher verbal than spatial scores) and a more masculine pattern when reared as boys (slightly higher spatial than verbal scores; Masica, Money, Ehrhardt, & Levis, 1969). It is important to remember, of course, that this finding is based on a small population with ambiguous sexuality. Nash's study does indicate that similar effects can operate in a more normal population.

Should we study sex differences?

Problems with the focus on sex differences
It may be valuable to summarize the reasons why some of those who are interested in gender do not concentrate on sex differences as an area of research.

1 The questions of sex differences are someone else's questions – They do not, of themselves, illuminate the mechanisms that create such differences. In fact, they may obscure the origin of such differences by leading us to believe that biological explanations are sufficient for understanding these behaviors. It is also important to remember that biological determinants which are used to distinguish between groups are sometimes chosen for other than objective, scientific reasons.
2 One cannot prove the null hypothesis, and anyway, the argument can just shift to another phenomenon.
3 Examination of sex differences obscures the examination of sex similarities. Sex similarities are not as dramatic and are less likely to be published than are differences. The fact that the sexes are similar in far more ways than they are different is not considered startling psychological news.
4 Analyses based on sex differences tend to imply a trait view of psychology that obscures the situational determinants of behavior. Under many conditions the constraints of the situation play a larger role in determining the individual's behavior in that context than do the psychological characteristics the individual brings to the situation (Wicker, 1969).
5 Studies of sex differences do not examine behaviors in which the rate is virtually zero for one sex. Thus, we do not

find studies in sex differences in rape, and until recently, there was no comparison of periodic male and female cycles. In a sense, therefore, studies of sex differences concentrate on those areas in which males and females are least different.

Some of these arguments could be used against the development of a field of gender differences if such a field were to come into existence. Researchers interested in gender, however, have tended to focus more on one or the other sex rather than on differences between them. Gender, like sex, may produce problems of its own for researchers, but it does have the advantage of possessing conceptual newness – requiring a reexamination of what is assumed to be true.

What do we study instead of sex differences?

It is always easier to criticize a particular position than to state positive alternatives. Nevertheless, researchers interested in the psychology of gender have made a number of conceptual advances in recent years. One such advance is related to the concept of androgyny, although it is not identical to the way androgyny is often used in research. Androgyny, as postulated by Sandra Bem (1974, 1975), is the simultaneous possession by an individual of an equal number of traits identified in our culture as strongly masculine and strongly feminine. Bem noted that this kind of personality constellation may facilitate effective behavior in a variety of social situations, rather than causing deficits in behavior due to confusion about sex role identity. What is important about this construct in the context of this article is the idea of independence between biological sex and the psychological components of sexual identity (gender). Although some main effects for biological sex have been found, males and females with the same psychological structure often function in similar ways. Thus, self-reports about gender may predict a person's behavior better than the person's biological sex does.

The effect of sex as a stimulus

Research in this area requires that we develop methods for contrasting sex and gender. There is a generalized belief that sex differences exist, and this phenomenon has been extensively investigated under the topic of sex role stereotyping. Using no stimulus materials other than the label *male* or *female*, investigators have found that the sex of the stimulus person alters people's criteria for mental health, affects their evaluation of the goodness and badness of performance, leads them to make differential attributions about the causes of someone's behavior, and induces differential perceptions about the values of others (Broverman, Broverman, Clarkson, Rosenkrantz, & Vogel, 1970; Deaux & Emswiller, 1974; Pheterson, Kiesler, & Goldberg, 1971; Unger & Siiter, 1974). These illusions about sex differences are held by both males and females and thus, in themselves, constitute a sex similarity rather than a sex difference.

Sex may also serve as a stimulus for the evaluation and appraisal of one's own behavior. Gender identity may be the major influence in producing sex differences in performance. The greatest number of sex differences are found in studies that use self-ratings as the measure of behavior in which the investigators are interested (Frodi, Macaulay, & Thome, 1977). Gender identity may also account for the fact that many more sex differences are found in field than in laboratory studies (Unger, 1981). Assumptions about the social desirability and normality of one's behavior may be more salient outside the laboratory.

It might be more valuable for the understanding of psychological processes associated with gender to examine those individuals who rate themselves as high or low in traits considered characteristic of a particular sex rather than looking at group differences between the sexes. Such a procedure would test the assumption that on any given characteristic, males and females usually form two overlapping distributions with a minority of people of either sex at the extremes. It would also permit us to determine whether sex or gender is the more important predictor of a given behavior. The degree of influence of biological and social factors will probably vary for different behaviors, but it is well to remember that even in behaviors considered highly specific to reproduction and even among more biologically determined lower mammals, no behavior unique to one sex has been found (Bermant & Davidson, 1974).

It is possible to trace the development of the concept of sex as a stimulus variable during the short history of the field presently defined as the psychology of women. First, researchers noted that psychologists studied women less frequently than they studied men (Carlson & Carlson, 1961). Next, they recognized that the sex of the experimenter or other evaluator of the subject's performance can affect that performance (Harris,

1971). The sex of the experimenter and the sex of the subjects may influence research in subtle ways. For example, some areas (e.g., aggression vs. attraction) have been considered more appropriate for research on males than on females (McKenna & Kessler, 1977). Some procedures (e.g., those that involve the measurement of active aggression in subjects) are considered more appropriate for males (Frodi et al., 1977). Aggression in females, in contrast, is more likely to be measured by pencil-and-paper methods. When queried on the subject, some researchers in the area of aggression have made statements about not wishing to use procedures that could be physically harmful to female subjects.[3] It is also noteworthy that areas in which males are defined as the most relevant subjects are also those that have until recently received the most attention by psychologists. One can cite as examples the relative number of studies on achievement versus those on nurturance, on aggression versus cooperation, or on the acquisition of mathematical versus reading skills.

Interest in sex as a stimulus variable has been stimulated by the demonstration of persistent evaluation biases in our society. The studies of Kay Deaux and her associates (Deaux, 1976) amply support the proposition that there is no such thing as identical male and female behaviors. Perhaps more important in its implications is the finding that women are evaluated on a narrower continuum than men (Deaux & Taynor, 1973). Women not only receive less credit when they excel but also receive less blame when they fail.

Evaluation biases are particularly difficult to eliminate because they are often subtle and show up only as interactions with other variables. A recent study, for example, analyzed the relationship between the ratings given by students to actual faculty members of either sex and their evaluations of the level of difficulty of that teacher.[4] Although there were no significant sex differences in perceived difficulty and though sex differences in perceived effectiveness of instructor failed to reach significance, the relationship between perceived effectiveness and difficulty was radically different for the two sexes. The two dimensions were independent for ratings of male teachers ($r = 0.05$), but they were negatively related for females ($r = -0.49$). This negative correlation indicated that women who were perceived as difficult graders received lower teacher-effectiveness evaluations relative to other women, whereas those who were perceived as easy graders received higher evaluations. The relationship appeared to be most marked for those women who were viewed as exceptionally difficult or exceptionally easy relative to the entire department. A more controlled laboratory study by Harris (1976) also revealed that instructors of either sex who were perceived as masculine in style were evaluated differently from those who were more feminine. Thus, taken together, these results suggest that suppositions involving gender may invade objective evaluation instruments, and these may measure social biases rather than subject biases.

Toward a new definition of biosocial variables
The problem of viewing sex as a stimulus or social variable appears to be compounded by the fact that the stimulus aspects of sex appear to be inevitably confounded with the biological aspects of sex differences. It is difficult to find a male control group who manifest some of the biological properties unique to females. Thus, male and female subjects alike infer that a woman's bad mood during the premenstrual and menstrual phases of her cycle is more attributable to her biology than are similar behaviors during the midcycle that are assumed to have a more situational cause (Koeske & Koeske, 1975). Males, nonetheless, are no less likely to attribute their moods to biological causes than are females.[5] It is also noteworthy that the five-day work week, two-day weekend sequence produces larger and more predictable cyclic variations in female behavior than does the periodicity of the menstrual cycle,[6] although this finding is not widely reported.

The menstrual cycle represents an excellent avenue of analysis of the way assumptions are made about the causal relationship between sex-characteristic behavior and the central nervous system. Parlee (1978) has clearly analyzed the nature of scientific thinking and lack of objectivity in this area. It is possible to argue that psychological change is a reflection of the social response to biological factors rather than a direct result of the biological variables themselves. Thus, Paige (1973) found that women who were heavy bleeders were more likely to manifest anxiety during the premenstrual phase of the cycle, no matter what their hormonal constitution, than were women with equivalent biochemical states who bled more lightly. Paige suggested that their negative affect represented fears about the social consequences of bleeding visibly and the discomfort and inconvenience that accompanied such heavy bleeding. Behaviorally, such women were more likely to abstain from sexual intercourse during this phase than were women who bled less.

It is possible that we have underestimated the effects of social judgments about physiological conditions unique to women. In a recent, novel experiment in this regard, Taylor and Langer (1977) found that both men and women (although men more than women) stand farther away from a pregnant woman, although they stare at her more than at a non-pregnant woman. Subjects also indicated that they liked a pregnant woman more when she was passive than when she was assertive. At the same time, they rejected the pregnant woman as a companion. The authors suggested that these unacknowledged social rejection mechanisms may be an important source of stigmatizing pregnancy. Internalization of behaviors considered appropriate for this state could then account for many behaviors considered characteristic of pregnancy that are usually attributed to high levels of female hormones.

Psychologists are beginning to recognize that some variables which mediate individual differences may also mediate social differences. Physical attractiveness is one such variable that has received considerable attention. Judgments based on physical attractiveness are considered more salient for females than for males. Size and strength may be more specific mediators of sex differences (Unger, 1976). In fact, one could offer a new definition of a biosocial variable – not one that is the result of biological and social causes, but one that produces effects because of generalized sociocultural assumptions about universal biological processes. Many biological processes are evident to an observer and may be the subject of his or her social judgments. A consideration of this kind of variable may help to explain why some sex differences in psychological function seem to appear universally. After all, the biological states on which the attributions are based are themselves universal.

New hypotheses may be generated by a redefinition of biosocial processes. Questions might include the following: To what extent may greater female concern with weight be due to periodic weight instabilities generated by the menstrual cycle? Is social responsiveness in females enhanced by their designation as the physically attractive sex? Within a sex, do larger children make more attempts to influence others, and are they more overtly aggressive than smaller ones? In other words, what is the association between external bodily characteristics and gender? This position does not deny that biological differences between the sexes may exist, but explanations based on them may lie elsewhere than in direct physiological influences on the central nervous system. Social processes can, of course, of themselves differentially affect the behavior of people of different sexes. There are, for example, considerable data that there are fewer positive connections between behavior and rewards for females than for males (Unger, 1979a).

Presumed sex differences, by this analysis, cannot be used to justify differential treatment of the sexes. Group data can never legitimately justify treatment of individuals, and characterization of behaviors as sex specific is particularly questionable in view of the abundant evidence that the social judgment process almost always results in the equations, *male = superior, female = inferior*. In sex, as in race, there are no separate but equal social categories.

The scientific value of redefinition

In sum, this article makes a case for partitioning sex in terms of the various ways it can function biologically and socially. The distinction between sex and gender can assist in the generation of research hypotheses that do not assume the former is necessarily the basis for the latter. The use of the term *gender* makes it less likely that psychological differences between males and females will be considered explicable mainly in terms of physiological differences between them. Those who study the psychology of women are often concerned with the stimulus functions of sex – the fact that the label *male* or *female* with no additional information provided greatly alters people's view of the stimulus person described. Gender refers to the traits and behaviors considered characteristic of and appropriate to members of each sexual category. Gender identity is more appropriately used when these attributions are made with oneself as the stimulus person. These terms, however, do not imply that we have any information on the origin of gender-characteristic effects. It is likely, in fact, that a number of factors – physiological, biosocial, and environmental – contribute to differences between females and males.

Consider a rainbow. Given the full spectrum of color, we perceive red and magenta as being similar. If, however, we eliminate all other hues, red and magenta are now perceived as being different. But the price of emphasizing this difference is the loss of the rest of the spectrum. Similarly, relationships relevant to both sexes have been obscured by the limitation of research to the difference between them. Many so-called sex differences may actually be gender differences. However, the substitution of gender for sex is not the solution to this problem. Both terms – appropriately defined – are necessary parts of our psychological vocabularies. I hope that gender will provide a useful tool for our ultimate understanding of people – sex unspecified.

Notes

1 Mossip, C.E. Hemispheric specialization as seen in children's perception of faces. Paper presented at the meeting of the Eastern Psychological Association, Boston, April 1977.
2 Parlee, M.B. Sex differences in perceptual field dependence: A look at some data embedded in theory. Manuscript submitted for publication, 1976.
3 Prescott, S., & Foster, K. Why researchers don't study women. Paper presented at the meeting of the American Psychological Association, New Orleans, August 1974.
4 Unger, R.K. The student teacher evaluation form as an instrument of sexism. Paper presented at the meeting of the American Psychological Association, San Francisco, August 1977.
5 Garcia, M. Fluctuations of mood in the menstrual cycle not confirmed. Paper presented at the meeting of the Eastern Psychological Association, New York, April 1975.
6 Parlee, M.B. From the known into the unknown: Sexual politics becomes science. Paper presented at the meeting of the New York Academy of Sciences, New York, 15 November 1976.

Reading 4

Through the looking glass: no Wonderland yet! (The reciprocal relationship between methodology and models of reality (Unger, 1983, pp. 9–16, 20–29)

It is difficult to find a title for an essay in an area that can encompass the whole of psychology. Hence, I take refuge in

Alice in Wonderland, since one can find an allusion to almost anything in its pages. Nevertheless, my title does relate to the content of this article. I am going to embark with you on a very adventurous journey – a voyage into the nature of the psychological reality with which we deal.

The purpose of this exploration is to examine the extent to which "methodological" issues are actually conceptual ones. Many of the issues to be discussed here have been raised about mainstream psychology, but are relevant to the psychology of women as well (see the growing discussion of methods in our literature, e.g., Brannon, 1981; Grady, 1981; Parlee, 1981; Unger, 1981; Wallston, 1981).

I propose to examine some issues that are usually considered philosophical or metaphysical and therefore irrelevant to us in psychology. I shall discuss how conceptual frameworks of which we may not be aware affect our methodology; how models of reality influence psychological research; how particular value structures have affected specific studies; how some aspects of the feminist value structure influence our own work; some of the factors determining whether or not paradigmatic change will occur; and why women may be uniquely suited to be agents of paradigmatic change. Finally, I will offer some suggestions for a more responsive psychology.

It is necessary first to consider some fundamental questions, such as

1   What is the nature of the human being we study?
2   How do the constraints of methodology influence what we see as the nature of that human being?
3   How do our ideology, our values, and/or our place in society influence our methods and the way we interpret them?
4   Contrariwise, how do our methods create our concepts?

These questions are basically epistemological, that is, they involve the nature of the truths we seek. It is not a mere semantic quibble whether we discover truths or create them or whether facts are absolute or relative. Arguments about methods frequently involve conflicts between different epistemological systems. We are *all* concerned about the valid means by which truth can be acquired. And, by now, we all understand how the nature of the search affects the very findings. It will clarify matters considerably if we deal with these issues as conceptual rather than methodological. For example, much of the argument about the relative value of quantitative versus qualitative methodology actually involves the issue of whether or not measurement can or should be divorced from evaluation.

Although such questions may be ultimately unresolved, an analysis of them will be helpful for the understanding of research trends in the psychology of women and may be helpful in the formulation of future work in the field.

The positivist empiricist model and its critique

The positivist empiricist model has been an important model for psychology and, despite occasional allusions to post-positivist science, it still guides much of the work in the field. In brief, this model restricts analysis to a few clearly observable units of behavior in order to avoid imposing one's own beliefs upon the organisms studied. The subject matter and method of investigation are conceived as independent of each other. In practice, although not in principle, behavior is removed to a laboratory in order to prevent extraneous variables (defined as anything other than the experimenter's manipulations) from influencing the behavior. This practice turns people into subjects by removing them from their situational and historical context.

Early waves of feminist psychologists concentrated upon the omissions produced by this approach. They focused attention on the neglect of women as subjects of research (Carlson & Carlson, 1961); on the effect of the sex of the experimenter or other evaluator of the person's performance (Harris, 1971; Pedersen, Shinedling & Johnson, 1968); on the tendency to make more generalizations to humans as a whole from all-male than from all-female data (Holmes & Jorgenson, 1971); and on the effect of sex biases in determining what kind of behavior gets studied with what sex (Frodi, Macaulay & Thome, 1977; McKenna & Kessler, 1977).

Such omissions, however, may be and are being remedied by feminists using traditional experimental methodology. It is the transformation of people into object-like subjects that is the essence of the theoretical critique of most empirical psychological work on humans. The ideological framework of positivist empiricism defines the relationship between researcher and subject as an impersonal one. The logic of these methods (and even their language) prescribes prediction and control. It is difficult for one who is trained in such a conceptual framework to step beyond it and ask what kind of person such a methodology presupposes.

It may be argued that the ideal subject of the psychological experiment is a narrowly calculating human being who adapts, conforms, and engages in self-interested behavior, rather than in action that has social as well as personal meaning (Elshtain, 1979). But to produce such a creature, a set of arbitrary and strongly simplifying assumptions have had to be set up; the behaviors examined have largely been restricted to those that are amenable to simple observation and/or categorization (and, therefore, devoid of much meaning to the subject); alternative behaviors have been eliminated (this is known as control); and, most importantly, those actions involving ideology and values have been defined out by fiat as operationally meaningless. Here I am reminded of one of Alice's encounters with Humpty Dumpty in *Through the Looking Glass*:

> "When *I* use a word," Humpty Dumpty said, in a rather scornful tone, "it means just what I choose it to mean – neither more or less."
>
> "The question is," and Alice, "whether you *can* make words mean so many different things."
>
> "The question is," said Humpty Dumpty, "which is to be master – that's all."

Control by definition is a key to understanding many of the issues in this area.

Given the context of observation, it is not surprising that the subject permits himself or herself to be manipulated by the experimenter's independent variables. The results of these studies may reflect not only people's desire to be helpful to the experimenter, but also the degree to which people experience themselves as overwhelmed by external conditions beyond their control.

We should not be surprised that the human element has a way of slipping through. It is characteristic of the unreflective nature of much research that the social nature of human experimentation has been seen more as a procedural problem than as an indication of a general conceptual crisis (Gadlin & Ingle, 1975). Like increased blood clotting due to the "pill," the social relationship between experimenter and subject is seen as an "unwanted side effect." Like the blood clotting properties of estrogenic substances, however, such effects are intrinsic. They are side effects only to the extent that they are not the ones desired.

It is not easy to document how many side effects due to the social relationship between subjects and researchers have been ignored. By definition, they are not an aspect for analysis. However, a study I came across recently provides an instructive example. In 1964, Berkowitz, Klanderman, and Harris published a study of subjects' productivity in a simulated work situation. When the subject and experimenter were of different sexes, the subjects worked harder for their unseen partner the sooner the experimenter saw their work, but when the subject and experimenter were of the same sex they did not do so. The investigators suggested that subjects worked harder for an opposite-sex experimenter's approval since the work would be learned about right away. This effect, however, "interfered" with the *real* purpose of the experiment, which was to determine whether effort expended on behalf of the partner varied depending on the length of time before which their effort would become known. Therefore, the sex-related effect was never followed up. Some time later, in fact, Berkowitz (1972) remarked: "In order to minimize S's desire to gain E's approval, all later experiments employed investigators of the same sex as the subject" (p. 72).

Many sex-of-subject/sex-of-stimulus-person effects are hidden away as factors that produce dilemmas for the experimenter (Unger, 1981). Such phenomena are characterized by terms such as experimenter bias, demand characteristics, or evaluation apprehension. What these phenomena actually demonstrate is that the experimental method cannot expunge human relationships. They demonstrate that the experimental method presupposes its own appropriateness and cannot adequately handle questions of its own efficacy (Gadlin & Ingle, 1975).

Sex-related effects are particularly problematic for experimental methodology for a number of conceptual reasons.

1   In traditional methodology sex is a nonmanipulable given or an independent variable. To assume that sex, or rather gender, is created by the measuring procedure involves assuming a different paradigm (Unger, 1979c).
2   Experimentation, with its ahistorical, asituational context, is not appropriate when the problem involves the person's sense of place in the world (Lana, 1976). As we are aware, it is virtually impossible to eliminate consideration of the role of status from any examination of the relationship between females and males (Unger, 1976, 1978a).

3   When women become involved in the research process,
either as subjects or researchers, it becomes impossible to
continue the fiction that knowledge is a matter of objective
observation. The actual and particular position of women
in the world cannot be suspended (Smith, 1979).

Models of reality and psychological research

As larger numbers of women (and minority and poor people)
have become involved in social science research and as more
matters of concern to them have become the objects of
research, it has become harder for social scientists to sustain
the illusion that knowledge is abstract and value-free. We have
become more and more aware that objectifying practices
conceal a particular vision of people and their world. Women
scholars are particularly likely to reach this conclusion because
we have been largely excluded from the processes through
which knowledge is obtained.

It might seem surprising that this exclusion of more than
half of humanity has gone unnoticed. The reason becomes
clear, however, when we recognize the implications of a view
of knowledge as the discovery of universals. As Sampson
(1978) has noted, such a view argues that a particular group
has no more valid claim to knowledge of their world than does
someone not in that group. This view of scholarship thus helps
support the existing balance of power and the interests of the
dominant minority.

The positivist empiricist model is, of course, not the only
epistemological model available to psychologists. Psychology
appears to have alternated its focus from time to time between
an objectified view of the person and a concentration upon the
person's subjective reality (Lana, 1976). Buss's (1978a) recent
analysis of the deep structure of this kind of paradigm shift has
been most useful to my thinking in the area. He suggests that
two prototype statements can be used for characterizing the
underlying structure of psychological paradigms: *either reality
constructs the person or the person constructs reality*. Psychological revolutions represent a shift from one to the other
paradigm. Thus, the most recent shift from behaviorism to
cognitive psychology represents a shift from a conceptualization that stresses how various factors in an individual's past or
present situation determine her or his actions (assuming an
objective past or present) to a conceptualization that stresses
how the individual's motivations and belief structures influence

what aspects of the psychological world are attended to, remembered, and utilized.

These two basic paradigms reflect different conceptions of reality. Both behaviorism and many theories about personality minimize the importance of rationality and human consciousness (Buss, 1978a). They see the individual as a consequence of certain aspects of an unchanging reality. Causality runs largely in one direction – responses to past and present stimuli direct present and future actions. There is little room in this kind of metaphysical reality for the awareness that people can change their circumstances and, therefore, potentially, themselves.

Current cognitive theory assumes that the objective conditions in a person's world fuse with his or her subjective view of these conditions (Berger & Luckmann, 1966). Although researchers in the area may disagree about the extent, they assume that some aspects of reality are socially constructed and that so-called objective reality is based upon various levels of agreement among individuals as they interact with each other. In this view, knowledge is clearly a matter of social definition.

Recent research in social cognition (*cf* Hamilton, 1979) has demonstrated that cognitive biases are very pervasive. It has recently been shown that people use much less information than is available to them (Major, 1980); that they form illusory correlations based upon statistically rare information and groups (Hamilton & Gifford, 1976); that they selectively seek information that confirms their naive hypotheses rather than disconfirming them (Hansen, 1980); and that they reconstruct memories based on stereotypic beliefs about members of groups other than their own (Snyder & Uranowitz, 1978). Any individuals who are distinctive within a group are most likely to receive extreme judgments (Taylor, Fiske, Close, Anderson & Ruderman, cited in Taylor & Fiske, 1978). And so-called normal behavior may be attended to and labeled as deviant when it is engaged in by a person who has received a socially deviant label (Langer & Imber, 1980). Erroneous relationships may be inferred and the beliefs maintained even when the initial evidential base is totally discredited (Anderson, Lepper & Ross, 1980). All of this work is noteworthy because it demonstrates the mechanisms by which sexist and racist biases may be perpetuated even after repeated scholarly demonstrations that no major differences between groups exist.

Since most people are uncritical or naive realists they are not aware of the extent to which they create the reality with which they deal. Psychologists who uncritically accept a positivistic empiricist model (reality constructs the person) may, in fact, deny that the world is dependent upon the observer's viewpoint. They see knowledge as discovered, not made. This unwillingness to accept a relativistic view of knowledge does not, of course, prevent such a view from having an impact upon their own operations on the world.

It is important to stress that it is not techniques of experimentation or quantification that I am criticizing here. They are potential tools that are devoid of much significance in themselves. What I am criticizing is our unawareness of the epistemological commitments we make when we use such tools unthinkingly. As Ruth Hubbard has written:

> We learn to examine the ways in which our experimental methods can bias our answers, but we are not taught to be equally wary of the biases introduced by our implicit, unstated, and often unconscious beliefs about the nature of reality. (1978, p. 10)

It is important to reiterate that our beliefs about reality also prescribe what we ignore or omit as well as with what we concern ourselves.

Philosophical concerns are relevant to contemporary psychology because questions about what is true are answered implicitly by the psychologist in the way she or he frames questions or phrases statements about observations (Eacker, 1972). As the information so gathered is strained through successive reworkings, psychologists come to agree that they are discovering phenomena and laws of the universe in the behavioral laboratory. For example, when a researcher writes that "the acquisition of sex-typed behavior is facilitated by reinforcement" this passive linguistic structure conceals the statement "someone is choosing to reinforce and thereby differentially change behavior in males and females." The linguistic convention omits such major questions as, reinforcement by whom? For what purpose? In whose interest? When we acknowledge the omitted questions, we realize that the phenomena and laws of behavior are of interest *only* in terms of their situational context and that this situational context is far larger than the laboratory in which they were observed.

Potential conceptual biases in feminist scholarship

Biological determinism seems to be particularly notable for its unwillingness to scrutinize alternative mechanisms for the effects obtained. Its intransigence may be explicable in terms of the role of ideology in the structuring of knowledge. Since the position appears to spring from a world view that assumes that certain aspects of physical reality construct the person, there may be difficulty encompassing a multicausal perspective, let alone one that postulates that causality operates "backwards" from the person to reality as well. Although lip service is frequently given to the concept of interaction, person-centred and situation-centred variables are rarely both examined in the same research study or even by the same researcher.

Again, I wish to stress that I am not arguing against the use of biological data. Biological variables, however, appear to possess some conceptual properties of which researchers may be unaware. For example, they are more likely to be perceived as irreversible than are social variables. Moreover, factors that operate early in the lifetime of the individual are also seen more as irreversible than are those that operate at a later developmental stage. I have reviewed a number of biological assumptions in my book *Female and Male* (Unger, 1979a) and so will stress only a few here. Important other assumptions include: the belief that female psychology is more dependent on biology than male psychology is; the belief that conditions that have a strong biological basis in women have no analog in men; and, possibly most importantly, the belief that behavioral characteristics associated with biological events occur by way of direct central nervous system regulation. Researchers are not required to specify what these hormonal or neural mechanisms are. Social perceptions and cognitions relating to such events are presumed to have little effect on behavior associated with them.

There is little empirical evidence to support these assumptions. They should be tested wherever possible. While it is important to continue to emphasize that sex differences operate in a context of interactions, it is equally important to recognize that many different kinds of interactionist hypotheses are possible that may have quite different emphases in terms of biology or culture. I am indebted to Nora Newcombe (1980) for her clear analysis of various forms of interaction. She notes that in the analysis of spatial ability it is equally interactionist to postulate:

> a. that a biologically given sex difference in spatial ability is potentiated and widened by cultural circumstances; b. that a biologically given sex difference in activity level leads to sex differences in experience, which produces sex differences in spatial ability; c. that

biologically given differences in genitals elicit different responses
from caretakers, and that these treatment differences lead to sex
differences in spatial ability. (Newcombe, 1980, p. 807)

Each of these hypotheses generates a distinct set of empirical
predictions and social implications. They are not, of course,
mutually exclusive. Acceptance of a biological explanation for
sex-related differences should not automatically result in the
conclusion that differences are immutable or independent of
social context.

It is also clear that sex differences, like race differences, are
often a matter of interpretation and focus. Has the research
looked at the behavior of the stimulus persons or at the reports
of individuals perceiving these stimulus persons? The problem
is further compounded because sometimes the persons
reporting the behavior are themselves the stimulus persons.
Far more self-reports of sex differences exist than do reports of
such differences when actual behavior is observed by others
(O'Leary, 1977; Sherif, 1979). We need to make clear the
distinction between self-reports based on social expectation and
those based on personal experience. Interestingly, our psychological vocabularies lack the clarity to make the necessary
distinctions.

Studies on sex differences probably also suffer from prejudice against the null hypothesis (Greenwald, 1975). It is
impossible to tell how many studies of sex similarities might
have been found if theoretical or conceptual frameworks had
justified their publication. Relabeling the area "sex comparisons" is only one step in making any finding in this area
salient.

We cannot assume that all conceptual confusions and dis-
tortions are the responsibility of "other" psychologists. Female
psychologists, in general, appear to share psychology's belief
in objectivism to a degree only slightly less than that of their
male counterparts (Coan, 1979). I have been attempting
recently to delineate the belief structures of feminist psychologists and have found, contrary to my initial hypothesis, that
my sample of activist people in the field is similar to my
colleagues and students at a state college in their belief in the
importance of non-conscious forces in the control of
behavior.[1] In other words, even actively feminist researchers
share the assumptions of the subdisciplines in which they
were socialized, regardless of whether these perspectives were
experimental, clinical, or social-cognitive.

Researchers in the psychology of women have often searched within the person to explain why women are different from men. Such explanations share a deep paradigmatic relationship to biological explanations. Society is seen as relatively unproblematic whereas individual behavior is seen as problematic (Israel, 1979). In both psychology of women and biology, the relatively permanent properties of people are seen to determine their behavior. Examples of concepts that derive from inside the person are fear of success and androgyny. Those who use these concepts are careful to emphasize that they arise from differential socialization of females and males and/or are supported within the individual by continual situational constraints. Nevertheless, they are commonly used as typologies by which to organize and predict other attitudinal characteristics (Wallston, 1981).

Androgyny has been viewed by some feminist theorists as a prescription for social health because of its potential for greater sex role flexibility. I have no basis with which to quarrel with this formulation. Nevertheless, the search for sources for social change within the person has many pitfalls, as we already know from reviewing the literature on race psychology. (See Caplan and Nelson, 1973, for an excellent critique of person-centred theories in terms of their latent ideological content.)

One can also argue that lack of androgyny has not yet been defined as a source of personal problems. However, aspects of traditional femininity have been so defined, placing women in yet another version of the double bind. The creation of the social myth known as the "Cinderella syndrome" is already in progress. The energy we spend on criticizing these myths cannot be used for creating our own.

Person-centred interpretations appear to derive from biases deeply imbedded in belief structures. These biases distort reality, although the distortion is neither conscious nor intentional. Again, person-centred research is not necessarily poor research. But feminist scholars must transcend the values, norms, and prejudices of their disciplinary structures rather than accept customary conceptual structures and simply test whether traditional constructs about women are or are not true.

Paradigm change and the sociology of knowledge

The number of instances in which critiques of traditional psychology have appeared in mainstream psychological journals is striking (e.g., Buss, 1975; Caplan & Nelson, 1973; Gadlin & Ingle, 1975; Koch, 1981; Levine, 1974; Sampson, 1978; Sarason, 1973). The critiques to which I refer do not simply involve the so-called crisis in social psychology or awareness of the ahistorical and acultural bias of traditional psychology. In one way or another, these critics have also maintained that methodological problems are often conceptual ones. They have offered example after example of what Koch (1981) has so aptly termed "epistemopathology."

Despite these critiques, there are forces that make change within any area of psychology difficult to induce. These forces have been discussed extensively within the area known as the sociology of knowledge; I will briefly describe some that are particularly relevant to scholarship by and about women.

It is well to remember that it is through the approval of members of our disciplinary community, not that of the target population affected by our work, that careers are made. Mary Payer (1977), a philosopher of science, has made the distinction between knowledge and scholarship that is an important one here. She notes that questions about knowledge include: "What is real?" "What is objective?" and "How do I know this to be the case?" Scholarship provides another set of questions: "What bodies of data are held to be significant?" "What are the criteria for their acceptance?" "Who sets these standards?" "In accordance with whose needs and interests?" And, lastly, "What constitutes valid criticism?"

In scholarship experiences are not only created but are legitimized by institutionalized vocabularies and practices. Mature institutions are seen as possessing a high degree of objectivity (Payer, 1977). They are seen as existing over and beyond individuals who happen to embody them at the moment. When institutions are experienced as having a reality of their own, we lose sight of the crucial elements of history and social context. We fail to take into account our own responsibility for our creations. As Payer states: "Consequently, it *makes* the world, both theoretically and practically speaking – when we say *not* this is one view or theory of reality *we* have developed, *but* this is the way that reality is" (1977, p. 32). The reification of institutions such as scholarship enables them to make claims for universality and objectivity that individuals would be unwilling to make for themselves.

It is also important to keep in mind that not all members of a community of scholars have an equal opportunity to define what is legitimate knowledge. Humpty Dumpty's assertions have more power than Alice's. Becker (1967) speaks of a "hierarchy of credibility." In any system of ranked groups, participants take it as a given that members of the highest group have the right to define the way things really are. Matters of rank and status have an almost moral quality. We are, if we are proper members of the group, bound to accept the definition imposed on reality by the superordinate group in preference to those definitions formulated by subordinates.

Women have less legitimacy than men even when they occupy supposedly equivalent positions (Unger, 1982). Women may sometimes do some of the naming. Nonetheless, the power to name the namers rests with men (Stimpson, 1979). It has been argued that the method of independent observations insures an objective reality. As we have seen, however, scientists do not think and work independently. Scholars have been predominantly university-trained white males from privileged social backgrounds. It is likely that their views about the nature of reality have been biased by their limited experiences and that their scholarly product tells us as much about the investigator as about the subject studied (Hubbard, 1978).

Women as agents of scholarly change

If scientific knowledge is held to be the superior or only way of knowing, it serves to devalue or invalidate much of people's daily experience. Since even those females involved in scholarship have had a different subjective reality from their male counterparts, it is not surprising that they focus on different aspects of experience and/or evaluate it differently. For example, Lisa Furby (1979) notes that by virtue of social class and sex in the United States, most psychological researchers have had more objective (actual) experiences of internal control than the average person. Thus, they have more subjective (perceived) experiences of internal locus of control and may have difficulty making a distinction between people's sense of personal control and their expectations about the degree of control permitted to them by society. This level of expectation or aspiration could be defined as a "knowledge" variable. Because, however, psychologists may not recognize the role of differential personal experience in determining what we know, they may have difficulty distinguishing knowledge from motivation.

Women's position as both the subjects and objects of their own research uniquely fits them to be agents of change.

Dorothy Smith (1979) makes the analogy to servants of the upper class in England who knew much about both their own lives and those of their masters, whereas the upper class had access only to their own lives. If, however, women make claims of special access to knowledge by virtue of our position in society, we must do so with the realization that paradigmatic shifts take a long time to accomplish. We must also remain aware that because of our inferior status in academia we are in a poor position from which to argue legitimacy issues. It is very easy to dismiss feminist arguments as "special pleading" or as examples of the poor worker who blames his or her tools. We cannot expect that arguments will be evaluated independently of who makes them.

These problems, of course, are not arguments that we should stop thinking. It is unlikely, however, that a paradigm will be discarded without another one to put in its place. Kuhn (1970) has documented many instances in which scholars have continued to ignore countervailing "facts" and have buttressed increasingly outmoded theories because there was no acceptable alternative model. Buss (1974–1975), working from Mannheim's theory about generations and social change, has argued that paradigm shifts are most likely to come about when a new generation without years of commitment to the existent ideology comes to power. In some ways, women scholars are in a position of being the younger generation whatever their ages. They may have less commitment to prevailing ideology both because they are in a good position to recognize its flaws and because they have not received many rewards for having been committed to it.

Toward a reflexive psychology

It is important that I do not conclude this article by simply reiterating the need to question *all* conceptual frameworks. I would rather present some ideas for breaking away from the fixations we have inherited from the psychology in which we were trained and socialized.

I am not arguing for a simple cognitive paradigm although, as I noted earlier, studies designed in terms of that paradigm appear to be very valuable to feminist psychology. Some of the flaws of a purely cognitive approach include its apparent inability to deal with the evaluative aspects of the self (Sherif, 1982) and confusion between the causes and reasons for behavior (Buss, 1978b; Eacker, 1972). These flaws reveal that the cognitive framework also has unexamined epistemological problems. For example, the question "why" appears to have different meanings for the observer and the actor. Simple informational hypotheses do not explain this problem.

Probably the most trenchant criticisms of the cognitive framework have been offered by Sampson (1981). He points out that by concentrating on subjective reality we may neglect the actual barriers various groups encounter. Perceptual and cognitive restructuring may also serve as a substitute for action. The uncritical acceptance of the social choices available at a given time fails to confront the issue of how such choices became available in the first place. Lastly, we may fail to consider the possible nonrationality or ineffectuality of any of the set of alternative behaviors available to some groups in terms of what a given social system has made available to them for their apparently rational selection.

I would like to join with others in arguing for a social science that admits values – not only as sources of bias, but also as means for evaluating all parts of the research process. We must accept as an assumption that to describe and to evaluate, to state what is and what ought to be, are not two entirely separable activities (Elshtain, 1979). Description is always from someone's point of view and hence is always evaluative. Description is always for a purpose. Because purposes may be unintentional or imbedded in a series of tacit unexamined prior commitments, scholars have never felt the need to defend them. Instead, critics of established views have always felt compelled to justify their "deviant" theoretical positions.

What form might a moral – i.e., value-imbued – social science take? I have borrowed some ideas from a variety of sources that may prove fruitful.

1 No particular methodology of psychology needs to be singled out for criticism. The major problem lies in unthinking acceptance of any methodology without ana-lyzing its underlying metaphysical framework. We should be particularly concerned about any methodology that makes unwarranted claims to be the sole source of truth.

2 I have devoted more time to a paradigm that stresses that the person creates reality, not because I feel this is the only way to proceed, but because it is relatively unexplored as a resource for feminist psychology. It is especially valuable to our field because of the particularist nature of the

realities it espouses. Just as it was important to criticize universal theories about humans based on studies of men, it is equally important to be aware that we are not ready to build universal theories about women. Some forms of knowledge may simply not be universal.[2] In fact, the idea that some psychological relationships exist only in a relatively limited context or under limited circumstances may be an important contribution of the psychology of women to the field of psychology as a whole.

3 We need to begin to consider a paradigm in which hypotheses about subject-object relationships will not be transformed whenever we reach an impasse in what we can learn by exclusive focus on the "objective" or "subjective" world. Recently, several theorists have discussed what they have termed the dialectical or reflexive nature of such a paradigm (Buss, 1978a; Elshtain, 1979; Gadlin & Ingle, 1975; Riegel, 1979). Its nature is too complex to be discussed at length here. One important element, however, is its emphasis on the reciprocal, interactive relationship between the person and reality. It emphasizes that although circumstances change people, people can also alter their circumstances.

4 A reflexive or dialectical view of understanding behavior probably also requires a different way of doing research. We must recognize that subjects' actions in a study are not different in kind from their actions in the so-called real world. Hence, experimenter and subject bias must be recognized as inevitable accompaniments of research and not as transient procedural contaminants. We can learn a great deal about the informal mechanisms controlling behavior in terms of sex and gender by examining such "biases" (Unger, 1981).

5 If we recognize that our subjects possess the ability to size up a situation and think about it, we may wish to enter into different research arrangements with them. For example, one could construct a study in which the subject is exposed to self-knowledge based on the experimenter's research findings (Buss, 1978b). This process might assist people in escaping from previously unconscious causal forces. Kenneth Dion (1975) has made use of a similar technique incorporating false feedback about a confederate's evaluation and his social biases, but I know of no studies that have provided subjects with accurate information about themselves.

It might also be possible for researcher and subject to attempt to determine the subjective meaning of the subject's behavior throughout the research process. Some efforts have been made to this end by asking respondents successive questions designed to get at different aspects of their reality (Looft, 1971). This technique is analogous to practices in clinical psychology, but is said to invalidate the research process.

6   Reflexivity assumes that the study of human behavior necessarily includes the behavior of the psychologist (Gadlin & Ingle, 1975). Any picture of reality must involve knowledge about the subject, about the researcher, and about knowledge itself. No one researcher can concern herself or himself with all aspects, but no claims about data should be made without taking into consideration all facets of the acquisition of knowledge.

7   We must build other criteria besides seeking the facts into our studies. One such criterion is the degree to which studies are helpful to the target population. This point does not mean we must do away with "pure" and only design "applied" studies. But, at the very least, we should attempt to make our subjects more self-aware than they were before they involved themselves in our procedures. It may be particularly valuable to teach as many people as possible that alternative explanations can be drawn from any set of findings. Recent social cognitive researchers (Anderson, Lepper & Ross, 1980) have suggested that the generation of alternative explanations may be the most effective means of getting people to alter preexisting cognitive biases. They suggest that it might even be possible to "innoculate" against the perseveration of erroneous beliefs by having people imagine all possible positive and negative connections that can be generated from information before being exposed to that information.

8   We must continue to be wary about proof. M. Brewster Smith (1980) has argued that many of the "classic" contributions to psychology have been valuable as exemplifications and demonstrations of important processes and relationships more than as starting points for cumulative parametric exploration. What accumulates from them is sensitization to and enlightenment about aspects of the contemporary human condition that we had not previously seen so clearly.

Sigmund Koch (1981) has recently noted that the quest for certainty is a major reason why psychology has failed to progress. This failure may spring both from the unwillingness to deal with complex conceptual issues and from the anxiousness of American psychologists to escape from their philosophical roots. It is an exemplification of the reflexive nature of the acquisition of knowledge that much of the material that I have drawn upon for this article was generated either by Canadian psychologists, by American males with a European background, or by females. We cannot share in the general unwillingness to acknowledge the existence of these epistemological issues or to regard philosophy as synonymous with pseudoscience if we wish to build a better scholarship. The questions will not go away. Koch (1981) has offered a quote from Bertrand Russell that appears to be most apt:

> Science tells us what we can know, but what we can know is little, and if we forget how much we cannot know we become insensitive to many things of very great importance. . . . Uncertainty in the presence of vivid hopes and fears is painful, but must be endured if we wish to live without the support of comforting fairy tales. It is not good either to forget the questions that philosophy asks, or to persuade ourselves that we have found indubitable answers to them. To teach how to live without certainty, and yet without being paralyzed by hesitation, is perhaps the chief thing that philosophy, in our age, can still do for those who study it (Russell, 1943, pp. XIII–XIV).

Or to conclude with a comforting fairytale – remember Alice's discussion near the red king as to who is the dreamer and who is the dreamed. We are the dreamers – Wonderland may yet be ours!

Notes

1 Unger, R.K. A preliminary analysis of the Attitudes towards Reality Scale. Unpublished data, 1981.
2 Parlee, M.B. Personal communication. March, 1981.

Reading 5

Imperfect reflections of reality
(Unger, 1990, pp. 122–31, 135–41)

Social constructionism as an alternative to social cognition

The acknowledgement of contradiction as a fundamental part of social reality is consistent with theoretical frameworks that make use of some form of social constructionism (cf. Gergen, 1985) or postmodernist philosophy (cf. Flax, 1987). Social constructionism, for example, stresses the way in which social categories or processes are produced by the use of language or the selective use of evidence – for example, what questions are asked as well as how the answers are interpreted. Social constructionism can be seen as an alternative to positivist epistemology, which asserts that realities are discovered rather than created.

A social-constructionist perspective within psychology differs from purely traditional approaches in several ways. Such a perspective argues, for example, that psychological phenomena must be understood in terms of their historical or situational specificity – that they have no abstract existence apart from the context in which they occur or are studied. Thus, it is meaningless to compile the results of many studies of what is presumed to be the same phenomenon, as in meta-analysis, in order to arrive at general statements about its existence. Social constructionists would also argue that several different definitions of important categories such as sex and gender can operate simultaneously in a particular situation. Differing perspectives can be present among the various participants in a social interaction or even within a single individual, depending on which aspects of these categories are salient at a particular time. Thus, researchers can expect to obtain different definitions depending on how they frame their questions or shape the context in which the questions are asked. These are not methodological flaws but an integral part of the processes by which sex and gender are continually redefined.

A social-constructionist approach to psychology also leaves room for feminist political analysis to influence theory and practice directly rather than by way of the selection of a content area or problem to be studied. Since phenomena can be interpreted only in terms of current circumstances, current social arrangements must enter into psychological analysis. This kind of formulation prevents us from believing that factors that influence choices and limit lives are "all in our heads" and helps to explain consistencies in female realities without resorting to biological explanations. Virtually all women exist within a social hierarchy in which "male is greater than female."

From a social-constructionist standpoint, sex and gender are complex descriptive and prescriptive processes. They are both internalized and communicated to others. Neither sex or gender, however, is integrally whole or internally consistent. The problem for feminist psychologists, therefore, is to determine under what conditions a particular definition is salient. When, for example, is a particular definition of gender a mechanism of social control that exerts influences on most individuals of a particular sex? What enables individuals to resist definitions of gender in particular circumstances? And why are only some social definitions of sex and gender incorporated into our views of ourselves?

These problems are at the heart of the relationship between the person and society. Psychologists have wrestled with these issues for many years without resolution. There is no reason why feminist psychologists should attempt to resolve them de novo. It might be helpful to examine conceptualizations developed by feminists in other disciplines. In a recent article, for example, Gerson and Peiss (1985) suggest that we study the societal function of gender in three areas: boundary maintenance, social negotiation, and domination and consciousness. These are mechanisms that regulate cross-sex interactions. Consideration of them might be helpful in delineating the different levels at which sex and gender can be defined.

On a societal level, for example, boundaries between the sexes are maintained by the sex-segregation of occupations. On a smaller scale, the sexes are separated by implicit rules about interpersonal gestures and styles. Women are expected to use a less assertive style than men and violators can be viewed as sexually aggressive rather than interpersonally assertive (Unger, 1979a). Perceptions and misperceptions about the meaning of nonverbal behaviors for women and men appear to function in a way that maintains power asymmetries between the sexes. It is surely no accident that one of the first and fundamental feminist insights in psychology involved interpersonal touching and the confounding of sex and status in our society (Henley, 1973).

On an interpersonal level, processes involving social negotiation appear to be very important in producing and maintaining sex differences. Men have control over a great share of resources and opportunities so that women's ability to negotiate for societal equity is restricted by their limited access to such resources. Negotiation for interpersonal equity is also restricted by social norms and punishments for gender deviance. Perceived penalties for deviance might account for the sex-related differences in public and private behavior discussed above. There seems to be increasing evidence that women will behave as competitively as men when rewards for doing so are available to them (cf. Keller & Moglen, 1987).

Societal arrangements that make women more responsible for everyday life can influence their consciousness of it. Women's supposedly more concrete and relational perceptions might be their response to the persistent need to negotiate for a place in a male-dominated world. Different worldviews also serve to separate the sexes. Feminist psychologists can contribute to our understanding of such processes by elucidating the psychological mechanisms by which gender exerts control at these various levels of analysis. Power is clearly an important part of the social context at each of these levels.

Gender and contradiction

Contradiction can be a particularly interesting area to explore in terms of a social-constructionist theory of consciousness. For example, an individual may be well aware that gender deviance will not be allowed even if only a few instances of gender-inappropriate behavior are punished. Widespread media attention to such cases as that of Mary Cunningham, an attractive Harvard M.B.A. who rose "too rapidly" in the Bendix Corporation, can make it clear to other women that high aspirations and physical attractiveness do not go together. For working-class women, magazines such as *True Story* include many (35 percent) stories about rape and attempted assault – which usually occur when the woman has been in the wrong place, has chosen not to accept advice, or has acted too independently (Cantor, 1987).

Feminist psychologists have begun to develop a typology of situations and circumstances in which gender-appropriateness is likely to be noticed and judged (cf. O'Leary, Unger & Wallston, 1985). This involves distinguishing contexts in which any female is seen to be out of place and when it is "only" her behavior that will be devalued rather than her presence (Unger, 1988b). For example, women are accepted in work environments in which women predominate but are more likely to report being sexually harassed in nontraditional jobs with highly unequal sex ratios (Gutek & Cohen, 1987). We still need, however, to identify the form and circumstances in which negative judgments about members of one's social category are incorporated into one's personal identity.

I have argued elsewhere (Unger, 1988b) that contradictions in terms of how and when gender is socially salient make it difficult to develop an accurate self-knowledge. A kind of tyranny of structurelessness makes it difficult for a woman to determine whether a negative response is a consequence of her social category or of her personal behavior. Since negative responses often occur in situations where women are isolated, they might find it impossible to validate their perceptions with others like themselves. Our very language has many more terms for differences in personal characteristics than for differences in situational constraints. Thus, women might be more likely to assume personal responsibility for their behavior and its consequences and, therefore, blame themselves rather than seek social explanations and social change.

Contradictions within definitions of femininity create double binds for women that do not seem to exist for men in our society. Socially acceptable feminine behavior has negative social consequences because it conflicts with perceptions of instrumentality and adulthood (Broverman, Vogel, Brover-man, Clarkson & Rosenkrantz, 1972). As noted above, however, feminine behaviors are demanded via the expectations of others and so-called self-fulfilling prophecies confirm these expectations.

Imagine a woman viewing her own behavior from the perspective of an outsider observer (although few or no other members of her social category are likely to be present under circumstances in which social mechanisms that create sex differences are most potent). She might see herself as confirming feminine stereotypes of dependency, oversensitivity to others, or emotional liability. Without observing other women behaving in a similar way under similar conditions, she might well explain her behavior as the result of her personal deficiency – the explanation fostered by cultural norms. It is important to keep in mind that her perception of her own behavior may be correct, but her explanations of it are wrong. It might be preferable for her self-esteem, however, to accept complicity in behaviors that can have harmful consequences rather than to see herself as controlled by others.

Experimental social psychology provides some useful techniques for analyzing gender as an interactional phenomenon. It provides some ways to evaluate the claims of theories that posit the existence of gender differences as opposed to those contending that gender differences are created. It is difficult to argue, for example, that so-called gender differences in conformity are the product of long-term socialization if they emerge or disappear as a function of whether people's behavior is observed by others. Comparison of behavior in private and public provides a way to bring social norms into the laboratory. It also provides a way to study the effect of social context while holding social roles constant.

It is important that we do not regard perceptions and cognitions about sex and gender as individualistic phenomena. People cannot alter their inadequate or inappropriate views of the world at will. It is also important that we not neglect the role of the social framework in creating these perceptions. Each of these caveats is important in light of psychologists' propensity for conceptualizing human problems on a personal level.

The construction of social reality

One way in which feminist psychologists can challenge psychology's tendency to accept difference as a given is to demonstrate the enormous extent to which both our professional and cultural categories are constructed. Examples can be found at every level of analysis. Historians of science have noted that throughout the nineteenth and most of the twentieth century, estrogen was called "the female hormone" despite the fact that the richest source of this hormone was the urine of stallions (Hall, 1977). Anthropologists tell us that not all societies have two genders derived from two sexes. In some kinship systems, age is the major differentiator, and words referring to gender have meaning only with reference to specific adult reproductive roles (Gailey, 1987). In other societies, it is possible for a female or a male to take on the role and the gender of the other sex. What differences in social organization emerge when gender is viewed as modifiable?

It is not necessary to go to other societies to find different cognitions about gender. Transsexuals, for example, appear to see their sex, but not their gender, as modifiable. Social psychologists have, however, been reluctant to study cognitive frameworks in a so-called deviant population. This unwillingness is partly a function of the fact that social psychology derives from a nomothetic tradition – it seeks to extract general rules for behavior rather than to examine the individuality of particular persons. It is probably also a function of our cultural definition of sex and gender as a highly correlated system, as unmodifiable, and as internally consistent. Other ways of defining sex/gender have been made to disappear (Flax, 1987).

Even among so-called normal males and females, perceptions involving gender vary with race, social class, and even geographic region. Black women, for example, generally expect that they will hold paying jobs as adults (Turner & McCaffrey, 1974) and are less likely than white women to see marriage and motherhood as incompatible with work outside the home (Murray & Mednick, 1977). It is important that we do not obscure the differences between particular groups of women in our examination of women's differences from men.

Dichotomies between male and female or masculine and feminine are constructed by selective research – by bias in our research methodology as well as in the populations chosen for research. Methods that allow subjects to respond freely indicate a much greater range of meanings for gender. In an extensive anthropological study of Southern college students, for example, Holland and Skinner (1987) found that both sexes had a complex, implicit categorization system for gender types that classified both the evaluator and those he or she evaluated. Females appeared to classify males in terms of how likely they were to use their position or attractiveness to females for selfish purposes; how ineffectual or unlikable they were; and how unusual their sexual appetites were. Males classified females in terms of their prestige as valued sexual possessions or companions; their tendency to be overdemanding or engulfing; and their sex appeal. Obviously, such typing has utility for the social system in which college students interact, but it has little resemblance to beliefs about males and females tapped by conventional psychological methodology.

When two sexes are not clearly demarcated, people seem to invent them. In a clever experiment designed to manipulate assumptions about gender rather than simply to measure them, John and Sussman (1984–85) asked subjects to take the role of a participant during several stages of a narrative involving a social interaction between two persons whose sex was unspecified. Sometimes "brown buttons" made assertive or initiative-taking statements and sometimes "gray buttons" did. The researchers found that subjects made assumptions about the heterosexual nature of the transaction even at the expense of role consistency or the integrity of the narrative. They also inferred role reciprocity so that when one participant was assumed to be male, the other automatically became female.

The applicability of social constructionism to psychology

It can be difficult for psychologists to accept the social construction of such an apparently basic phenomenon as gender. This is partly because of a continuing positivist epistemology within the field as well as a confusion between sex and gender. Variables that have physical reality such as neurons, hormones, and physiological sex appear as more *real* than purely psychological processes. It has been suggested that psychology suffers from "physics envy."

It is probably no accident that Naomi Weisstein, author of a pioneering constructionist critique of psychology's treatment of women in 1968, is also well known for her research on the neural bases of optical illusions. Using the figure-ground illusion – an ambiguous situation in which two perceptions alternate although the physical stimulus remains the same – she has shown that discrimination of an additional faint stimulus imposed on the illusion is better within the figure than the ground irrespective of where that figure may be at the time (Wong & Weisstein, 1982). Weisstein (1970) has also demonstrated that adaptation to an entire grid of lines (so that the intensity of stimulus required to perceive all parts of the grid is greater) occurs even when part of that grid has been blocked by a cube. She has suggested that this phenomenon represents a kind of symbolic activity in neurons – a neuronal awareness that something is at the back of something else.

Although these studies would appear to have nothing to do with gender, they demonstrate that some forms of subjective construction take place at a very basic physiological level.

Such findings have no place in a theory that states that physiological mechanisms reflect reality. They demonstrate, however, that constructionist explanations can be useful at all levels of psychology and that constructionist processes are not any less real than other psychological phenomena.

An additional barrier to understanding the constructed nature of gender in our society is the continuing tendency of psychologists to dichotomize both sex and gender. As noted above, this is probably a reflection of the kinds of questions psychologists ask and the methods they use to analyze the answers. But dichotomies are also metaphors for the way we structure reality. The terms *male* and *female* carry with them beliefs about good and evil, rational and irrational, and so forth. Some of these metaphors can be extracted by psychological methodology that permits subjects to choose their own categories when they are making evaluations about the sexes. Such techniques applied to gender reveal a "dark side" to stereotypes that reflect implicit assumptions about dominance and sexuality not unlike those voiced by Southern college students described above (Ashmore, 1981). Beliefs about male hardness and female softness probably exert as much social control over the sexes as do societal prescriptions about appropriate gender-role behavior. Indeed, these negative beliefs can exert even more powerful social control because they are subject to neither conscious scrutiny nor public debate.

Feminism and the issue of comparisons

In several points I have discussed the concept of the comparison group as a major factor in our decisions about whether a particular sex difference exists. The ability to offer meaningful comparisons is an important contribution that feminist psychologists can make to feminists in other disciplines. Since, however, comparisons require that some differences must be ignored, it is easy to misunderstand the role of comparison in psychology and to charge that researchers interested in quantification have oversimplified and overgeneralized findings about males and females. Nevertheless, comparison can be the fundamental tool by which feminist scholarship can escape a kind of radical relativism – in which we can make no generalizations at all.

Feminist psychologists will have to transcend the current dichotomy between an approach that focuses on the specific qualities of each woman (and thus permits only description) and an approach that focuses on generalities (and thus permits global statements about sex differences). To do so, we must generate studies that simultaneously compare groups in a number of different ways. Instead of simply comparing women to men, we need to compare black women to white women, heterosexual women to lesbians, and working-class women to affluent women. But we also need to compare groups of men and women that we believe to be similar in various ways. Comparisons of this sort in terms of occupational roles suggest that men and women are not particularly different (Powell, 1987). What is important here is that we specify ahead of time why each comparison is useful.

Who we compare to whom is a fundamental question in the psychology of sex and gender. In an early paper in this area, Parlee (1981) pointed out that conclusions about whether males and females differed in health were affected by whether the group chosen for comparison with affluent, well-educated, successful males was their sisters (who were presumably biologically similar but in different social roles) or unrelated females in comparable occupational roles. Datan (1986), in a reappraisal of her important work on midlife transition of women from various subcultures in Israel, noted the failure to investigate the husbands of her respondents because funding agents at the time were primarily concerned with the consequences of what they defined as a strictly biological event – menopause. Both of these studies illustrate implicit assumptions about the importance of biological determinants – assumptions that influenced the comparison groups selected and thus influenced their results.

Experimental psychology is based on comparisons. Reliability, for example, refers to a comparison of the same research population to itself to determine whether a measure shows consistent effects over time. Validity has many meanings but generally refers to comparisons between psychological instruments believed to measure similar aspects of behavior. Replicability – the cornerstone of empirical investigation – involves comparisons of independent studies to see if the same results are produced. These concepts are limited by their assumption that people remain constant over time and place and do not react to being examined by different researchers. Nevertheless, they give us a framework on which generalizations can be examined. For example, the failure of projective measures of achievement to predict the achievement-related behavior of women in the same way as that of men (a failure of validity) led to the development of the concept of fear of success and an extensive literature on gender and achievement. Similarly, inconsistency between various measures of androgyny (a failure of reliability) has led to questions about the meaning of the concept. Failures in replicability have also led to questions about the existence of sex-related differences in moral development.

The useful comparisons for feminist psychologists include:

1 A comparison of the same behaviors in different social contexts. Eagly (1987) has suggested that the laboratory environment of psychological studies can produce a greater amount of gender differentiation because it strips participants of other social roles. It could be, however, that the role of subject overrides gender awareness and can reduce some sex-related differences (Unger, 1981). The laboratory as a social context deserves special attention.

2 A comparison of behavior carried out under public scrutiny as compared to behavior believed to be private. Studies summarized earlier suggest that the presence of others causes an invasion of social norms that enhances gender differentiation.

3 A comparison of sex-ratios in groups, as well as comparisons between transient and permanent groups. Dion's (1985) preliminary analysis of group processes suggests that these two variables together produce either gender assimilation or distinctiveness. People appear to emphasize distinctiveness when their place within a group is secure (such as within the family or classroom), whereas they minimize gender differences when they are in a minority in transient groups. We need to pay special attention to the position of token as the most extreme example of being a minority in any kind of group.

4 A comparison of what people say about themselves in terms of sex and gender and what they say about others. Spence and Helmreich (1978) report that there is no relationship between how people rate their own instrumental and affective qualities and the extent to which they generate sex stereotypes about these qualities for others. People appear to perceive themselves as less sex-typed than they perceive others. If so, estimates of sex differences in some characteristics associated with gender will vary depending on whether the referent is the self or others.

All of these comparisons involve investigating gender as a phenomenon rather than gender as a difference. The universality of gender differences can, however, also be tested by comparisons between people of different races, social classes, and ethnic backgrounds. Investigation of the constructions of gender in different cultures and subcultures is, of course, fundamental as is the development of research techniques that permit us to go beyond dichotomization. One such technique is the Q sort, in which people are permitted to rank a variety of statements in terms of their importance or relevance. Kitzinger (1987) used this methodology to evaluate the meaning of lesbianism for a group of self-defined lesbians. She found that lesbianism had a range of meanings from a source of self-fulfillment and inner peace through political self-definition to a self-definition based on belief in personal inadequacy or failure. This methodology provides a rich picture of important differences within groups and could certainly be used to understand differences between them. But as Kitzinger warns, it is, like any research strategy, at the mercy of the researcher's judgment, since she has selected the statements or categories to be sorted.

Any method using comparison must ignore many important differences among individuals. It is the reliance on some form of categorization that has led feminists outside of psychology to accuse psychologists, including feminist psychologists, of context stripping and ignoring the unique features of individuals. But comparisons carefully done, with the criteria for group selection made explicit, can focus the debate in terms of what is truly unique to women and to men, or, more correctly, careful comparisons can focus the debate on the question, What aspects of gender produce the particular qualities being measured at this time? Unfortunately, because methods involving multiple comparisons often involve what is seen by those outside the discipline as arcane statistical manipulation, they will be less easily integrated with feminist scholarship as a whole than are the narrative techniques discussed below.

Feminist psychology and the individual's story

A promising and quite different avenue of research involves the growing concern of feminist psychologists with various forms of narrative and personal stories. Such studies place the individual within her time and place. Although some of these analyses are akin to literary ones, substituting experience for text, psychological concepts are used to illuminate the material. Thus far, these integrations appear to have been most successful in analyzing developmental issues for women. Helson (1984–85), for example, has used Jungian theory to elucidate critical points in the lifespan of individual women. She points to correspondences between changes in the work of creative women and age-related changes in their life circumstances. Stewart (1987) has used the concept of historical cohort to explain personality dynamics in successive generations of women. She suggests that unique historic events that were important at critical periods in women's development influence what is important to them at a later stage. Thus, it is meaningless to compare women of the same age across generations unless we take into account the historical events that occurred at critical points in their lives.

One means of integrating narrative measures with more conventional psychological measures involves comparing structured and nonstructured questions. In nonstructured cases the respondents provide the narrative to be analyzed. Sanders and her colleagues (Sanders, Steil & Weinglass, 1984–85), for example, gave traditionally religious women vignettes in which married career women made decisions that had a negative impact on their careers. They found that although their respondents apparently favoured choices that "preserved the family" when measured by objective scales, these women also showed considerable anger about such choices when their subjective responses were evaluated. In contrast, Crawford (1988) found that sex differences in humor production were the same whether she used structured or less-structured methods. These varied findings suggest that we do not yet know enough about psychological methodology to prescribe or proscribe a particular kind of research.

Feminist psychologists are also attempting to make their involvement with their research more explicit and reflexive. This process has been termed *conscious subjectivity* (Wilkinson, 1986). Dialogue by the researcher both with the participants in the research and with its hypothetical audience illuminates the way that the researcher's assumptions have constructed the particular reality being examined. Thus, Fine (1983) shows us how her beliefs about effective coping following rape are a product of her white middle-class position in society. In her account of an extended conversation in a rape crisis center, she reveals as much or more about herself than she discloses about the black woman who has just been raped. Similarly, Marshall (1986) shows us how she became more feminist and more accepting of qualitative research as she progressed through her research on the experiences of women managers. Last, Lykes (1989) illustrates some of the problems produced when the researcher and participants have different constructions of reality. She analyzed the response of Guatemalan Indian women to an informed consent form regularly used by psychologists to insure ethical treatment of their subjects. Use of a written form, however, violated the oral tradition of the Indian women and resulted in a loss of trust. Each of these narratives portrays the intrusion of the researcher into her research and thus explodes the myth of objective science.

The use of narrative opens up as many problems for feminist psychologists as it resolves; for example, what criteria do we use to determine whose story should be told? What yardsticks do we use to measure the reliability of personal reality when we know that people constantly reconstruct themselves as their personal circumstances and awareness change? If everyone has his or her own version of reality, what criteria do we use to determine the most useful definition of reality? Of course, the key question here is: Useful to whom?

5

Ideology, epistemology, and other covert agendas

Philosophy re-enters psychology

The term 'epistemology' had long been absent from psychology when I first used it in my presidential address to Division 35 in 1981 (Unger, 1983). Muzafer and Carolyn Sherif, who were in the audience, liked the talk, but thought the term was too metaphysical, would not be understood by the audience, and probably should not be used more than once at the most. Ironically, the term has become something of a cliché in feminist scholarship today. It is still not clear, however, if psychologists use it in the correct philosophical sense or whether we all mean the same thing when we use the term.

Epistemology has had a long history within philosophy where it is used to refer to theories about what constitutes knowledge. Psychologists of my generation have a love–hate relationship with philosophy. It represents our intellectual roots, but we were taught to eschew its ways of thinking as contrary to scientific thought. As an undergraduate and graduate student the only philosophy I encountered within a psychology course was logical positivism. We were taught that the nature of human behavior (never human thought) could be understood if we carefully operationalized our definitions, kept independent and dependent variables separate, and followed rigid rules for experimental design. Although my final year at Harvard was spent in an office in the William James Building, we were not often reminded that he was one of our progenitors.

The rules of logical positivism worked fairly well for my early studies on the caudate nucleus of rats and the hypothalamus of cats. They even worked fairly well for my first studies in social psychology in which I was interested in people primarily as cues for misperception and stereotyping. Even then, however, I was interested in the way in which people extracted meaning from such cues. One of our early studies, for example, looked at the inferences people made about others' values based on the kind of clothing that they wore (Unger and Raymond, 1974).

At this point, however, my concerns were more about stereotypes than about epistemology. I was still in the process of making the transition from physiological to social psychology. Aside from moving from animal to human subjects, this transition also involved changes in basic assumptions. For example, I could not assume that my subject population would be unaffected by the awareness that I was manipulating them. This led to questions about the demand characteristics of experiments (Raymond, Unger and Stone, 1972) and to the exploration of unobtrusive methods of investigation (Unger, 1981).

Possibly because my own viewpoint had changed so drastically, I became and have remained interested in how our frame of reference influences our assumptions. My early studies were rather naive. We asked students to rank themselves, their peers, and their parents using Rokeach's instrumental value scale (Unger and Fishbein, 1973). We found, of course, that they misperceived their parents much more than they did their peers, whom they saw as much like themselves. Later we went on to use this technique to test the accuracy of their perceptions of the values of members of the same and opposite sex (Unger and Siiter, 1974).

Social cognition and feminist psychology

I now recognize that we were, in a crude way, manipulating cues that people use to make inferences about their own and others' beliefs and behaviors. Our procedures were akin to the many studies of attributional processes that were published in the 1970s. Social psychologists such as Kay Deaux and Sara Kiesler recognized early that attributional processes could be used to explain some of the differential beliefs about women and men. For example, an early study by Gail Pheterson, Sara Kiesler and Phillip Goldberg (1971) found that people did not discriminate against the work of women if they believed that it had received official sanction, for example, it had won an award. Kay Deaux and Tim Emswiller (1974) found, moreover, that identical performance by men and women did not always produce similar beliefs about their work. What was skill in a man could be seen as luck in a female. Later, Kiesler and her colleague (Feldman-Summers and Kiesler, 1974) found that women were seen to exert more effort than men for an equivalent achievement. They titled their paper 'Those who are number two try harder'.

Research demonstrating differences in attributional patterns about males and females with identical performance has continued. In my view, the most compelling research in this area has been done by Jacqueline Eccles and her students on sex-related differences in attributions about mathematical performance (cf. Eccles and Jacobs, 1986). She has found that parents make differential attributions about their sons' and daughters' excellent mathematical performance similar to those found earlier on other tasks. They are more apt to see their sons' performance as due to talent and their daughters' to hard work. Differential attributions induce different expectancies. Thus, when the going got tough, boys (who were assumed to have more stable qualities related to mathematical aptitude) were advised to persevere.

Other social psychologists have shown that attributions may depend upon how much information people possess. People possess more information about their own than about others' behaviors. Thus, they see themselves as exceptions to any kind of group categorization. They do not appear to be aware, however, of the inconsistencies between what they say about themselves and what they say about others although, from an observer's perspective, they appear to be in identical circumstances. This selective awareness, also known as the fundamental attribution error, produces some very contradictory views about agency and control.

Faye Crosby (1982, 1984) pioneered work on the ways in which women use selective awareness to deny personal discrimination. For example, she has consistently found that women and members of other groups that suffer economic and societal disadvantage report that they, personally, are doing well although they recognize discrimination against other members of their social category. I believe this work helps to elucidate some of the mechanisms by which people internalize negative views about people like themselves.

Much of this work was done by mainstream – albeit female – social psychologists. In the 1970s there was relatively little professional contact between these researchers and those of us who identified primarily with the psychology of women. In fact, at least one prominent woman social psychologist who had done extensive research on differential perceptions of women and men had to be persuaded to join Division 35. She felt that her work was on both sexes and the division's name did not adequately define it. She was persuaded that many of us had reservations about the name and that she could make a feminist statement by joining the division.

Because of this split in disciplinary allegiance, feminists doing work in similar areas did not always know about each other. I met Faye Crosby because of our mutual involvement in the Society for the Psychological Study of Social Issues (SPSSI) and found that some of my research paralleled her findings on women's denial of discrimination. We had focused, however, on cognitive contradictions as barriers to societal change rather than on attributional processes within the individual (Unger and Sussman, 1986).

This study came about serendipitously as a result of my efforts to develop a scale which would measure personal epistemology (discussed later in this chapter). I could not decide whether to word items in the first or third person singular so I did both in a preliminary study and compared the results. We used similar statements that could be answered either for oneself or for others. Students appeared to believe that they themselves were more in control of their actions and its consequences than others. The most dramatic example of this process was demonstrated by a statement worded: 'At the present time, people are recognized for their achievements regardless of race, sex, and social class' versus 'At the present time, I am recognized for my achievements regardless of race, sex, and social class'. Comparable groups of students disagreed strongly with the first statement and agreed just as strongly with the second.

I have employed this logical inconsistency in class demonstrations to illustrate some of the difficulties involved in helping people to become aware of the need for social change. As we noted in the conclusion to this study:

> These findings also suggest that there is no reason to believe there is a strong connection between personal change and social change. Individuals may accept their own gender-related characteristics and still view them as deviant in others. Similarly, divergence between epistemology about the self and epistemology about the world in general permits the use of different "yardsticks" when evaluating personally relevant or irrelevant information. It may even permit an individual to disregard information about societal biases against groups of which he or she is a member. Thus, persons can come to share societal assumptions that are oppressive to themselves. (Unger and Sussman, 1986, p. 635)

Studies on implicit assumptions would not have been possible in social psychology until the so-called cognitive revolution made it possible to consider mental processes as well as behaviors. At one time (Unger, 1983–4), I believed that the shift from behavioral to cognitive paradigms would resolve our problems with sex as a psychological variable. At that time, I stressed the growing numbers of studies that showed sex-related effects were highly correlated to status differences; group context had a great effect on whether a sex-related difference would appear; and, in general, sex as a label had a greater impact on people's behavior than one would expect, given the long-term socialization of maleness and femaleness in our society.

Although I still believe that an important role of social psychology is to elucidate the mechanisms through which gendered behaviors are developed and manifested, I now recognize that the cognitive social view of sex and gender also has flaws (cf. Sampson,

1981; Unger, 1989b). The most important flaw is the apparent inability of most social psychologists to recognize the systemic and pervasive nature of oppression in our society.[1] The behavioral mechanisms of prejudice and discrimination may be expressed by individuals, but the targets do not appear to be a matter of individual choice. Moreover, the kind of laboratory research engaged in by most social psychologists does not lend itself well to a consideration of their own covert assumptions about the world and the meaning of their methodology.

Ideology and epistemological dualism

As I became more and more interested in the role of viewpoints I began to recognize that they influence many aspects of the way we perceive the world. My radical shift from physiological to social psychology forced me to think more about multiple criteria for making judgments than I might have if I had not changed fields. While on sabbatical during the 1980–81 academic year, I did a lot of reading on the relationship between ideology and behavior. Since I had not been formally trained as a social psychologist, I was not constrained to read only those works that had been sanctioned by the field. Indeed, the critiques I found most cogent came from psychologists interested in either the philosophy or history of science.

I became aware of a small but important literature which indicated that psychologists' ideology had an influence on their choice of a specialty within the discipline (Coan, 1979). I also found studies that indicated that social origins influenced what questions psychologists asked in research (Samelson, 1978) and, especially, what conclusions they drew from their data (Sherwood and Nataupsky, 1968). I drew on much of this literature for my presidential address to Division 35 (Unger, 1983).

I also became intrigued by a theoretical position developed by Alan Buss (1975, 1978a). He argued that psychological paradigms shift between two basic forms whose deep structure can be characterized either as: *reality constructs the person* or *the person constructs reality*. Buss recognized that psychology as a discipline needed to transcend this dualism, but subsequently retired from the field. I have made great use of Buss's insights. For example, I have used his distinction to classify apparently disparate psychological theories and to analyze some of the underlying similarities between them especially in terms of sex and gender (Unger, 1989b). (See Reading 6 at the end of this chapter.)

Attitudes About Reality Scale

I also used Buss's theoretical framework to construct a scale designed to measure individuals' views about the relationship between the person and reality. I reasoned that just as psychology as a field has flip-flopped between two sides of an epistemological dualism, so, too, might individuals in their efforts to understand the world. It was this reasoning that led me to construct what is now known as the Attitudes About Reality Scale (Unger, Draper and Pendergrass, 1986).

I had never constructed an attitude questionnaire of any kind before. Had I known how difficult it is to do, I probably would never have tried. We went through what seemed like an infinite number of revisions until we finally settled on a forty-item scale. Its two end points mirrored Buss's dualism, but in more individualistic terms. We characterized people with a predominant 'reality constructs the person' orientation as (logical) *positivists* and people with a predominant 'the person constructs reality' orientation as (social) *constructionists*.[2] A positivist world view was defined as structured around belief in the validity of a materially based external reality and the legitimacy of external authority. In contrast, constructionists were defined by their tendency to see external reality as historically and situationally determined; to accept individual efforts to change society as legitimate; and to prefer social explanations to biological ones.

The biggest problem with this scale was how to validate a philosophical construct. In other words, what behaviors would be associated with either a positivist or a constructionist orientation? We settled on an analysis based on known groups. For example, we evaluated scores on the scale in terms of political preference, religion, and religiosity. Our hypothesis that positivists – who value external sources of authority in explaining how the world works – would be more conservative in both their politics and their religion than constructionists was confirmed.

We also found that personal epistemology appeared to predict the behavior of students in terms of course selection. Positivists were more likely to be found in traditional courses within the discipline, whereas constructionists were more likely to be found in courses with a social issues focus. To a limited extent, social issues courses such as those on women and gender also fostered constructionist thinking in their students (Howe, 1985; Unger, Draper and Pendergrass, 1986).

We had believed that a constructionist view of the world with its emphasis on the belief that reality is malleable, that many social problems have primarily environmental explanations, and that the status quo is unjust or unfair would appeal to those groups of individuals who are marginalized in our society. To our surprise, we found no important sex-related differences in scores on this scale. Later, we found that, as a group, African-American students were somewhat more positivist than their Anglo-American counterparts (Unger and Jones, 1988).

Subjective versus objective 'reality' and feminism
In an attempt to understand more about the relationship between epistemology and ideology, I began to explore the attitudes about reality of feminist and other socially activist scholars. At this time I was a member of a faculty seminar at Rutgers University on the construction of the self and society led by Alison Jaggar, a feminist philosopher, who held a visiting chair in women's studies. I believed this group would be an ideal audience (and research population) for my concerns with the relationship between covert beliefs and behavior.

Again to my surprise, the group as whole was sympathetic neither to my theoretical perspective nor to my methodology. They cooperated in answering the questions in the scale, but denied that I would find anything meaningful. One of the members of the seminar even argued that feminists had no systematic biases. The majority believed that psychologists would never get anywhere using this kind of context stripping methodology. Nevertheless, this group (as well as subsequent groups of feminist and socially activist leaders within psychology) proved to be far more constructionist in their view of the world than any other populations I have ever studied (Unger, 1984–5). When I returned some weeks later with these data, the group claimed to admire my persistence, but did not change its mind about the value of my methods.

This disagreement bothered me a great deal at the time and continues to concern me today. Most of the members of the seminar were scholars in the humanities. I was the only psychologist and there were two sociologists in the group. Some of the dispute was due to differences in what various disciplines consider to be evidential sources. But the conflict was deeper than that. Some of the feminist scholars present appeared to have a very deep distrust of the concept of quantitative measurement.

Ironically, despite their disbelief in the methodology, these feminists' critical view of science was evident in some of their responses to particular items on the scale. I believe this hostility has contributed to an interdisciplinary split within women's studies in which feminist empirical psychologists contribute little to its ongoing dialogues. Other empiricist psychologists with whom I have discussed this matter have also given me examples of the same kind of hostility directed against their work.

Explanations for this distrust are not hard to find. Quantitative measurement (especially by psychologists) has often been used to 'prove' that women are abnormal or deficient. It is seen by some as a tool of patriarchy. Nomothetic methods – which attempt to generalize across individuals – are especially questionable in terms of postmodernist theories which argue that there is no 'truth' and only the individual's story is important. These theories question the existence of a stable self. If even identity is socially and temporally situated, how can one make statements about the general properties of any group?

Feminist theory is, in general, constructionist. It provides a useful antidote to positivist theories about the essential qualities of maleness and femaleness; masculinity and femininity. However, the unwillingness of postmodernist feminist theory to come to grips with some issues has produced biases too. And ideological biases can produce blind spots for feminists as well as positivists.

Feminism and the problem of science

Many feminist scholars have a peculiar ambivalence about scientific data. Feminist theoreticians of science such as Evelyn Fox Keller, Ruth Hubbard, and the late Ruth Bleier are rightfully applauded for their trenchant critiques. But these scholars do not put theory into practice and it is difficult to figure out what 'good' applied feminist science would be like. Hobbled with suspicions about quantification, generalization, and the context-stripping nature of experimental methodology, it is difficult for women to be both feminists and working scientists. Moreover, a lack of concern about evidential criteria has produced a kind of 'rampant relativism' that makes it difficult for empirical feminists to marshall evidence against sexist science.

It is extremely important that some feminists exist who can speak the language of science. Despite my background, I had believed I no longer had the expertise in physiological psychology to do so. In 1993, however, I was invited to participate in a NATO-sponsored conference on the development of sex similarities and differences in behaviors. One of the organizers had read a version of 'Toward a redefinition of sex and gender' that had been translated into French and thought that I could provide a theoretical counterpoint to some of the data on sex differences. Most of the other thirty-two participants were neurobiologists or physiological psychologists. Many were women, but I was one of only three feminists invited to participate in the conference.

Many feminists have tended to reject the possibility of a bio-logical contribution to some sex-related behaviors. I chose another strategy. I developed a paper that looked at alternative mechanisms by which sex-related differences can be created (Unger, 1993a). I reviewed evidence from feminist scholars who had studied: cultural differences in the definition of sex and gender; humans with various sexual anomalies to determine whether there are any biological factors that are necessary for the expression of sex-related behav-iors; and the ways social systems convey meanings based on external characteristics.

Using evidence primarily from biological and anthropological sources, I tried to deconstruct sex rather than gender. I concluded:

> It is clear that there are a great many sources of variability associated with the apparently simple word "sex." As noted at the beginning of this paper, sex is used to refer to our reproductive category, physiological properties, reproductive and nonreproductive behaviors, and, in human beings, our sense of who we are, physically and psychologically. It also refers to a system of categories that differ from one culture to another. We will probably never be able to determine one single variable that causes a person to be male or female. The language of dimorphism leads us into searching for causal dichotomies. How would our analyses be affected if we used the concept of "many sexes" rather than just two? (Unger, 1993a, p. 472)

The scientists at this meeting had never encountered such data before. They do not read feminist scholarship and some were genuinely pleased to learn about some of these studies. I do not know whether I convinced anyone there. Some of the more regressive scientists chose to see me as an exception – a kind of talking platypus – because they believed that most feminists did not know as much about their subject as I did (I had boned up for the meeting). I was pleased to be able to write a chapter for the conference proceedings (Haug et al., 1993) that provided an alternative viewpoint to the pervasive biological determinism of the group. I hoped it would provide ammunition for those who are not willing to accept neural 'hard-wiring' without question.

Feminist negativity toward biological theories is quite under-standable. Biological arguments have often been used against both women and people of color. Biologically based arguments do not disappear for long, but reappear regularly under different guises (cf. Shields, 1975a; Gould, 1981; Russett, 1989). There is also an essential sameness to biological arguments, no matter what group is targeted. The repetitive nature of these arguments may have its roots in unexamined epistemological assumptions.

About fifteen years ago several articles appeared in the *American Psychologist* which led me to believe that behavioral scientists were beginning to recognize the importance of the relationship between values and science (Kimble, 1984; Krasner and Houts, 1984). These articles led me to offer some preliminary results from my first study using the Attitudes About Reality Scale which were also published in the *American Psychologist*. I noted that individuals who identified themselves as republican or conservative were more likely than individuals who identified themselves as democratic, liberal, or independent to agree with the following items on the scale:

● Science has underestimated the extent to which genes affect human behavior.
● Most sex differences have an evolutionary purpose.
● Biological sex, sex role, and sexual preference are highly related to each other in normal people.
● A great deal can be learned about human behavior from studying animals.

None of these items would seem to have an obvious connection to political attitudes. I argued for an implicit connection that accounted for the historical relationship between political conservatism and biological determinism and concluded:

> The relationship between political conservatism and beliefs about bio-logical determinism may account for the consistent reappearance of biology in controversies involving the empowerment of formerly disenfranchised groups. The assumption of whether a racial or sexual entity is a biological or a social category is fundamental to both political and scientific paradigms. Thus, the shift from a biological position (the study of sex differences) to a social position (the examination of gender) was a necessary step in the development of a new psychology of women.
>
> Biologically determinist arguments are often used to answer political and social questions although there is no necessary overt connection between them. Evidence of a connection by way of deeply embedded implicit ideology is, therefore, exciting. We need to examine this connection before we can deal with it. Awareness of our assumptions is only a necessary first step. (Unger, 1985a, p. 1414)

Despite this promising beginning, however, most behavioral psychologists remain unwilling to examine their socio-political assumptions or to believe that these have anything to do with the way they practise science. Studies in this area seem to disappear very quickly.

Ideology and behavior in Israel and elsewhere

I believe the connection between covert assumptions about biology and political–social behavior is one of the keys to understanding intergroup conflict. I have continued to explore the relationship from a variety of perspectives. For example, I have been interested in finding out whether the connection is based on particular beliefs within North American society (from which I generated the scale) or whether there are more fundamental connections based on the way people think about the world.

I sought and was awarded a Fulbright fellowship for research and teaching in Israel during the 1988–9 academic year. I was particularly interested in exploring attitudes about reality in Israel because of its diverse population and its intense religious and political conflicts. In particular, I wanted to find out whether implicit ideology had similar effects cross-culturally – independent of the particular religious and political context of the eastern USA.

My year in Israel was both exciting and enlightening. The intifada had already begun, but the University of Haifa (where I was a visiting faculty member) still maintained tolerable relations between its majority of Jewish students and the roughly 20 percent Israeli Arab population who also attended. This latter group included Christian, Moslem, and Druse students. The Jewish student population ranged from orthodox to completely secular in religiosity. It included students who had recently immigrated from other countries in the Middle East as well as students whose ancestors had lived in Israel for several generations. The diversity of this population was a social psychologist's fantasy.

For obvious reasons, Israelis are also passionate about politics. Dinner parties come to a halt when the news is turned on. I encountered difficulties in constructing political identification questions to be used with the Hebrew version of the Attitudes About Reality Scale because, at the time, there were eighteen political parties in parliament. Nevertheless, we found a relationship between positivism and religious and political conservatism among Jews and Arabs in Israel similar to that found in the USA (Unger and Safir, 1990).

Despite myths about sexual equality, Israel is a deeply sexist state. It has a patriarchal state religion and a strong military establishment. Sexism is firmly embedded in the Hebrew language itself. Unlike European languages, both nouns and verbs have a masculine and feminine form. The collective plural is, of course, masculine. One ongoing 'grammatical' argument concerned the question of how small the proportion of males in a group would have to be to permit the use of the collective feminine form. I taught a course in the psychology of women and found it difficult to make the distinction between sex and gender for a group whose language did not then have a word for gender.[3] In Hebrew, even nouns and verbs had a 'sex'.

Several Israeli political scientists had suggested that women are more interested in peaceful solutions to the Arab–Israeli conflict than are men. Although I had found no significant differences between men and women in terms of covert ideology in the USA, sex-related differences were not unexpected in Israel. We found such differences among secular, but not religiously observant Jews (Unger, 1992). As a group, secular Jewish women were more constructionist than either their secular male counterparts or religious women or men (who did not differ from each other).

Epistemological position also helped to predict which political group individuals chose as the one they most disliked. Positivists were significantly more likely to select Israeli supporters of the Palestine Liberation Organization (PLO), whereas constructionists were more likely to choose Kach (a right-wing militant movement). However, ideology did not predict tolerance toward members of one's most disliked group. Once they had selected a group, positivists and constructionists were equally intolerant. Women and men, moreover, did not differ in terms of their political tolerance toward members of groups whose ideology they most disliked.

These findings suggest a relationship between ideology and politics that transcends the values of a particular culture. Ideology proved to be a better predictor of political attitudes and behaviors than a person's sexual category. We have also found that covert ideology, as measured by the AAR Scale, was a better predictor of a person's attitudes about the Gulf War than sex or self-label as a Republican or Democrat (Unger and Lemay, 1991).

The neglect of subjectivity

Unfortunately, psychologists appear to ignore philosophical constructs in their attempts to understand human behavior. For example, Lawrence Wrightsman, a prominent social psychologist who has been president of two APA divisions, published a philosophies of human nature scale in 1964. I was unaware of this scale when I constructed the AAR and, in general, Wrightsman's scale has received relatively little attention. He has recently published a second edition of a book based on research with the scale (Wrightsman, 1992), but I suspect it will also receive little attention from psychologists.

Psychologists focus on biological categories at the expense of subjective ones because of disciplinary conservatism. Because psychology has rejected philosophy in favor of so-called objectivity, it has neglected subjectivity as well. Part of subjectivity consists of deeply held assumptions which may not be consciously acknowledged and are rarely discussed with others. The label 'feminist' or 'lesbian' may actually be more predictive than 'sex' because they are markers of subjective identification. People who accept these labels identify with a constructed social grouping rather than a biological category (cf. Unger, 1984–5; Unger and Jones, 1988; Ricketts, 1989).

One of the things that Israel reinforced for me was the importance of subjectivity in our claims for truth. The tragedy of the conflict between the Palestinians and the Israelis is that everyone has evidential support for their legitimate demands. However, what is considered valid evidence depends upon one's point of view. Israel taught me yet again that methodology cannot substitute for judgment. For example, one can easily count the number of years that Jews and Moslems have lived in Jerusalem, but at what date does one determine that occupancy constitutes 'ownership'? The date which is chosen – the first century, the date of first crusade, 1948 (the date of the founding of the Israeli state), and so on – obviously depends on one's other assumptions.

Although it had not been planned to function this way, the Attitudes About Reality Scale works differently than most Likert-type measurement scales. It is not simply agreement or disagreement with particular statements that produces its effects, but the fact that some statements, at least, may be interpreted differently by people with constructionist or positivist epistemologies. For example, how one responds to the statement 'The facts of science change over time' depends on whether one defines a fact as an 'enduring truth' or a 'probablistic conjecture'. Although the evidence is not as clear-cut as we might like, we have collected some support for the idea that constructionists and positivists do prefer different synonyms for some key words in the scale (Smith-Brinton and Unger, 1992–3).

Epistemology and self-awareness
Since people do not usually talk about the bases for what they believe they know, they are largely unaware when these bases change. I was forced to confront some of these changes in my own epistemology when *Feminism & Psychology* did a reappraisal of Naomi Weisstein's work and asked me to participate. This paper was much more self-revealing than most of the formal papers I have written. I began with the following paragraphs.

Naomi and I were in related departments in the same graduate school at the same time when there were few women enrolled in either program, yet we did not know each other very well. The departments had a very contentious relationship with each other. They had at least one thing in common, nonetheless. Women were treated very badly (when we were not being completely ignored).

Studies on tokenism indicate that there are only a few ways that one can handle this kind of hostile environment (cf. Laws, 1975). One can identify with the aggressor (and hope to be treated like an "honorary man") or one can try to make the system live up to its stated rules including its claims to be a meritocracy. I chose the former route whereas Naomi challenged the system. Individuals who do this are often stigmatized as deviants and avoided by others who do not wish to be so labeled (Wolman & Frank, 1975). Because of this, I cannot say that I knew Naomi in graduate school. It took me a lot longer to identify the fundamental sexism of psychology and in academia as a whole. (Unger, 1993b, p. 211)

Later in this paper, I tried to analyze why I did not challenge the system at that point in my life.

Naomi Weisstein and I were physically in the same place at the same time. Nevertheless, we were intellectually in very different places. She understood the social construction of gender well before I even recognized that gender was an important issue. I believe this difference can be attributed to differences in our personal epistemologies with respect to how we were treated and the treatment of women in general. I personalized the sexism in the system and believed that it was "my fault." Naomi realized that if sexism could be directed at her, it could be directed at any woman. She recognized the existence of women as a social class and herself as a member of that class.

The special social circumstances of token individuals often make it very difficult for them to recognize how they are influenced by their circumstances. They may be rewarded for their personal competence while members of their social category are overtly or implicitly denigrated. These conflicting processes help explain why many women and members of other marginalized groups in our society deny personal discrimination although they are aware of discrimination against their group as a whole. (Unger, 1993b, p. 215)

It was very difficult to make these admissions.

There are various terms for this kind of phenomenology. Anna Freud called it 'identification with the aggressor'. Feminists know it as 'the internalization of oppression'. In an important paper in this area, Erika Apfelbaum (1979) has pointed out that once systems of inequality are internalized, the overt use of coercive techniques is no longer necessary. Marginalized individuals will accept their own inferiority.

Awareness of discrimination is a key to change in this area. For example, if victims of discrimination are made aware that their judges are biased against members of their group, they are more able to resist the devastating psychological effects of negative judgments (Dion, 1975; Dion, Earn and Yee, 1978).

I have gradually learned to name my oppressors. I have also come to believe that most feminists who resist the 'gendering processes' of our society do so by embracing rather contradictory epistemological viewpoints. They possess a kind of 'double vision' of reality. They recognize that there is more randomness in our lives than determinist philosophies would acknowledge. They also accept the idea that identities are fluid and that they act out a multitude of historically and socially situated roles. Nevertheless, they also believe that their own actions can change the world.

I have known a number of activist resistors besides Naomi Weisstein. They do not have an easy time. It is often easier for others to do what I did at Harvard – to accept dominant norms, to deny the need for resistance, and take comfort in a limited access to the meritocracy. Acceptance of the dominant ideology, which involves the derogation of marginalized groups can, however, be self-destructive. Fayneese Miller (1990), using a simplified version of the AAR Scale, has found, for example, that positivism in adolescents of color is associated with hopelessness.

How do people acquire a constructionist epistemology about the world and a positivist one for themselves? Or, in other words, where do resistors come from? It is not easy to predict who will become a feminist and when they will do so. Personal experiences of discrimination will not have an impact unless the individual recognizes the systemic nature of the experiences. It is possible, however, that systemic belief structures may be transferred across group categories. Naomi Weisstein has described herself as a 'red diaper baby'. And many other early feminists in psychology have described the social activism of their parents (Unger, 1998). It is probably not accidental that many of these early activists are/were Jewish, working class, or both – other categories besides femaleness that can lead to systematic discrimination in our society.

Consciousness and feminism

Most people, however, are not likely to recognize systematic factors unless they share information with others like themselves. The second wave of the feminist movement was based on mechanisms for sharing such information. The term 'consciousness-raising' referred to the collective examination of individual women's experiences to determine their similar core. Consciousness-raising was supposed to help energize collective action as the phrase 'the personal is political' would suggest. However, as the movement became more popular and diffuse, consciousness-raising 'degenerated' into a mechanism for personal rather than social change (Rosenthal, 1984).

Some of us are concerned that feminism is the product of a specific historical context and worry about the relatively few young women who appear to be attracted to social activism in the 1990s. This makes the question of how people become feminists even more important. A few years ago I conducted a 'fishing expedition' designed to clarify some of the developmental and social factors involved. I am reluctant to term this project a 'study' because it was very open-ended and I was unclear about what I expected to find.

I have never published any of the data from this investigation, but did present it at an APA symposium on creativity and humor in honor of Nancy Datan. What I was looking for in this investigation were the sources that feminist leaders in psychology had used to construct their feminist identities. In particular, I was interested in their past and present heroes. I believed this work was particularly suitable for a symposium memorializing Nancy because I believe that she constructed herself many times and, to the last, she possessed a clear, unique feminist voice (cf. Datan, 1989).

One of my major sources of recreational reading both as a child and an adult is speculative fiction. I have known several other feminist psychologists who are interested in this genre and, when I was president of Division 35 I appointed a task force to develop a bibliography of materials in this area in terms of its usefulness for feminist psychology (cf. Fine, Kidder and Boell, 1989). I believed that readers who explored alternative realities might be more ready to reject our own than those who read more realistic fiction.

Feminist psychologists were not, however, particularly likely to read speculative fiction although they were nearly all voracious readers. Their childhood 'hero' was most likely to be Nancy Drew who was the protagonist in an endless series of 'potboilers' designed for adolescent and near-adolescent girls. She would not appear to be a likely hero for a budding feminist. But, as I was reminded by my respondents, Nancy Drew had her own car and solved mysteries with little or no help from males or from society as a whole. She was also 'the best we could get' in those days.

The current heroes or role models in this group were most likely to be each other. These activists continued to construct their own heroes rather than accept those designated by society. But to do so they had to have a group with which they could identify and from which they could draw their sources of energy and inspiration.

All of these studies and observations have led me to some tentative conclusions. Feminist awareness involves a collectivist epistemology rather than simply a personal one. Our assumptions about causality will alienate us unless we have others to share them with. We will question our beliefs if there is no one else around with whom to validate them. And it is very easy for social systems to isolate those with deviant views.

All this means that we need a collective identity in order to think about social change. But is our feminism meaningful for the generation of women who are coming of age today whose circumstances have been changed by the feminism of the 1970s? Perhaps the question needs to be changed. It may not be 'How can we help more young women to accept a feminist identity?' Rather, we need to ask 'What issues do women today believe they need to resolve and can they do so collectively?' We need to acknowledge the historical and social roots of our current epistemological dilemmas. If feminism was epistemologically inevitable in the 1970s, what epistemology is the most useful now?

Notes

1 Exceptions include recent work on aversive racism (Gaertner and Dovidio, 1986) and ambivalent sexism (Glick and Fiske, 1997).
2 Originally the scale was anchored by the terms now in parentheses, but because of the specific meaning of logical positivism for philosophers of science and a desire for clarity, I have omitted these modifiers in my recent papers.
3 Recently, a word for gender was entered into the official Hebrew lexicon.

Reading 6

Sex, gender, and epistemology (Unger, 1989b, pp. 17–24, 29–32)

It has been argued by Buss (1975) and others that psychology as a discipline tends to alternate between two basic paradigms explaining the relationship between humans and their environment. These two basic conceptual paradigms are: (1) reality constructs the person, and (2) the person constructs reality. Paradigm (1) postulates a model of a reality that is stable, irreversible, and deterministic. It further postulates that this reality is discoverable through the proper application of scientific methodology and that individual differences are a result of the impingement of that reality on the developing organism. This deep structure underlies such diverse schools of thought as behaviorism, psychoanalysis, and sociobiology. These theoretical frameworks do not question that reality exists. They differ merely on the aspects of reality they stress as having the most impact on individual behavior.

Recently, psychology appears to have undergone a "cognitive revolution" (Gardner, 1985; Neisser, 1967). The former paradigm has been replaced by a keen interest in the active role of the individual in constructing his or her own reality. This model postulates that reality is largely a matter of historical and cultural definition (Gergen, 1985). It emphasizes the power of ongoing social negotiation in the creation of individual behavior and is more willing to take a less deterministic view of causality in general. Those who espouse a strong social constructionist viewpoint appear to be more likely to attribute individual differences to chance (nonpredictable or noncontrollable events) and, in the most extreme views, despair of the possibility of any generalizable laws of human behavior at all.

Although the social constructionist viewpoint is much more congenial for feminists in psychology (Unger, 1984–1985), I shall argue that sex and gender pose problems for both paradigms. I shall review briefly some of the major strengths and weaknesses of each in terms of sex and gender research, discuss what I see as some important conceptual and methodological trends in the area, and, lastly, discuss some of my own research and theorizing that bears on attempts to integrate apparently dichotomous views.

Reality constructs the person

Behaviorism, sociobiology, and psychoanalysis share a commitment to a fixed past as a major determinant of the individual's current behavior. They differ in the phenomena or processes they stress as the most important creators of that past. However, the explanatory power of schedules of reinforcement, genes, or familial psychodynamic processes is based on sometimes unstated assumptions about their connection with basic psychobiological mechanisms.

In these theoretical frameworks, sex is a biological given or an organismic variable. This assumption, of course, is stated

explicitly by sociobiologists who assume that current differences between men and women are evolutionarily adaptive
and interfered with by society at our peril. This view is most
clearly spelled out in the title of the book *The Tangled Wing:
Biological Constraints on the Human Spirit* (Konner, 1981).

Classic psychoanalytic theory and even some of its more
feminist derivatives, however, also assume psychobiological
mechanisms. Biology is introduced by the universal fact of
motherhood and the inevitable conflicts produced by the
relationship between the custodial parent (almost always the
mother) and the developing child. Feminist psychodynamic
theories appear to differ from classical Freudian ones by
stressing power rather than sexual-erotic mechanisms, and by
their belief that the psychodynamic consequences of the basic
human family structure are not primarily due to the gender of
the chief custodian. They tend to argue that the role of
primary childrearer (linked to females, to be sure, by the
biological necessity of childbearing) is the major determinant
of gender-related differences between the sexes.

Behaviorism seemed to avoid biological assumptions. In its
classic form, it tries to avoid the need to utilize variables from
any other level of disciplinary discourse. Its essence is to restrict
psychology to a few simple, easily observable and categorizable
behaviors in order to facilitate the examination of the
relationship between behavioral output and its outcomes (so-
called reinforcers). In so doing, however, it has limited itself to
behaviors that are devoid of much meaning for the human
subject – of either sex – and has had to examine these subjects
in a controlled environment – a situational context that
eliminates any opportunity for the organism to select alternative behaviors. As a "science" that seeks to establish universal
"laws of behavior" from an examination of the behavioral
similarities between pigeons, rats, and humans, it has had little
to say about the similarities or differences between various
groups of human beings. In theory, behaviorism has ignored
sex as a variable. In practice, even the rats were male.

What, if anything, have we learned about sex and gender
from schools of thought emanating from reality constructs the
person assumptions? Sociobiologists have compiled a long list
of supposed sex differences based on the adaptive value of sex-
specific behaviors for the survival of males and females of
various species. They have little to say about the rich variability
of sex-related behaviors in human cultures of the past and
present. And they offer us little in the way of specific

mechanisms to explain sex differences (other than their primary notion of relative reproductive economy for mammalian males – who may scatter their plentiful sperm widely – and mammalian females – who produce relatively few eggs and must cherish their scarce offspring).

Unfortunately, the area of psychology that has had the most to say about sex differences – the subfield of individual differences – is also the area that is most intellectually and historically akin to sociobiology. It has been noted that Galton, the founder of this field, was a strong believer in social Darwinism. He viewed women and colored people as inferior to men and the British (Buss, 1976). The area of individual differences has produced little in the way of a theoretical rationale for its data on differences between various groups and, in fact, has given us little explanation as to why some "causal" variables (such as sex, race, and class) should be studied, whereas others (such as height, physical appearance, or hair color) can be ignored.

The area of individual differences has remained a virtual catalog of behavioral phenomena with the mechanisms left unspecified. Since no systematic theory exists, it has been left to the user of this data base to determine when and why a specific sex difference may be cited. The consequences are obvious when one looks at various introductory textbooks in psychology written by authors with various theoretical perspectives. "Sex differences" in an almost infinite variety of behaviors are cited. There is, however, little consistency in whether or not a particular behavior is cited in different texts, and there is no agreement about what comprises a usable sex difference – in terms of statistical size, generality of occurrence, or cross-situational consistency.

Unfortunately, many early feminists in psychology took this data base seriously (Rosenberg, 1982; Shields, 1975a). Early researchers worked to demonstrate that many so-called sex differences could not be verified empirically. Since the list of potential sex differences is potentially infinite, however, they may have spent their lives on issues that later psychologists regard as of no particular importance. The number of possible sex differences is not an important issue in the current feminist agenda. Much more pressing is the issue of how sex difference as a conceptual tool is deployed and manipulated.

Since behaviorism excludes questions about sex and gender entirely, the only other area utilizing this paradigm within which we may look for information is psychodynamic theory.

It is noteworthy that this is the area from which feminist scholars outside psychology derive most of their inspiration. It has been largely ignored, however, by the majority of researchers within psychology, who primarily derive from a social psychological framework.

An extensive critique of psychodynamic theories about sex and gender would be tangential to the main thrust of this chapter. I shall therefore limit my discussion to a few remarks about what I see as the major problems of the psychodynamic view of women and men, as well as some benefits feminist social psychologists can derive from the theory. The major problem of the psychodynamic perspective for social psychology is the unexamined psychobiological connections discussed above. It is not clear what causal mechanisms best explain gender differences in the developing child. It is also not clear what role cultural prescriptions about gender-appropriate characteristics for boys and girls, and fathers and mothers, play in the development of such gender-related behaviors as intimacy, relatedness, individualism, or aggression.

Psychodynamic theory roots the individual in a historical time and place. I believe it is this aspect of the theory that makes it attractive to feminist scholars in other academic disciplines. They tend to find the logical positivist underpinning of traditional experimental psychology sterile because they are unwilling to conceptualize human beings devoid of their situational context (Unger, 1983). They also question the morality of the subject-as-object relationship specified by traditional psychology and deny the possibility that researchers can divorce themselves from their subject matter in order to measure human phenomena in an objective manner. They may also resent the arrogance of psychologists in defining themselves as the "measurers" of human beings. While these are all valid criticisms, some of the lack of communication between feminist scholarship and feminist psychology may be attributed to lack of awareness of the former about paradigm shifts within psychology as a discipline. In particular, there appears to be little knowledge about those aspects of the psychology of sex and gender that utilize the "person constructs reality" paradigm.

The person constructs reality

As in the case of the "reality constructs the person" paradigm, there are a number of ways researchers can deal with phenomena having to do with sex and gender using "person constructs reality" assumptions. All these perspectives involve a formulation of human beings as consciously aware individuals who actively select and influence their environment, as well as being influenced by it. This positing of human subjects as agents of their own reality underlies the various perspectives influenced by the "cognitive revolution" within psychology.

In the new psychology of sex and gender, maleness and femaleness are seen as social stimuli that provide valuable information for organizing reality to both actors and observers (Deaux & Major, 1987). Observers use information about sex to determine whether the individual is behaving in a role-consistent manner. Identical male and female behaviors are rarely evaluated similarly, because sex and role are highly confounded in our society. In the absence of disconfirming information, individuals are evaluated in terms of the gender consistency of their behavior. Deviation from normative gender/role prescriptions has a major impact on how the individual is perceived by others. It is difficult to tell, in fact, how often, and to what extent, negative judgments of women's behavior in certain social contexts are due to their role deviance, rather than their gender deviance.

The observer's beliefs about sex as a social reality are confirmed by gender-characteristic styles of self-presentation and by the differential distribution of females and males into roles with divergent degrees of status and power. Individuals may maintain gender-characteristic behaviors because of both intrapsychic needs for self-consistency and pressure from others to behave in a socially desirable manner. Ultimately, the individual may lose sight of distinctions between herself and her role. She may become the person society prescribes.

What evidence supports this theoretical framework for sex as a cognitive variable? The analytic methodology of social psychology is very useful here. For example, it can be demonstrated that sex is a salient social category even under the most impersonal of circumstances and even when it may be useless or counterproductive as a source of information about the person (Grady, 1977). Very few individuals appear to question what makes sex such an apparently useful source of information.

There is evidence, moreover, that people use sex-related information differently, depending on whether they are making judgments about themselves or others (Spence & Sawin, 1985). Males and females also use different categories in evaluating their own gender identity: males use *attributes*, such as strength or size, and females use *roles*, such as mother or wife. Neither group, however, appears to regard either sex or gender as anything other than a simple, unitary "fact of life."

One of the most difficult questions in understanding sex as a cognitive variable is determining when it is salient for the individual and when it is not. Sex-related effects do not appear in every possible social context. They have a "now you see them, now you don't" quality, which makes analysis difficult (Unger, 1981). Some important work has been devoted to developing typologies of contexts in which sex-related effects appear. A number of intriguing findings have emerged.

First, sex appears to be an important cue for behavior when the individual is a member of a statistically rare category for the social context in which he or she appears. This condition applies to sex both as a self-label (McGuire, McGuire, & Winton, 1979) and as a label used by others (Taylor, Fiske, Etcoff, & Ruderman, 1978). It is possible that statistical deviance heightens the expectation of role deviance.

Second, sex-related differences in social behaviors appear to be maximized when such behaviors are subject to public scrutiny, as compared to situations in which individuals believe that their behaviors are private and anonymous (Eagly, Wood, & Fishbaugh, 1981; Kidder, Belletirie, & Cohn, 1977). Public behavior appears to conform to sex-stereotypic assumptions much more than does private behavior. What is particularly important about these findings is that they derive from one of the very few methodologies that permit social scientists to manipulate societal norms within a laboratory context. The difference between public and private represents a difference in assumptions about the probability with which others will evaluate one's behavior. For example, males are found to be more concerned with equity and justice in public than in private (Kidder et al., 1977). It is difficult to argue that long-standing personality traits underlie sex-characteristic behaviors that are so easily influenced by social comparisons.

Third, sex-characteristic patterns of behavior can be made to conform to the expectations of others. Laboratory models of the "self-fulfilling prophecy" have demonstrated that gender-linked "personality traits" (such as "sociability") of the target person may be altered by changing the expectations of the individual with whom they are interacting. Effects are produced by manipulating the beliefs of the observer about other gender-relevant characteristics of the target individual, such as her physical attractiveness (Snyder, Tanke, & Berscheid, 1977).

Physical attractiveness is associated with assumptions of further gender-appropriate characteristics for both males and females. Handsome males are seen as particularly likely to possess masculine characteristics, and beautiful females are seen as possessing feminine attributes (Lemay & Unger, 1982). In contrast, lack of attractiveness is associated with perceptions of social deviance in a variety of situational domains. For example, less attractive males and females are seen to be more likely to be campus radicals than are their more attractive counterparts (Unger, Hilderbrand, & Madar, 1982).

Fourth, developmentally and culturally consistent patterns of behaviors directed toward males and females can be identified that may be related to sex-related differences in personality. For example, the most persistent contexts in which females are helped more than males are those involving travel outside the home (Piliavin & Unger, 1985). Young girls are helped more than boys when they request assistance from their teachers or adult mentors (Serbin, Connor, & Citron, 1978). Interestingly, girls also request more help when they are placed in the kind of structured activities that preschool girls appear to prefer (Carpenter, Huston, & Holt, 1986). Together, these data suggest that social and environmental constraints induce helpless or dependent behaviors in females that are frequently attributed to personality traits or even biological determinants.

Although this kind of constructionist paradigm has produced some very interesting information about sex and gender, there are dangers as well as strengths in the cognitive paradigm. Problems will probably emerge more clearly as the territory is further explored, but a few "traps" are already evident. One major problem is how to distinguish compliance with a gender-prescriptive reality from the actual self as actor. A useful tool in this regard is the methodological distinction between public and private behavior discussed above. One may assume that private behavior is less constrained by social desirability and therefore more closely represents the self as actor.

A more serious problem for cognitive theories about sex and gender involves the search for general laws that regulate behavior. Research has already shown that people use different information about sex and gender to organize their own behavior as contrasted to the behavior of others. Males and females may also use different sources of information to answer identical questions about their gender-relevant attributes (Spence & Sawin, 1985). The "same" information about sex and gender may be used differently by children of different ages (Katz, 1986). We therefore have every reason to believe that such information will also be used differently by individuals of different cultures, social classes, or ethnicities. We must be as wary of overgeneralizing a "female" consciousness as we have been of overgeneralizing from males to females or from the American middle class to everyone else. The search for truly general laws must be conducted with acute attention paid to the influence of transitory contextual variables.

On the other hand, the analysis of reality as individually constructed and highly subjective also carries traps with it. If everyone constructs their own reality, what criteria do we use to test the validity of their constructs? Some personal realities appear to be more functional than others, but utility may come at the cost of the individual's excessive compliance with societal norms. Functional analyses of both intrapsychic and behavioral coping may be greatly influenced by the values of the evaluator (Fine, 1983–1984). Middle-class investigators may too easily blame the victim and ignore the constraints of environments unfamiliar to them.

A focus on events that take place "inside one's head" may also make it easier to ignore external realities that are not under the person's control. For example, current analyses of stereotyping consider stereotypic perception as a normal variant of information seeking and cognitive processing. In a sense, stereotypes offer a kind of cognitive economy for the individual who needs to evaluate information about a wide assortment of different people. Stereotypes provide an easy way to select and remember information about others (Deaux, 1985; Hansen, 1980; Snyder & Uranowitz, 1978). These analyses, however, tend to ignore the fact that this kind of cognitive economy is not helpful to those individuals who are grouped as members of target populations. Nor do social analyses based on information processing explain individual differences in the extent and kind of stereotypes produced. Lastly, our fascination with the more powerful segments of society has produced little work on the consciousness of the victims of prejudice. Faye Crosby's (1982) and Kenneth Dion's (Dion, 1975; Dion & Earn, 1975) excellent work in this area are notable exceptions.

In sum, the "person constructs reality" paradigm as currently applied to sex and gender has both pluses and minuses.

It takes a big step forward by providing psychologists with a theoretical rationale for measuring perceptions and cognitions about females and males. It also places explanations for sex-related differences within the framework of social reality rather than physical or biological reality. However, cognitive psychology does not explain how social reality is translated into individual reality. We need to explain when and why people are different as well as when and why they are similar. Some questions that need to be resolved include: Why do perceptions and cognitions about males and females appear to be consistent across a wide variety of times and places? Why do females concur with a social reality that is harmful to themselves as individuals? How do we explain those individuals who appear to be "invulnerable" to sex-characteristic attributions about themselves or others?

There is also a difference between a cognitive and a feminist perspective on sex and gender. Perhaps the greater danger of a cognitive perspective is that psychologists will come to believe that all the questions about sex and gender can be answered within that paradigm, and we will forget that there are real societal forces that impact on the individual's ability to influence his or her own reality. The major social fact that has been ignored is the differential nature of social power (Unger, 1986a). People of some social groups have more ability to impose their definitions of reality than do others. Their definitions influence the extent to which members of oppressed groups make use of resources theoretically available to all (Sherif, 1982). We need to understand how individuals incorporate an inegalitarian reality into their personal identities. But we also need to recognize that society is inegalitarian and that systems as well as individuals must change.

The problem of inconsistency

What are we to make of all this complexity? Clearly, we cannot view sex and gender as holistic concepts, despite the fact that individuals in our society rarely examine their underlying assumptions for either others or themselves (Spence & Sawin, 1985). Assumptions about the sexes are also clearly tied to a complex network of assumptions about how the world works and which strategies are most useful for dealing with that world. Since we pay little attention to our underlying belief structures, we have little opportunity to examine them for inconsistencies or to alter them in the face of conflicting evidence.

Personal epistemology appears to be relatively consistent over a large variety of conceptual domains and fairly stable over time (Unger, Draper & Pendergrass, 1986). People appear to establish systematic belief structures similar to those found among established scholars before being trained in a particular discipline's epistemological assumptions (King, 1980). Social constructionist epistemology appears to be associated with social marginality in such areas as religion and sexual orientation, as well as gender ideology.

Although we have not yet done analyses for other groups, active feminists appear to be able to incorporate an ideology that insists on the possibility of both societal and personal control (Unger, 1984–1985). I would argue that such a paradoxical epistemological position is particularly adaptive to a contradictory reality. Feminists recognize the power of consensually defined social reality, while at the same time recognizing that individuals have the power to evade sex-biased definitions of their behavior. It is possible, for example, that female supervisors may exchange structural criticisms of established corporate policy when among females of equal company rank but frame the same issues in more guarded, individualistic terms when among subordinates or males of any rank. Judith Laws (1975) suggested such a dual consciousness in her early and important work on academic tokenism, but I know of no clear empirical test of this hypothesis. Proof of such contradictory patterns may necessitate the selection of social contexts in which alternative verbal and nonverbal definitional processes apply.

In the examination of the evasion of sex bias, however, the irony of trying to avoid the pitfalls of either logical positivist or constructionist models becomes evident. Social constructionists cannot ignore the fact that the power to define reality is more in the hands of some social groups than others. The governing groups tend to enforce and apply their own epistemological position. Thus the evidence we generate to support the social construction of gender-based reality will be evaluated in terms of both professional and personal epistemology. I have provided data to suggest that feminist epistemology is quite distinct as a constructionist way of looking at the world. Nevertheless, the methods that I have used to demonstrate this point are clearly logical positivist. How am I to deal with this inconsistency?

Scholars in a number of disciplines have attempted to avoid the assumptions of logical positivism by using various deconstructionist techniques. Such methodologies involve letting each person construct her own reality. Personal reality is seen as having no meaning apart from its historical and cultural context of the personal circumstances of the individual's life. Evidence about shared reality is provided through a comparison of shared stories.

This kind of methodology, however, is inconsistent with the desire of most psychologists to find generic predictors of human actions. Feminist social psychologists therefore must live with even more inconsistency than other feminist scholars. Any self-assessment method, as contrasted to psychodynamic or phenomenological approaches, appears to strip behavior from its historical and cultural context. What is the relationship between the response to items on a paper-and-pencil scale and the response to similar issues of effectiveness and merit in the context of personal evaluation? I can measure generic consistency in social constructionist beliefs only by using a measure that may strip these beliefs of their social meaning.

Some of these same kinds of inconsistencies emerge in attempts to analyze the ongoing perceptual dynamics in the relationships between individuals. Double binds are constructed by means of unexamined and contradictory definitions of normative female behavior (Unger, 1988a; Wood & Conrad, 1983). They are effective largely because they are invisible to the participants in a social transaction. Not only do we lack a vocabulary to describe these social constraints, but attempts to bring them into awareness will probably cause them to disappear. Ironically, the "Heisenberg principle" is a concept shared with physics that psychologists have been less willing to acknowledge than operationalism or experimental methodology. Physicists recognize that they cannot predict the behavior of single electrons, but psychologists are less willing and less able to abandon the individual. Our apparent inability to deal with the subjective without losing the objective and vice versa is exemplified by psychology's endless cycling between the two basic paradigms with which I introduced this chapter. It has split psychologists into "two cultures" (Kimble, 1984) and threatens to tear apart the field as a unitary discipline.

The uses of paradox

It is easy for psychologists to get caught in dualisms (c.f. Coan, 1979, for a list of some of the dualisms uncovered by his

Theoretical Orientation Scale). Contradiction, however, may be used to avoid some apparent dichotomies. The person versus situation controversy may be resolved, for example, by noting that persons bring symbolic constraints to situations (in terms of the way they perceive and define the world). These cognitive frameworks influence how they perceive and explain the mechanisms of interpersonal control found within most relationships between the sexes outside the home. We need to integrate findings on contradictory perceptions about men and women and about self versus others in identical circumstances. Unexamined contradictions in such perceptions help explain how people acquiesce to social schemata that are potentially harmful to them.

Similarly, dualisms involving internal versus external causality can be transcended by looking for methods that vary the extent of social coercion in apparently identical behavioral contexts. Private versus public behavior is one method by which societal prescriptions may be varied. Other methods may involve alternation of the "rules" for socially desirable behavior or the imposition of salient stimulus persons who embody particular gender-prescriptive norms. For example, work by Mark Zanna and his associates (von Baeyer, Sherk, & Zanna, 1981) has demonstrated differences in self-presentation style based on women's assumptions about an interview with a sexist or nonsexist employer.

A final duality involves the person versus society. Research on feminist epistemology indicates that a belief in the efficacy of the person may be linked to identification with a reference group whose consensual validation of reality resembles one's own. Some kinds of research questions can be formulated only if we accept the validity of a number of definitions of personal reality and are able to measure the discordance between various constructs. Thus, our American belief in individualism and the meritocracy may be possible only if those who construct this reality benefit from it and are able to discount the realities of others who do not. More communal analyses of social welfare may be easier for those who define human society more inclusively and who find the status quo less personally beneficial or rewarding.

Philosophers value the study of paradox because it prompts questions about the nature of a given belief system that can produce such conceptual "traps." A more familiar analogy for psychology is the study of optical illusions, which are "perceptual paradoxes" in the sense that identical physical stimuli produce several different sensory responses. When we find an optical illusion, we do not question the nature of physical reality. Instead, we analyze neural and perceptual mechanisms to see how the multiple reality is created. Similarly, the study of social paradoxes can lead to a richer conceptualization of what must be known.

Social contradictions exist because people either accept several conflicting definitions about the same person or differ as to when particular definitions should be applied. Psychology lacks the criteria to determine whose definitions are more valid, or even if "validity" has any meaning in consensually defined reality. Our yardsticks cannot be merely methodological – they must be conceptual and moral as well. We need a different, transcendant model for human beings. Perhaps the kind of person who functions best in a socially constructed world is one who can live in each reality as though it were the only one, but who knows that it is possible to stand outside them all.

6

Thinking it over

In the process of writing this book I have been forced to reconsider many aspects of my research and my professional and personal life. Just as I did not plan to study the psychology of women, I did not plan to do extensive programmatic research either. This has been the positive side of having had very little external research funding during my career. Because of this, I have been able to ask questions because I am interested in the answers. It is perhaps fitting, therefore, that most of this final chapter is also devoted to questions.

Many of the issues that I have examined have been of interest to the field as a whole. I have tried to illustrate how research questions are a result of an interaction between collective history and personal experience. As I have tried to show throughout this book, the psychology of women developed as a collective enterprise through the work of a critical mass of women who shared both an intellectual tradition and the constraints of being marginalized within that tradition. From this perspective, it appears almost inevitable that certain questions would be addressed.

This is not the way science is supposed to work. The official prescription for research states that hypotheses proceed logically from theory and from the results of earlier research. However, research does not necessarily follow such a programmatic formula. Brewster Smith (a past president of SPSSI and of APA) has argued that many of the classic contributions to psychology have been valuable as exemplifications and demonstrations of important processes and relationships more than as starting points for cumulative parametric exploration (Smith, 1980). What accumulates from them is sensitization to and enlightenment about aspects of the contemporary human condition that we had not previously seen so clearly. Much of the feminist research discussed in this book meets these criteria.

As noted in earlier chapters, feminist research on prejudice and discrimination and on power had its roots in women's experiences within academic and other hierarchies. Our experience and training might also help explain why critiques of methods and theory came somewhat later. We may have been reluctant to challenge systems of knowledge which gave us some, albeit limited, access to power in the academic world. Conversely, our experiences may have also helped us to define what we did *not* consider problematic. For example, much early feminist research in psychology was on achievement rather than motherhood, whereas fatherhood and the family have been major concerns of psychologists within the men's movement.

Is/was a developmental sequence predictable?

It is always easy to have twenty-twenty hindsight. Nevertheless, my observations of the psychology of women compared with more recent developments in the psychology of sexual orientation, race, and ethnicity suggest that scholarship in these areas follows a predictable sequence. First, researchers recognize that they have the power to name the subject rather than accepting others' definitions. This first venture at naming often has an essentialist quality. The focus is on women, Blacks, gay men[1] and lesbians, etc. as categories although researchers attempt to change psychological definitions of these groups as problematic or inferior (cf. Crawford and Marecek, 1989 for a discussion of such stages in the psychology of women).

At first, researchers waver between examining the internal versus the external properties of members of the named group. Thus, the contents of the earliest texts in the psychology of women emphasized women's biology and their intrapsychic processes. Even when researchers focused on external factors, however, it was the cue properties of individuals from target groups rather than their situational context that was seen as most important. This kind of research helps psychologists shift focus – from the internal properties of the targets of prejudice to the characteristics of those who discriminate against them (cf. Samelson, 1978).

Once it is renamed, the group may be moved from being defined as a problem to being considered superior. It is easy to trace this process in some forms of feminist theory as well as in the Black power movement. And it is occurring today in the area known as 'queer studies'.

In bringing a formerly neglected group from 'margin to center' (hooks, 1984), researchers who are members of that group also empower themselves. Empowerment has several consequences. Most importantly, it permits the recognition that there is an intimate relationship between the personal and political in all scholarship. Therefore, the research questions of members of any particular target group cannot be dismissed as merely 'self-interested'. However, empowerment can also foster a belief that one's own personal experiences make one especially sensitive to the concerns of one's group. It is an easy step from this belief to the idea that only group members can do effective studies in the area.

In-group biases have tended to produce rather insulated groups of scholars. For example, few men have contributed to the psychology of women. There exists, moreover, a body of literature called 'men's studies', which has had little contact with its sister field. Few women have contributed directly to the area and studies from the psychology of women are rarely cited by its practitioners (Addelston, 1995). Most of the active men in this field are more interested in men's intrapsychic distress than in social or political analysis.

The psychology of women also suffers from in-group bias. Race/ethnicity, sexual orientation, and class have been neglected in most studies. Although some African-American psychologists have contributed much to feminist psychology (cf. Reid, 1988, 1993; Landrine, 1995), few citations to the *Journal of Black Psychology* can be found either in texts or journals in the field. A similar statement may be made about lesbian psychology with a few exceptions such as Laura Brown (1989) and Celia Kitzinger (1991, 1996) whose articles appear in more 'mainstream' feminist books and journals as well as lesbian sources. Class has been virtually ignored by psychologists in the USA. It has been of more interest to British feminist psychologists.[2] In-group bias has meant that as each group becomes the focus of attention, it has done so in relative isolation without learning from the development of other allied areas.

As each of these areas has developed, scholars have begun to move away from essentialized categories and to explore the systematic nature of sexism, racism, homophobia/heterosexism, etc. This emphasis on socio-structural variables rather than intrapsychic ones can help to merge formerly isolated areas of scholarship. For example, some years ago I argued for the value of a course on the psychology of social issues that would look at scholarship across a number of areas (Unger, 1988c). Recently, I have come across a description of a more focused course developed by an African-American psychologist, Aaronette White, entitled 'The psychology of oppression'. She designed the course to help students 'understand the factors that undermine the appreciation of multiculturalism and other forms of diversity in society' (White, 1994, p. 17).

Such courses make use of a social constructionist framework for the understanding of groups that have been marginalized in our society. Social construction appears to be a later phase in the development of scholarship in these areas. In addition to its use in scholarship about gender, one can now find titles such as *The Social*

Construction of Lesbianism (Kitzinger, 1987) and *White is a color!* (Roman, 1993). Disability may also be viewed as a social construct (Roth, 1983).

I am concerned that the term 'social construction' is being overused and misinterpreted. The social construction of gender is beginning to be confused with the socialization of gender. But social construction is not simply an argument for the environmental origin of gendered traits: 'Rather, the constructionist argument is that gender is not a trait of individuals at all, but simply a construct that identifies particular transactions that are understood to be appropriate to one sex' (Bohan, 1993, p. 7). These transactions both construct and maintain gender and may be independent of the individual's actual biological sex. In this sense, one could argue that gender is a 'verb' rather than a 'noun' (Unger, 1988b).

Social constructionists also argue that psychological categories such as gender or race have no abstract existence apart from the context in which they occur or are studied (Unger, 1990). Moreover, several different definitions of these categories may coexist within the 'same' social interaction or within a single individual depending upon what aspects of his or her identity/social category are salient at the time. Social construction differs from social psychology because it recognizes the power of contradictory definitions (Unger, 1988b). Such contradictions can exist either between individuals in the 'same' social interaction or as unacknowledged inconsistencies within an individual. Social construction also extends the meaning of 'context' to consider the important role of history and culture in determining the relative salience of the many social categories each individual occupies at any given time.

Social construction is particularly valuable if we focus upon similarities in the ways in which societies construct marginality for groups with low power within them. Cues to marginality that are not historically rooted – such as physical appearance – may be particularly useful in this regard. Researchers are, for example, beginning to examine the politics of skin color (Russell, Wilson and Hall, 1992). They have found that like the cue of physical attractiveness, skin color can predict occupational success, salary, and social desirability within as well as outside of the African-American community. These studies show how oppressive beliefs can be internalized and shared by stigmatized individuals as well as marginalized groups.

Examination of constructionist processes can help us to avoid the 'politics of identity' in which various groups' oppressions are measured against each other to determine relative need. This is because the societal context rather than the individual's experience becomes the focus of our scrutiny. But social construction can also produce conceptual problems if we do not recognize that every group (including those with power) is socially constructed. Fortunately, a scholarly literature is beginning to develop that looks at the social construction of 'whiteness' (cf. Fine et al., 1997; Frankenberg, 1993; Roman, 1993) as well as other hegemonic categories such as masculinity or heterosexuality (Wilkinson and Kitzinger, 1993).

This scholarship recognizes that it may be impossible to view different groups without taking into account their relationship to each other. As Glenn (1992) has pointed out, categories such as male/female, Anglo/Latino are positioned and gain meaning from each other. The experiences of white women and women of color are not just different, but are connected in systematic ways. Privileged women's lives are often purchased at the cost of the exploited labor of women (and men) in subordinated race and class locations (Zinn, 1994).

It is possible that this is the next step in the development of feminist psychology. It involves a recognition that feminism is not just about the empowerment of women, but that we need to involve ourselves in coalitions concerned with social change. Such coalitions move us beyond the recognition that groups of women of differing race, ethnicity, sexuality, disability, or class have differing experiences.

There is no doubt that the recognition that a variety of factors operate simultaneously will make our theories more complex. Cultural diversity will also make our theoretical perspectives less essentialist (cf. Spelman, 1988). What may not be as clear is that cultural diversity will make our perspectives more fluid as well. Situational questions result in situational solutions and if we recognize that our answers are proximate (as is all knowledge), we will recognize that our solutions must also change over time (cf. McGrath, 1986).

The previous analysis appears to suggest some sort of stage theory of feminist development. I have always avoided stage theories because, inevitably, comparisons are made that suggest earlier stages are inferior to later ones. This kind of value judgment is poor scholarship for a number of reasons. First, as I have tried to show throughout this book, it is important to recognize the social and historical context from which a research question is generated. This context has influenced our own feminist questions as well as the questions of others that we see as naive or offensive.

Stage theories also seem to assume that earlier phases stop evolving once a later stage is reached. I was dissuaded from this position by a book by Stephen J. Gould (1989) entitled *Wonderful*

Life, which is cited much less often than *The Mismeasure of Man*. In this book Gould pointed out that very early organisms already had the complexity considered to be characteristic of later evolution. He also pointed out that early 'primitive' organisms have continued to evolve even after more complex organisms developed from them; for example, the lungfish of several hundred million years ago did not stop evolving just because one of its group may have become an amphibian.

So, too, feminist psychological views of discrimination have continued to evolve. We have moved, for example, from questions about whether discrimination against women exists to a recognition that sexism functions at a variety of levels (cf. Deaux and Major, 1987; Unger and Saundra, 1993). These richer theoretical frameworks lead to studies that look for subtle as well as blatant forms of discrimination against women.

Sometimes theoretical change is accompanied by changes in nomenclature that make continuities harder to trace. Some feminist clinicians such as Jean Baker Miller (1976), for example, began with discussions of power and control while others talked about dominance and subordination or patriarchy (Chesler, 1972). Such apparently dualistic positions may be reconciled, however, by the recognition that systems partially maintain dominance by colonizing individuals' minds. Thus, feminist psychologists have begun to investigate systemic and contextual factors that enhance people's sense of entitlement as well as their feelings of powerlessness (Gilbert, 1994; Major, 1994).

Our recognition of the subtle impact of institutionalized oppression means that we cannot assume that even apparently equal environments will produce either identical experiences or equitable outcomes. For example, Abigail Stewart's longitudinal studies of women who had attended Radcliffe in the early 1960s (Stewart and Ostrove, 1993) found that working-class women had felt more alienated there than their middle- and upper-class peers. The impact of social class persisted for many years after graduation. These women regarded the marital role with more suspicion than their more privileged classmates and reported that the women's movement had confirmed and supported their skeptical views of middle-class gender norms. I do not think it is an accident that many feminist psychologists are from working-class backgrounds.

Current studies of the impact of single-sex and single-race education in the USA also support the idea that legal equality does not always produce social equality. Sadker and Sadker (1994) have amply documented the ways in which teachers treat boys and girls differently. Recent fine-grained analyses indicate that Black girls, in particular, must negate their cultural differences from the Anglo norm in order to be successful in school (Fordham, 1993). Unwillingness to divest themselves of their cultural identity appears to contribute to the dropping out from high school of intellectually able African-American girls (Fine and Zane, 1988).

These results provide feminists with a dilemma. Many of us fought hard and long for educational equity only to find out that achievement may be maximized within segregated educational contexts. I am still trying to resolve this dilemma for myself, but I recognize that it can provide us with an opportunity to learn. For example, the existence of this dilemma illustrates clearly a point I made earlier in this chapter – solutions need to be reconsidered when circumstances change.

This dilemma also teaches us that feminist solutions will not allow us to transcend contradiction. Equitable education is an advance because segregated schools were often inferior; because it makes a statement that all social groups within a society deserve equal opportunity; because it provides role models from *all* social groups; and because it provides an opportunity for such groups to interact in a context of relative equality. However, we now also know that dominant groups do not give up their power readily and may use it to harass and exclude members of marginalized groups within these so-called equal environments.

What are the questions in feminist psychology today?

Barbara Wallston's (1981) presidential address to Division 35 was entitled 'What are the questions in the psychology of women?' We have learned by now that the hard questions do not just get answered and go away. These difficult questions may not be resolvable because any solution raises new questions for feminists as well as for society.

I have argued that feminists need to learn to live with contradiction (Unger, 1988b). Now I would like to discuss some of these contradictions in the major areas of psychology to which feminist scholars have contributed over the past twenty-five years. These are: prejudice and discrimination; power; critiques of theory and method; and epistemology. Feminist scholarship has contributed to our understanding in each of these areas, but has also raised more questions. Some of these questions are contributing to current controversies among feminist scholars because we continue to believe that there is a 'right' or a 'wrong' answer.

Has the level of discrimination against women decreased?
While it is clear that some obvious forms of discrimination against women have declined, more subtle forms can still be documented (cf. Caplan, 1993). Moreover, forms of sexism that were unexamined in the 1970s have come to the fore. Feminist scholars have, for example, documented a high incidence of acquaintance rape as well as other forms of violence against women (Koss, 1990). These studies often focus on women's stories of their experiences and the aftermath. Some critics have, however, found it difficult to reconcile a psychology which focuses on so-called victims with feminist goals of self-empowerment, growth, and social change (Tavris, 1993).

Part of the dilemma appears to be due to unstated assumptions about the nature of the informant and the meaning of the information obtained. Those who study experiential accounts of women who are the targets of violence have contributed greatly to our knowledge about sexual violence. They have found, for example, that experiences which others would define as rape are often not acknowledged as such by those who survive them (Kahn, Mathie and Torgier, 1994). They have found that sexual harassment is a more common phenomenon, even in high school, than society had recognized (Larkin and Popaleni, 1994). And they have found that rape and other forms of sexual violence are a much greater health hazard globally than anyone could have believed (Koss, Heise and Russo, 1994).

Some critics have complained about the focus of this research on women's victimization. They ask whether sexual incidents, that are not defined as harassment or violence by their target at the time it occurred, should be defined as violence. They also complain that researchers in the area do not find it necessary to explain or define why one person's experiences are more important than another's or why one kind of experience is more important than another. They ask by what criteria are survivors' stories more important than those who have been more successful (or lucky) in avoiding such violence. Probably their most cogent criticism is to what extent do such experiential accounts change the social systems that sustain violence.

Social psychologists who study violence are also subject to dilemmas. They often use standardized and objective questionnaires that may minimize the level of societal violence reported. For example, many women did not name forced sexual contact as rape. Changing norms about what is acceptable coercion may have contributed to the perception that the rate of sexual assault has increased in recent years.

However, the use of physical force as a form of discrimination may have increased in response to the perceived threat of the women's movement. Social psychologists may exaggerate perceptions of women's agency and efficacy because their usual subjects – white, middle-class, college students – are largely unaware of the various forms of oppression in society and appear to be functioning well. Their research is not likely to delve into the private as well as the public aspects of these women's lives. Thus, social psychological studies may minimize both the extent and the personal costs of sexual violence.

Some feminist critics have also argued that a focus on women as victims can create a self-fulfilling prophecy. Women may internalize their perceived lack of efficacy and develop fewer ways of actively coping with an oppressive society. More agentic women, on the other hand, may deny women's oppression and blame other women for their own victimization.

I have presented many sides of the argument here to demonstrate how the problem of violence against women presents a double bind for feminists. If we focus on the advances that women have made, we risk ignoring the inequities of a society whose privileges we share. If, however, we focus on continuing oppressions within society, we risk ignoring women as agents of personal and social change.

There is no easy resolution of this dilemma. Probably there are more possibilities available to some women today than there were twenty-five years ago. These increased opportunities are certainly not available to all women. To some extent, whether one stresses that the glass is half empty or half full probably depends upon one's definition of feminism. But that position is also influenced by one's own status and power.

Feminists within psychology, at least, have been reluctant to discuss how and why their feminisms differ from each other. But our position in society surely influences the degree of sexism that we perceive. Senior women can become 'honorary men' and less subject to the sexism of academia. I do not know, however, whether we then acquire a vested interest in denying such sexism or are simply less aware of it. Self-labeling as marginal seems to have helped some senior feminists to avoid this trap (Unger, 1998).

What is the relationship between sex differences and power differences?
Obviously, social position is highly related to power and status. In the early 1970s feminist scholars were very interested in these areas. However, the concern with status and power among feminist

psychologists has begun to wane. Although Arnold Kahn and Janice Yoder guest edited a special issue of the *Psychology of Women Quarterly* on women and power in 1992, many of the articles were on perceptions of power and influence strategies rather than on systemic forms of oppression.

A few psychologists such as Brinton Lykes and her colleagues have been interested in the systematic nature of oppression. They have studied the plight of women under conditions of state-supported violence (Lykes et al., 1993). Others such as Michelle Fine (Fine and Zane, 1988) have looked at the behavioral consequences for African-American and Latina adolescents educated in schools that practice both racial and gender oppression. It is notable that both Fine and Lykes have largely looked outside psychology for their collaborators (who appear more likely to be found in departments of sociology or in schools of education or law). Their work is not seen as integral to the psychology of women by many researchers in the USA. Except for these individuals and a few feminist psychologists of color (Wyche and Graves, 1992; Reid, 1993; Ginorio et al., 1995), even feminist examinations of power have remained within the laboratory 'safely' labeled as social influence or need for control (cf. Unger, 1986a).

Even more problematic for feminist psychology, the confounding of power differences with sex differences continues to be ignored by some feminist scholars. Interestingly, researchers such as Carol Gilligan and Deborah Tannen are extremely popular with the media and their books are widely read by the general public. Repeated critiques from the scholarly community (cf. Crawford and Unger, 1990; Tromel-Ploetz, 1991; Torres, 1992; Crawford, 1995) arguing that their work ignores the fact that males remain the more powerful sex in virtually every behavioral transaction have gone unheard.

Neither Gilligan nor Tannen have attempted to control systematically for the effect of power and status, despite the fact that repeated laboratory studies have shown that power differences are more predictive of behavior than gender differences (cf. Unger and Crawford, 1996). Conversational interruptions, for example, are not neutral with respect to power. In a recent study, Marianne LaFrance (1992) found that when a lower status person interrupted a higher status partner, he or she was seen as more disrespectful than when status differentials were maintained. Women who interrupted men were also seen as more disrespectful than men who interrupted women. These women received more opprobrium because they used a social privilege that they were not acknowledged to possess.

The link between gender and power presents another double bind for feminists. To assume, for example, that direct and coercive forms of power are largely the property of males denies women both their agency and their complicity in maintaining unequal power relationships between groups. But power and status differentials operate even within groups of feminist scholars (cf. Kitzinger, 1991).

We are presented with other dilemmas whenever we focus too exclusively on either personal or institutional power. Yoder and Kahn phrased this dilemma very well in their introduction to their special issue on gender and power: 'It seems myopic to discuss individual empowerment when the root of much gender-based oppression is societal. Similarly, it seems overwhelming to concentrate exclusively on societal oppressions when the building blocks of social change are committed individuals' (Yoder and Kahn, 1992, pp. 385–386).

The relationship between group identity and personal responsibility is a key area of controversy among feminists today as well as others committed to social change. This relationship may be particularly problematic for individuals who have been personally successful in our society while the group with which they identify remains culturally marginalized and financially impoverished (cf. McCombs, 1986; LaFromboise et al., 1995). They may be marginalized within their own group as well as within mainstream society. Thus, they may lack the ability to make the informed choices that are considered fundamental for mental health. If they lack other similar individuals with whom to identify and/or a language that analyzes the socio-structural nature of their problems, they may blame their own personal deficiencies for their lack of fit. A younger generation (raised on stories of individual women's empowerment) may not even recognize when they are in such situational contexts (cf. Neuborne, 1995).

How important is methodology in understanding feminist scholarship?

Difference is not a neutral concept in our society. Whether or not a difference is seen as important helps to determine social policies. While empirical evidence does not influence governmental decision-making as much as academics would like, it can have an impact. However, feminist empiricists within psychology are often in conflict with feminists in other disciplines because of our methodology. For example, critics of Carol Gilligan's work on purported gender differences in moral orientation point out that her findings have not been replicated by researchers outside her network of students and collaborators. Others dismiss these criticisms as mere methodological quibbles.

Differences about methodology often mask differences in models of reality (Unger, 1983). When once feminists believed that questions about sex differences would disappear as researchers demonstrated that such differences were relatively small, inconsistent, and contextual in nature, questions about sex-related differences have re-emerged. One of the factors responsible for renewed interest in the area is the development of meta-analysis as a tool to examine findings in a large number of independent studies. Feminists may differ, however, about the implications of the same effect size (cf. Unger and Crawford, 1989). Such disagreements demonstrate that methodological advances do not remove the necessity for making conceptual (and, therefore, value-laden) decisions about the results of our work.

Feminist psychology in the USA has been little touched by some of the other developments in methodology that are favored by feminists in other disciplines such as discourse analysis. Discourse analytic methodologies have had a much greater impact internationally. A high proportion of the papers submitted to *Feminism & Psychology* use this kind of methodology (Wilkinson, personal communication, October 1997).

US feminists are caught in a double bind when they use innovative, qualitative techniques. They may, at best, be accused of being obscure or using methodology that is not relevant to 'real' (so-called scientific) psychology. This kind of anti-qualitative bias is illustrated in a review of a book by Mary Crawford (1995) called *Talking Difference*. This book discusses research on language from a variety of methodological perspectives including discourse analysis. Although very positive reviews of the book were published in a number of mainstream journals, the reviewer in *Contemporary Psychology* (the official book review journal of APA) suggested that the book was written for only a 'small band of readers' (Tomarelli, 1996). She further argued that the book was likely 'to offend feminists who dislike science and scientists who dislike feminism' (p. 20). The reader was led to infer that only a small group of people exist who, like myself, value both viewpoints.

The development and use of innovative methodology is particularly important for feminist psychologists because they may bridge some of our conflict over the relative importance of nomothetic and idiographic methods of research (cf. Unger, 1990). Nomothetic methods involve quantifiable procedures which permit generalization across groups whereas idiographic methods such as case histories focus on a single individual's experience. Quantification is seen as synonymous with empirical for many within the mainstream psychology community. While I believe that both methodologies have something to contribute, it is important to recognize that they are valued differentially by the two communities with which feminist psychologists identify – mainstream psychology and feminist studies.

Even feminist psychology journals are less likely to publish idiographic studies than those which use traditional nomographic research techniques (Fine, 1985; Lykes and Stewart, 1986).[3] On the other hand, scholars of women's studies clearly prefer idiographic studies which concentrate on the individual's story. Feminist journals outside of psychology rarely publish nomothetic studies. Few feminist empiricist psychologists are involved in the National Women's Studies Association or serve on the editorial boards of feminist journals such as *Signs*.

Signs has neglected nomothetic scholarship and sometimes appears hostile to it. In one case in which I was personally involved, the editors declined to publish brief versions of the papers from the symposium that eventually became the book *Making a difference* (Hare-Mustin and Maracek, 1990), despite the fact that they had solicited the manuscripts in the first place. They decided that our discussions of measurement issues would not be of general interest to their women's studies audience.

This double bind is particularly distressing for feminist psychologists who identify with experimental psychology in some form. To the extent to which the work we do is acceptable to mainstream psychologists, it is rarely recognized as valuable by feminist scholars. And if we do cutting-edge feminist work, it is not seen as psychology. Some feminist psychologists have reacted to this dilemma by advising the abandonment of psychology as a discipline altogether. I am reluctant to urge this route because feminists in psychology do possess a power base from which to challenge the field and because I do not know what tools could replace the empirical psychological methods with which I am familiar (cf. Unger, 1996). By trying to straddle the two viewpoints, however, I often feel that I exist in the trough between two 'normal' curves.

I wish I could believe that any kind of empirical research will provide *the* answers. However, empiricism is also a double-edged sword for feminist psychologists. We want to use it and critique it at the same time. We can only do so if we recognize that empiricism is only one of many possible techniques for knowing about the world.

Feminists can do empirical research if we recognize its limitations. It will neither give us absolute answers nor certainly the 'truth'. On the other hand, empirical research about the 'right' questions can be used as a form of argument for social change (Unger, 1996). Feminist empiricist research seems to be particularly well suited for the sensitization and enlightenment of others who are not yet convinced by feminist ideology.

How much impact have feminists had on psychology?

Like many of the other issues discussed in this chapter, the answers to this question are somewhat contradictory. I will discuss evidence of legitimization in several areas separately because the situation is not the same in each.

Psychology of women journals

There are now several journals focusing either wholly or in large part on scholarship in the area such as *Sex Roles*, *Psychology of Women Quarterly*, and *Feminism & Psychology*. Many of the citations in this book come from these journals. Unfortunately, they are not always to be found in institutional libraries, especially those of more 'elite' universities. Courses in the area are also less likely to be taught in such schools too. At Harvard, for example, the psychology of women is taught in its extension division.

The existence of journals that focus on women and gender is an enormous advance compared to where we were 'forced' to publish in the early days of the field. In fact, one of the original purposes of this book was to bring together ideas from some of my publications in obscure journals which are not likely to be found in most university libraries.

Like all advances, however, the existence of these journals can produce dilemmas for the feminist researcher. If one publishes in them, one will reach an audience of feminists, but it is less likely that the work will be read widely by people outside the field. The work will probably be considered to possess less scholarly merit by promotion and tenure committees than that published in a more mainstream journal. Fortunately, many established feminist scholars are committed to publishing in 'our' journals.

Of course, academic publishing is also subject to political forces. Scholarly legitimacy appears to be based on the cumulative impact of professional networks and may take a long time to develop (Unger, 1982). Political legitimacy can, however, enhance scholarly legitimacy as well as detract from it. For example, the major source for feminist citations within psychology, other than feminist journals, is the *American Psychologist* – the official journal of record of APA. Nearly 25 percent of the 'classic' feminist articles reprinted by

Janis Bohan (1992) were first published in this journal, as well as many other articles which represented cutting-edge feminist scholarship at the time.

I would like to be able to argue that these articles were accepted by a journal known for its extremely high rejection rate because of their excellence. However, the review process, like everything else in scholarship, is not free of potential bias. Much of the gatekeeping that editors perform is determined by two practices: the reviewers to whom they send a manuscript and the decisions they make about mixed reviews. When a field is small, knowledgeable editors may be aware of the theoretical position of various reviewers and can 'save' or 'kill' a manuscript by judicious selection. When reviews are mixed or ambivalent (as they often are), editors can make a positive or negative decision based on their own biases or decide to send the paper to another reviewer.

Researchers (Peters and Ceci, 1982) have found that a paper submitted from a prestigious institution is more likely to be accepted for publication than the same paper from a less well-known source. Similarly, papers from well-known people in the field are likely to be seen as more credible than if the individual is unknown. We all know that evaluation bias against the work of women is widespread. When I submitted my own paper to the *American Psychologist* in 1978, I was neither well known nor from a prestigious institution. However, I did know the consulting editor from professional meetings. I believe this lent more credibility to my so-called radical feminist views than they might have received from an editor with whom I was not acquainted. When my professional acquaintance received mixed reviews, he invited me to 'tone down the feminism' and resubmit the paper.

The representation of sex and gender in textbooks
Surprisingly, feminists' active involvement in APA and their numerous publications in prestigious APA journals have not yet greatly influenced the field as a whole. One way of determining impact is to examine what is said about sex and gender in textbooks. Textbooks transmit ideas about what is legitimate knowledge to the next generation of psychologists. Peterson and Kroner (1992) recently conducted an extensive content analysis of current textbooks in introductory psychology and human development. They concluded that although there has been some decrease in sex-stereotyped language and in gender-biased content since 1975, representation of the work, theory, and behavior of males continues significantly to exceed the representation of the work, theory and behavior of females.

A brief examination of introductory texts favored by members of my own department also indicates that these texts remain both ethnocentric and androcentric (Unger, 1997). The 'worst' offenders (if it is possible to rank order such high levels of bias) are those texts that purport to present a scientific view of the discipline (cf. Gleitman, 1992; Zimbardo, 1992; Weiten, 1994). An analysis of their subject indices indicated that, as a group, these three texts had a total of 12 pages with a reference to gender and no pages devoted to either race or ethnicity. These findings are particularly disheartening because the Zimbardo text is in its thirteenth edition and, during my term on the board that constructed the Graduate Record Exam in psychology, I learned that Gleitman's text was the favorite resource of the 'experts' who construct it.

One of these texts (Weiten) has an additional 8 pages devoted to gender differences. This latter finding is consistent with Mary Brabeck's observation (personal communication) that although most current introductory psychology texts cover Maccoby and Jacklin's (1974) ground-breaking work on sex differences, they highlight the few differences found between the sexes rather than the many similarities among them.

Introductory textbooks written by psychologists with a social or developmental perspective appear to be more aware of recent feminist research. For example, a recent edition of Myers' text (1992) had 22 pages noting gender in its subject index and 8 pages noting race and/or ethnicity. However, even this text had 22 pages where the term 'gender difference' appeared.

The original edition of Myers (1986) included a chapter on gender, but this was changed in a later edition to a chapter on social diversity. I am not sure how to evaluate this change to greater inclusiveness because I am somewhat uncomfortable with its rationale. As one of the reviewers for the earlier version, I know that the change was due, in part, to the unwillingness of many introductory psychology instructors to consider gender to be a legitimate part of a first course in psychology. I do not know if they are more comfortable with the current theme of cultural and gender diversity.

Feminist impact on mainstream psychology

Stephanie Shields (1994) has pointed out that over the past twenty-five years contemporary feminist psychologists have developed an impressive variety and range of empirical work and theory. She offers a long list of texts and methodological and theoretical critiques to support her argument as well as an inventory of previously unexamined questions with important social implications that have been addressed. The latter list includes a large range of topics such as sex bias in language, women's adult development, and date rape.

But she also points out that the insights of feminist psychology have remained invisible to psychology as a whole. Feminist scholarship is largely omitted from psychology textbooks at any level. Most mainstream psychologists are unaware of any feminist perspective and, at best, embody it only in the persona of the few feminist psychologists who can be found in a given department. Such perspectives remain, of course, 'ghettoized' within courses on the psychology of women and gender.

Courses in the psychology of women and/or gender have gradually become part of the standard psychological curriculum in the USA. Surveys by APA find, for example, that 51 percent of all colleges and universities currently report that they include such a course (Women's Program Office, 1991). Of course, this also means that nearly 50 percent of all institutions of higher education do not have one. Those of us who have been teaching a course on the psychology of women for more than twenty years are surprised when we learn that many curricular committees remain hostile to its existence.

I believe that more and 'better' scholarship will not make such committees less hostile. This problem requires political and activist solutions. For example, when Barbara Wallston and I served back-to-back terms on the advisory board for the Graduate Record Exam in psychology, we made it a point to include some questions on gender in every exam. Committees that make site visits to accredit graduate programs can make the point that these programs are deficient if they do not include courses that examine gender and race. Finally, since most of our undergraduate and graduate students are female, we can help them to understand the importance of such a course and how to agitate for its existence. I never recommend that any of my students matriculate in a graduate program that does not have a course on women and gender. These policies do not, of course, preclude introducing gender issues into every course.

Early leaders

Many of the women who have been active in feminist scholarship over the past twenty-five years are friends and acquaintances and I have followed their careers with great interest over the years. As I noted earlier in the book, some of them have disappeared from psychology. Joann Evansgardner, for example, was never able to get a permanent job at an academic institution and has remained a grass-roots feminist activist. Some of them have left the field. Several friends died prematurely – Carolyn Sherif, Barbara

Wallston, and Nancy Datan. Major awards from Division 35 and the Southeastern Psychological Association memorialize the first two scholars. Nancy, whose work was more idiosyncratic and who was less connected to feminist networks, has yet to receive the institutionalized credit she deserves although I recently edited a reappraisal of her work in *Feminism & Psychology* (Unger, 1995b).

The surviving past presidents of Division 35 have done relatively well. Many of them have become academic administrators (Helen Astin, Florence Denmark, and Virginia O'Leary). Their pattern of continued institutional leadership is quite clear. Several early Division 35 presidents and AWP activists (including myself) have served terms as director of women's studies at various institutions. They include: Nancy Henley (at UCLA), Martha Mednick (at the University of Connecticut), Irene Frieze (at the University of Pittsburgh), Ellen Kimmel (at the University of South Florida), and Nancy Russo (at Arizona State). Unlike the feminists of a previous generation, they have had the opportunity to train graduate students in both feminism and psychology. Nevertheless, none of these is regarded as being among the most prestigious US research institutions.

All of the past presidents of Division 35 became full professors or the clinical equivalent. So why do I say that they have been only relatively successful? In part, it is because their work remains underutilized by both mainstream psychologists and mainstream feminists. In part, it is because our scholarship has not been acknowledged in the bastions of academic power. And in part, it is because success can only be determined by what comes later. Will our work be used by younger scholars and those who are still students in the field?

The next generation of feminist scholars
Academic generations are very short so it may be possible today to look at the next generation of feminist scholars – those who came of age in the late 1970s and early 1980s. This group of women appears to be less connected with feminist organizations within psychology than my own generation. When they have formal organizational affiliations within APA, they seem to be more likely to be with SPSSI than with Division 35. Other feminist scholars from this generation appear to have no organizational involvement at all within APA.

Why are these women relatively uninvolved in the leadership of a division on women's psychology? There are so many more women now in psychology that they may feel less need to identify with women as a marginalized group. Indeed, many of the women in the younger cohort have a deep commitment to social justice for many diverse populations. For example, Michelle Fine and Adrienne Asch (1988) edited an excellent book on women and disability which received an AWP publication award. Abigail Stewart coedited an issue of the *Journal of Social Issues* on sexism and racism in the lives of Black women (Smith and Stewart, 1983). Michelle Fine, Brinton Lykes, and Pamela Reid have participated in action research with oppressed women in the USA and elsewhere.

Their research is much more contextualized than that of the previous generation of feminist scholars. It appears to deviate even more from recent mainstream psychological work on women and gender which has largely focused on social cognitive models and meta-analyses. It is difficult to see how a rapprochement between these two groups of researchers will be reached. Nevertheless, one sign of the success and maturity of the field is that we now admit to a wide range of views and feel safe enough to permit our differences to be aired publicly (cf. Wilkinson, 1996).

Toward a synthesis of the personal and professional

I think my own life and professional career illustrate some of the trials and triumphs of my generation of feminist psychologists. I have been a full professor at Montclair State for many years and director of its undergraduate honors program from 1986 to 1996. I have, however, also encountered double binds in my personal and professional life. It has been difficult to be both a 'good feminist' and a 'good psychologist'.

On occasion, I have, for example, tried to move elsewhere. At one large research university, the women's studies program liked me, but the psychology department found even a social psychologist too radical for a department which was evenly split between clinical and experimental psychologists. In another, the psychology department was so anxious to hire me that my interview consisted of selecting which office would have the best view. However, the women's studies program was dominated by postmodernist cultural theorists who decided that a semioticist 'would be better at explaining to the administration the cutting-edge of feminist scholarship'.

I have also learned that it is sometimes impossible for any woman to be 'good enough'. During the early days in the field, both Barbara Wallston and I were told by interviewers that we would be hired if we would 'just do more research like that of Elaine Hatfield'. When I met Elaine years later and told her this story, she laughed and said, 'That's funny, I had trouble getting a new position too'. Conversely, at the University of Haifa, while they learned to respect my approach to the field, they insisted I was a 'social' rather than a 'feminist' psychologist.

I am still married to my first and only husband and we have raised two daughters who have become more feminist as they grow older. Our older daughter has always taken particular joy in hoisting me by my feminist principles. For example, she drives a motorcycle and a truck rather than more conventional vehicles. She works with computers and believes that she is one of the few female systems administrators that most people have met.

I have always felt very lucky that my professional interests and political commitments have meshed so well. This association has given me the energy to juggle research, writing, teaching, and familial responsibilities. My organizational activities have given me the opportunity to make a great many friends that I would not have had otherwise. These friendships include people with whom I have collaborated extensively and those whom I see once or twice a year at professional meetings. They have been more satisfying than finding citations to something I have written (although I like to know that I have had that kind of impact too). As I have said before, the professional, is the political, is the personal.

The reason I have written this book is because the synthesis of my intellectual, political, and emotional life has been an important part of my experience as a feminist in psychology. Many of the stories that I have told here have been recounted around dinner tables or in late night conversations at professional meetings. But they will not be available to younger women who do not have good professional mentors to tell them to go to conferences or who are less assertive than I have always been. I would not like to see such stories disappear from history – leaving us with a view of things as they are supposed to have happened rather than the way they really did. I hope this book will encourage others to tell their stories too.

It is easy to become paralyzed out there in the outer margins. Other people's published work looks better than our own, reputable feminist scholars are seen as too important to talk to, and we believe our small amount of political investment will have little payoff. I have written this book because we all think others' work is better than our own. I have also seen noted scholars such as Jessie Bernard eat alone at a professional conference because everyone was afraid to talk to her. And a few years ago during a dinner conversation at a conference with a past president of APA, a past president of SPSSI, and another past president of Division 35, I found out that we all feel marginal.

It would be difficult for any of us to defend our sense of marginality in any objective sense although, when pressed, we could all find some justification based on familial experiences. I do not know how many comparable men have the same feeling or would admit it if they did. However, I believe our feeling of marginality is what gives us the energy to persevere despite doubts about our personal lives, our political choices, and our intellectual underpinnings. Perhaps, if one is never quite sure one is in the right place, one is less afraid to be in the wrong one.

Beyond personal epistemology: toward social change

Has the field of psychology been changed by our work? Somewhat – but some issues just do not go away. The gender difference question has re-emerged for other reasons besides methodological advances. As I noted earlier in this book, ideas about group differences have frequently been tied to theories involving biological causality. Susan Faludi (1991) has pointed out that theories about the biological difference and inferiority of women have tended to become popular during periods when women have become politically threatening. We seem to be in another such period of backlash today.

But as I stated nearly twenty years ago (Unger, 1979c), feminist scholars cannot deal with the issue of biological differences by simply trying to 'disprove' them. Moreover, psychologists' concern over resolving the 'nature–nurture conflict' masks another more critical problem involving difference – the relationship between social difference and societal equality. As Joan Scott has stated:

> When equality and difference are paired dichotomously, they structure an impossible choice. If one opts for equality, one is forced to accept the notion that difference is antithetical to it. If one opts for difference, one admits that equality is unattainable. . . . Feminists cannot give up "difference"; it has been our most creative analytic tool. We cannot give up equality, at least as long as we want to speak to the principles and values of our political system. But it makes no sense for the feminist movement to let its arguments be forced into preexisting categories and its political disputes to be characterized by a dichotomy we did not invent. (Scott, 1991, p. 142)

Feminist psychologists have been more enmeshed in difference arguments than feminists in other disciplines because of the individualistic focus of the field. We have internalized psychology's epistemology and only a few scholars have attempted to transcend the terms of this debate. These scholars recognize that arguments about difference have obscured and protected institutional arrangements of privilege and stratification (Fine and Addelston, 1996).

Psychologists who write about institutionalized oppression often seem to be writing 'out of their field'. They are not often published in 'mainstream' feminist psychology journals – at least not in the USA. Their epistemology conflicts too much with the customary ways with which feminists, as psychologists, structure their work. It tends, for example, to undermine conventional ideas about the distance between subject and investigator. Many of such activist feminist scholars are involved in participant–observer relationships or in even more personal collaborative alliances with their 'subjects'. Their work is qualitative and subjective and often passionately militant.

These researchers are not unknown. But they have had little impact upon feminist empiricists within psychology because we find it difficult to change our 'starting point'. We have difficulty making the system rather than the individual our object of scrutiny. Clinical psychologists also have difficulty with this scholarship because they have been trained to change the individual rather than the system.

A view of reality that recognizes the overwhelming nature of gender, race, and class oppression can be debilitating unless it includes a view that the individual can be an agent of change. But the alternative postmodernist view that rejects the idea of reality in favor of an array of equivalent culturally distinct voices may produce political paralysis. One critic (Carby, 1992) asks compellingly:

> Have we, as a society, successfully eliminated the desire for achieving integration through political agitation for civil rights and opted instead for knowing each other through cultural texts? (Carby, 1992, p. 17)

Just as there is no evidence to support the idea that personal insight produces personal change, there is no evidence that cultural knowledge empowers the drive for social change.

How do we transcend our own epistemology? I wish I could end with this question rather than trying to resolve it – even partially. I think its resolution lies in our recognition of a collective identity similar to Brinton Lykes's (1985) concept of 'social individuality'. In her concept, there is no separation between self, other selves, and society. They constitute each other in an inextricable whole. Although not stated explicitly, this was an ideal of second-wave feminism. The 'personal was political' in the sense that what happened to each woman happened to all women and that change would empower us all.

What happened to this ideal? It is important to recognize that the forces of a competitive, individualistic society conspire to destroy the unity of marginalized groups. The work of Michelle Fine and her colleagues at the University of Pennsylvania Law School shows what can happen as a result of such forces (Fine and Addelston, 1996; Guinier, Fine and Balin, 1994). They found that women entered this elite institution with equivalent qualifications to men, but with a greater interest in social welfare than their male peers. They found that both white women and people of color described themselves as alienated during their first year of law school. By the second year, complaints about harassment and the dehumanizing environment had disappeared. So too had the women's interest in working for social justice. They had become more like the men, but at a cost. Despite equal credentials, these women did not perform as well as men during their law school years.

Sexist and racist institutional policies create a sense of entitlement in the white men for whom they are designed. Women and people of color who are 'let into' elite institutions 'pay' for their partial sense of entitlement by abandoning their group identities and their concern for social change. The price of becoming 'honorary men' appears to be a loss of a sense of agency as well as problems with emotional health. I can very much identify with these findings. After receiving my PhD, it took me over five years to return to writing professionally again. I started when I met other feminists and became involved in efforts to create professional change.

We have come full circle. The professional is political as well as personal. It is time to take collectivity seriously again. A number of feminist psychologists have, like myself, sounded clarion calls for a renewed concern with feminist coalitions and collective action (Tavris, 1993; Weisstein, 1993). But the coalitions, this time, must extend across a number of marginalized groups (Unger, 1995a). A focus on individualism and subjectivity has led to passivity in the past decade. Our history tells us that change is not always progress and that progress takes a long time. But it also tells us that progress can be cumulative and activism can be personally rewarding. A critical mass of women is now available to influence psychology's direction – if only we can get back to our earlier visions of collective change.

Notes

1 There has been an unpredicted return to theories of biological causality by some gay scholars (cf. Levay, 1993). These individuals appear to believe that their sexual orientation will receive less opprobrium from conservative society if it can be demonstrated that same-sex orientation is not a matter of choice. However, religious conservatism has been found to predict both less and more prejudice against homosexuals. Whatever the empirical connection turns out to be, this theoretical trend illustrates the close connection between our personal needs and the scientific questions we explore.

2 See, for example, the special issue on class in *Feminism & Psychology* edited by

Valerie Walkerdine (1996). Class is less likely to be confounded with race/ethnicity in Europe than in the US.

3   This has begun to change in recent years. For example, Mary Crawford and Ellen Kimmel have recently edited a special issue of the *Psychology of Women Quarterly* on innovative methods for feminist research (1999). It is noteworthy, however, that a number of the contributions for this issue came from scholars from outside the United States.

Appendix

Division 35 Presidents

Year	Name	Institution when elected	Area of PhD
1973–1974	Elizabeth Douvan	University of Michigan	Personality
1974–1975	Helen Astin	UCLA (University of California at Los Angeles)	Education/counsel
1975–1976	Florence Denmark	Hunter College	Social
1976–1977	Martha Mednick	Howard University	Personality
1977–1978	Annette Brodsky	University of Alabama	Clinical
1978–1979	Barbara Wallston	George Peabody College	Social
1979–1980	Carolyn Sherif	Penn State	Social
1980–1981	Rhoda Unger	Montclair State	Experimental
1981–1982	Michelle Wittig	Cal. State-Northridge	Developmental
1982–1983	Mary Parlee	CUNY (Graduate Center of the City University of New York)	Experimental
1983–1984	Irene Frieze	University of Pittsburgh	Social
1984–1985	Hannah Lerman	Private practice	Clinical
1985–1986	Jacqueline Eccles	University of Michigan	Social
1986–1987	Virginia O'Leary	Boston University	Social
1987–1988	Ellen Kimmel	University of S. Florida	Experimental
1988–1989	Nancy Russo	Arizona State	Developmental
1989–1990	Lenore Walker	Private practice	Clinical
1990–1991	Bernice Lott	Rhode Island University	Social
1991–1992	Pamela Reid	CUNY (Graduate Center of the City University of New York)	Developmental
1992–1993	Natalie Porter	University of New Mexico	Med. Social/clinical
1993–1994	Janet Hyde	University of Wisconsin	Behavioral Genetics
1994–1995	Norine Johnson	Private practice	Clinical
1995–1996	Cheryl Travis	University of Tennessee	Social
1996–1997	Laura Brown	Private practice	Clinical
1997–1998	Judith Worell	University of Kentucky	Counseling

Titles of presidential addresses

1974	Elizabeth Douvan	'Modeling in women's development'
1975	Helen Astin	'Role of higher education in the development of adult women'
1976	Florence Denmark	'Styles of leadership'

1977	Martha Mednick	'Now we are four: what should we be when we grow up?'
1978	Annette Brodsky	'Decade of feminist influence on psychotherapy'
1979	Barbara Wallston	'What are the questions in psychology of women: a feminist approach to research'
1980	Carolyn Sherif	'Needed concepts in the study of gender identity'
1981	Rhoda Unger	'Through the looking glass: no Wonderland yet! (The reciprocal relationship between methods and models of reality)'
1982	Michelle Wittig	'Metatheoretical dilemmas in the psychology of gender'
1983	Mary Parlee	'Psychology of female reproduction: menstruation, pregnancy, and menopause'
1984	Irene Frieze	'Gender roles, gender schema, and reactions to victimization'
1985	Hannah Lerman	'From Freud to feminist personality theory: getting here from there'
1986	Jacqueline Eccles	'Women's achievement: an alternative perspective'
1987	Virginia O'Leary	'Sex and gender in social context: towards a feminist psychology'
1988	Ellen Kimmel	'The experience of feminism'
1989	Nancy Russo	'Women and psychology: history, status, and future'
1990	Lenore Walker	'Feminist contributions to professional psychology'
1991	Bernice Lott	'The social learning of gender – a feminist perspective'
1992	Pamela Reid	'Poor women in psychology: shut up and shut out'
1993	Natalie Porter	'Teaching, supervising, mentoring: feminist pedagogies'
1994	Janet Hyde	'Women and maternity leave – empirical data and public policy'
1995	Norine Johnson	'Feminist frames of women's strengths: visions for the future'
1996	Cheryl Travis	'Sexuality and society: perspectives on women'
1997	Laura Brown	'Giving away feminist psychology: How and to whom?'
1998	Judith Worell	

References

Addelston, J. (1995) The construction of masculinity. PhD dissertation, Graduate Center of CUNY.

Alpert, J. (1978) The psychology of women: What should the field be called? *American Psychologist, 33,* 965–969.

Anderson, C.A., Lepper, M.R. and Ross, L. (1980) Perseverance of social theories: The role of explanation in the persistence of discredited information. *Journal of Personality and Social Psychology, 39,* 1037–1049.

Apfelbaum, E. (1979) Relations of dominance and movements for liberation: An analysis of power between groups. In W.G. Austin and S. Worchel (eds) *The social psychology of intergroup relations.* Monterey: Brooks/Cole (pp. 188–204).

Apfelbaum, E. (1993) Norwegian and French women in high leadership positions: The importance of cultural context upon gendered relations. *Psychology of Women Quarterly, 17,* 409–429.

Ashmore, R.D. (1981) Sex stereotypes and implicit personality theory. In D.L. Hamilton (ed.) *Cognitive processes in stereotyping and intergroup behavior.* Hillsdale, NJ: Erlbaum.

Ashmore, R.D. (1985) Thinking about the sexes: From sex-role stereotypes to gender belief systems. Paper presented at the Second Interdisciplinary Conference on Sex and Gender, Nags Head, North Carolina.

Astin, H.S. (1969) *The woman doctorate in America.* New York: Russell Sage Foundation.

Bardwick, J.M. (1971) *Psychology of women: A study of bio-cultural conflicts.* New York: Harper & Row.

Becker, H.S. (1967) Whose side are we on? *Social Problems, 14,* 239–247.

Bem, S.L. (1974) The measurement of psychological androgyny. *Journal of Consulting and Clinical Psychology, 42,* 155–162.

Bem, S.L. (1975) Sex role adaptability: One consequence of psychological androgyny. *Journal of Personality and Social Psychology, 31,* 634–643.

Bem, S.L. and Bem, D.J. (1970) Training the woman to know her place: The power of a nonconscious ideology. In D.J. Bem (ed.) *Beliefs, attitudes, and human affairs.* Belmont, CA: Brooks/Cole.

Berger, P.L. and Luckmann, T. (1966) *The social construction of reality.* Garden City, NY: Anchor.

Berkowitz, L. (1972) Social norms, feelings, and other factors affecting helping and altruism. In L. Berkowitz (ed.) *Advances in experimental social psychology,* vol. 6. New York: Academic Press.

Berkowitz, L., Klanderman, S.B. and Harris, R. (1964) Effects of experimenter awareness and sex of subject and experimenter on reactions to dependency relationships. *Sociometry, 27,* 327–337.

Bermant, G. and Davidson, J.M. (1974) *Biological bases of sexual behavior.* New York: Harper & Row.

Bernard, J. (1981) *The female world.* New York: Free Press.

Bernstein, M.D. and Russo, N.F. (1974) The history of psychology revisited: Or, up with our foremothers. *American Psychologist, 29*, 130–134.

Blau, P.M. (1975) Structural constraints of status complements. In L.A. Coser (ed.) *The idea of social structure.* New York: Harcourt Brace Jovanovich.

Block, J.H. (1976) Debatable conclusions about sex differences. *Contemporary Psychology, 21*, 517–522.

Bohan, J.S. (ed.) (1992) *Seldom seen, rarely heard: Women's place in psychology.* Boulder, CO: Westview Press.

Bohan, J.S. (1993) Regarding gender: Essentialism, constructionism, and feminist psychology. *Psychology of Women Quarterly, 17*, 5–21.

Brannon, R. (1981) Current methodological issues in paper-and-pencil measuring instruments. *Psychology of Women Quarterly, 5*, 618–627.

Brodsky, A.M. and Hare-Mustin, R.H. (eds) (1980) *Women and psychotherapy: An assessment of research and practice.* New York: Guilford Press.

Broverman, I.K., Broverman, D.M., Clarkson, F.E., Rosenkrantz, P.S. and Vogel, S.R. (1970) Sex-role stereotypes and clinical judgments of mental health. *Journal of Consulting and Clinical Psychology, 34*, 1–7.

Broverman, I.K., Vogel, S.R., Broverman, D.M., Clarkson, F.E. and Rosenkrantz, P.S. (1972) Sex-role stereotypes: A current appraisal. *Journal of Social Issues, 28*, 59–78.

Brown, L.W. (1989) New voices, new visions: Towards a lesbian/gay paradigm for psychology. *Psychology of Women Quarterly, 13*, 445–458.

Buffery, A.W.H. and Gray, J.A. (1972) Sex differences in the development of spatial and linguistic skills. In C. Ounsted and D.C. Taylor (eds) *Gender differences: Their ontogeny and significance.* London: Churchill Livingstone.

Burman, E. (1990) Differing with deconstruction: A feminist critique. In I. Parker and J. Shotter (eds) *Deconstructing social psychology.* London: Routledge (pp. 208–220).

Buss, A.R. (1974–1975) Counter-culture and counter-psychology. *Interpersonal Development, 5*, 223–233.

Buss, A.R. (1975) The emerging field of the sociology of psychological knowledge. *American Psychologist, 30*, 988–1002.

Buss, A.R. (1976) Galton and sex differences: An historical note. *Journal of the History of the Behavioral Sciences, 12*, 283–285.

Buss, A.R. (1978a) The structure of psychological revolutions. *Journal of the History of the Behavioral Sciences, 14*, 57–64.

Buss, A.R. (1978b) A conceptual critique of attribution theory. *Journal of Personality and Social Psychology, 36*, 1311–1321.

Buss, D.M. (1989) Sex differences in human mate preferences: Evolutionary hypotheses tested in 37 cultures. *Behavioral and Brain Sciences, 12*, 1–49.

Buss, D.M. (1995) Psychological sex differences: Origins through sexual selection. *American Psychologist, 50*, 164–168.

Cantor, M.G. (1987) Popular culture and the portrayal of women: Content and control. In B.B. Hess and M.M. Ferree (eds) *Analyzing gender.* Newbury Park, CA: Sage.

Caplan, N. and Nelson, S.D. (1973) On being useful: The nature and consequences of psychological research on social problems. *American Psychologist, 28*, 199–211.

Caplan, P.J. (1993) *Lifting a ton of feathers.* Toronto: University of Toronto Press.

Caplow, T. and McGee, R.J. (1961) *The academic marketplace.* New York: Science Editions.

Capshew, J.H. and Lazlo, A.C. (1986) 'We would not take no for an answer': Women psychologists and gender politics during World War II. *Journal of Social Issues, 42,* 157–180.

Carby, H. (1992) The multicultural wars. *Radical History Review, 54,* 7–20.

Carli, L.L. (1990) Gender, language, and influence. *Journal of Personality and Social Psychology, 59,* 941–951.

Carlson, E.R. and Carlson, R. (1961) Male and female subjects in personality research. *Journal of Abnormal and Social Psychology, 61,* 482–483.

Carpenter, C.J., Huston, A.C. and Holt, W. (1986) Modification of preschool sex-typed behaviors by participation in adult-structured activities. *Sex Roles, 14,* 603–615.

Carroll, L. (1960) *Alice's adventures in Wonderland and through the looking glass.* New York: Signet.

Cartwright, D. (1959) Power: A neglected variable in social psychology. In D. Cartwright (ed.) *Studies in social psychology.* Ann Arbor, MI: University of Michigan Press (pp. 1–14).

Cherry, F. and Deaux, K. (1978) Fear of success versus fear of gender-inappropriate behavior. *Sex Roles, 4,* 97–101.

Chesler, P. (1972) *Women and madness.* New York: Doubleday.

Chesler, P. (1995) A leader of women. In P. Chesler, E.D. Rothblum and E. Cole (eds) *Feminist foremothers in women's studies, psychology, and mental health.* New York: Haworth Press.

Coan, R.W. (1979) *Psychologists: Personal and theoretical pathways.* New York: Irvington.

Cole, J.R. and Zuckerman, H. (1975) The emergence of a scientific specialty: The self-exemplifying case of the sociology of science. In L.A. Coser (ed.) *The idea of social structure.* New York: Harcourt Brace Jovanovich.

Cole, S. (1975) The growth of scientific knowledge: Theories of deviance as a case study. In L.A. Coser (ed.) *The idea of social structure.* New York: Harcourt Brace Jovanovich.

Crawford, M. (1988) Humor in conversational context: Beyond biases in the study of gender and humor. In R.K. Unger (ed.) *Representations: Social constructions of gender.* Amityville, NY: Baywood Publishing.

Crawford, M. (1989) Agreeing to differ: Feminist epistemologies and women's ways of knowing. In M. Crawford and M. Gentry (eds) *Gender and thought.* New York: Springer-Verlag.

Crawford, M. (1995) *Talking difference: On gender and language.* London: Sage.

Crawford, M. (1997) Claiming the right to know: A personal history. In M. Crawford and R.K. Unger (eds) *In our own words: Readings on the psychology of women and gender.* New York: McGraw Hill (pp. 5–9).

Crawford, M. and Kimmel, E. (eds) (1999) Innovative methods for feminist research. Special issue of the *Psychology of Women Quarterly.*

Crawford, M. and Marecek, J. (1989) Psychology reconstructs the female, 1968–1988. *Psychology of Women Quarterly, 13,* 147–165.

Crawford, M. and Unger, R.K. (1990) Review of *Mapping the moral domain* edited by Carol Gilligan et al. *Contemporary Psychology, 35,* 950–952.

Crosby, F.J. (1982) *Relative deprivation and working women.* New York: Oxford University Press.

Crosby, F.J. (1984) The denial of personal discrimination. *American Behavioral Scientist, 27,* 371–386.

Crosby, F.J. and Herek, G.M. (1986) Male sympathy and the situation of women: Does personal experience make a difference? *Journal of Social Issues, 42,* 55–66.

Datan, N. (1980) Days of our lives. *The Journal of Mind and Behavior, 1,* 63–71.

Datan, N. (1986) Corpses, lepers, and menstruating women: Tradition, transition, and the sociology of knowledge. *Sex Roles, 14,* 693–703.

Datan, N. (1989) Illness and imagery: Feminist cognition, socialization, and gender identity. In M. Crawford and M. Gentry (eds) *Gender and thought.* New York: Springer-Verlag.

Deaux, K. (1971) Honking at the intersection: A replication and extension. *Journal of Social Psychology, 84,* 159–160.

Deaux, K. (1976) *The behavior of women and men.* Belmont, CA: Brooks/Cole.

Deaux, K. (1985) Sex and gender. *Annual Review of Psychology, 36,* 49–81.

Deaux, K. (1993) Sorry, wrong number – a reply to Gentile's call. *Psychological Science, 4,* 125–126.

Deaux, K. and Emswiller, T. (1974) Explanations of successful performance on sex-linked tasks: What's skill for the male is luck for the female. *Journal of Personality and Social Psychology, 29,* 80–85.

Deaux, K., Kite, M.E. and Lewis, L.L. (1985) Clustering and gender schemata: An uncertain link. *Personality and Social Psychology Bulletin, 11,* 387–397.

Deaux, K. and LaFrance, M. (1998) Gender. In D. Gilbert, S. Fiske and G. Lindsey (eds) *The handbook of social psychology* (4th edn). New York: McGraw-Hill.

Deaux, K. and Lewis, L.L. (1984) The structure of gender stereotypes: Interrelationships among components and gender labels. *Journal of Personality and Social Psychology, 46,* 991–1004.

Deaux, K. and Major, B. (1987) Putting gender into context: An interactive model of gender-related behavior. *Psychological Review, 94,* 369–389.

Deaux, K. and Taynor, J. (1973) Evaluation of male and female ability: Bias works both ways. *Psychological Reports, 32,* 261–262.

Denmark, F.L. (1974) Who discriminates against women? An overview with editorial license. *International Journal of Group Tensions, 4,* 3–5.

Denmark, F.L., Russo, N.F., Frieze, I.H. and Sechzer, J.A. (1988) Guidelines for avoiding sexism in psychological research: A report of the APA ad hoc committee on nonsexist research. *American Psychologist, 43,* 582–585.

Dimond, S.J. (1977) Evolution and lateralization of the brain: Concluding remarks. *Annals of the New York Academy of Sciences, 299,* 477–501.

Dion, K.L. (1975) Women's reaction to discrimination from members of the same or opposite sex. *Journal of Research in Personality, 9,* 294–306.

Dion, K.L. (1985) Sex, gender, and groups: Selected issues. In V.E. O'Leary, R.K. Unger and B.S. Wallston (eds) *Women, gender, and social psychology.* Hillsdale, NJ: Erlbaum.

Dion, K.L. and Earn, B.M. (1975) The phenomenology of being a target of prejudice. *Journal of Personality and Social Psychology, 32,* 944–950.

Dion, K.L., Earn, B.M. and Yee, P.H.N. (1978) The experience of being a victim of prejudice: An experimental approach. *International Journal of Psychology, 13,* 197–214.

Doherty, W.J. and Baldwin, C. (1985) Shifts and stability in locus of control during the 1970s: Divergence of the sexes. *Journal of Personality and Social Psychology, 48,* 1048–1053.

Eacker, J.N. (1972) On some elementary philosophical problems of psychology. *American Psychologist, 27,* 553–565.

Eagly, A.H. (1978) Sex differences in influenceability. *Psychological Bulletin, 85*, 86–118.

Eagly, A.H. (1987) *Sex differences in social behavior: A social-role interpretation.* Hillsdale, NJ: Erlbaum.

Eagly, A.H. (1993) Sex differences in human social behavior: Meta-analytic studies of social psychological research. In M. Haug, R. Whalen, C. Aron and K.L. Olsen (eds) *The development of sex differences and similarities in behavior.* Dordrecht: Kluwer (pp. 421–436).

Eagly, A.H. (1994) On comparing women and men. *Feminism & Psychology, 4*, 513–522.

Eagly, A.H. (1995) The science and politics of comparing women and men. *American Psychologist, 50*, 145–158.

Eagly, A.H. and Wood, W. (1985) Gender and influenceability: Stereotype versus behavior. In V.E. O'Leary, R.K. Unger and B.S. Wallston (eds) *Women, gender, and social psychology.* Hillsdale, NJ: Erlbaum.

Eagly, A.H., Wood, W. and Fishbaugh, L. (1981) Sex differences in conformity: Surveillance by the group as a determinant of male nonconformity. *Journal of Personality and Social Psychology, 40*, 384–394.

Eccles, J.S. and Jacobs, J.E. (1986) Social forces shape math attitudes and performance. *Signs, 11*, 367–389.

Elshtain, J.B. (1979) Methodological sophistication and conceptual confusion: A critique of mainstream political science. In J. Sherman and E.T. Beck (eds) *The prism of sex: Essays in the sociology of knowledge.* Madison, WI: University of Wisconsin Press.

Erikson, K.T. (1962) Notes on the sociology of deviance. *Social Problems, 9*, 308.

Erikson, K.T. (1966) *Wayward puritans: A study in the sociology of deviance.* New York: Wiley.

Faludi, S. (1991) *Backlash: The undeclared war against American women.* New York: Crown.

Feldman-Summers, S. and Kiesler, S.B. (1974) Those who are number two try harder: The effect of sex on attributions of causality. *Journal of Personality and Social Psychology, 30*, 846–855.

Fidell, L.S. (1970) Empirical verification of sex discrimination in hiring practices in psychology. *American Psychologist, 25*, 1094–1098.

Fields, R.M. (1974) The status of women in psychology: How many and how come? *International Journal of Group Tensions, 4*, 93–121.

Fine, M. (1983) Coping with rape: Critical perspectives on consciousness. *Imagination, Cognition, and Personality, 3*, 249–267.

Fine, M. (1985) Reflections on a feminist psychology of women. *Psychology of Women Quarterly, 9*, 167–183.

Fine, M. and Addelston, J. (1996) Questions of gender and power: The discursive limits of sameness and difference. In S. Wilkinson (ed.) *Feminist social psychologies; international perspectives.* Milton Keynes: Open University Press (pp. 66–86).

Fine, M. and Asch, A. (eds) (1988) *Women with disabilities: Essays in psychology, culture, and politics.* Philadelphia: Temple University Press.

Fine, M. and Gordon, S.M. (1989) Feminist transformations of/despite psychology. In M. Crawford and M. Gentry (eds) *Gender and thought: Psychological perspectives.* New York: Springer-Verlag (pp. 146–174).

Fine, M., Kidder, L. and Boell, J. (1989) Imaging feminist visions: Comments on a bibliography. In R.K. Unger (ed.) *Representations: Social constructions of gender.* Amityville, NY: Baywood (pp. 299–308).

Fine, M., Weis, L., Powell, L.C. and Wong, L.M. (eds) (1997) *Off white: Readings on race, power, and society.* New York: Routledge.

Fine, M. and Zane, N. (1988) Bein' wrapped too tight: When low income women drop out of high school. In L. Weis (ed.) *Dropouts in schools: Issues, dilemmas, solutions.* Albany, NY: State University of New York Press.

Fiske, S.T., Bersoff, D.N., Borgida, E., Deaux, K. and Heilman, M.E. (1991) Social science research on trial: Use of sex stereotyping research in Price Waterhouse v. Hopkins. *American Psychologist, 46*, 1049–1060.

Flax, J. (1987) Postmodernism and gender relations in feminist theory. *Signs, 12*, 621–643.

Fordham, S. (1993) 'Those loud black girls': (Black) women, silence, and gender 'passing' in the academy. *Anthropology and Education Quarterly, 24*, 3–32.

Forward, J.R. and Williams, J.R. (1970) Internal–external control and black militancy. *Journal of Social Issues, 26*, 75–92.

Frankenberg, R. (1993) *White women, race matters: The social construction of whiteness.* Minneapolis, MN: University of Minnesota Press.

Freeman, J. (1975) How to discriminate against women without really trying. In J. Freeman (ed.) *Women: A feminist perspective.* Palo Alto, CA: Mayfield.

French, J.R.P. and Raven, B. (1959) The bases of social power. In D. Cartwright (ed.) *Studies in social psychology.* Ann Arbor, MI: University of Michigan Press (pp. 150–167).

Frieze, I.H., Parsons (Eccles), J.E., Johnson, P.B., Ruble, D.N. and Zellman, G.L. (1978) *Women and sex roles: A social psychological perspective.* New York: Norton.

Frieze, I.H. and Ramsay, S.J. (1976) Nonverbal maintainence of traditional sex-roles. *Journal of Social Issues, 32*, 133–141.

Frodi, A., Macaulay, J. and Thome, P.A. (1977) Are women always less aggressive than men? *Psychological Bulletin, 84*, 634–660.

Furby, L. (1979) Individualistic bias in studies of locus of control. In A.R. Buss (ed.) *Psychology in social context.* New York: Irvington.

Furumoto, L. (1979) Mary Whiton Calkins (1863–1930): Fourteenth president of the American Psychological Association. *Journal of the History of the Behavioral Sciences, 15*, 346–356.

Gadlin, H. and Ingle, G. (1975) Through the one-way mirror: The limits of experimental self-reflection. *American Psychologist, 30*, 1003–1009.

Gaertner, S. and Dovidio, J. (1986) The aversive form of racism. In J. Dovidio and S. Gaertner (eds) *Prejudice, discrimination, and racism.* New York: Academic Press (pp. 61–89).

Gailey, C.W. (1987) Evolutionary perspectives on gender hierarchy. In B.B. Hess and M.M. Ferree (eds) *Analyzing gender: A handbook of social science research.* Newbury Park, CA: Sage.

Gardner, H. (1985) *The mind's new science.* New York: Basic Books.

Gentile, D.A. (1993) Just what are sex and gender anyway? A call for a new terminological standard. *Psychological Science, 4*, 120–122.

Gergen, K.J. (1985) The social constructionist movement in modern psychology. *American Psychologist, 40*, 266–275.

Gerson, J.M. and Peiss, K. (1985) Boundaries, negotiation, consciousness: Reconceptualizing gender relations. *Social Problems, 32*, 317–331.

Gilbert, C. and Bakan, P. (1973) Visual asymmetry in the perception of faces. *Neuropsychologia*, *11*, 355–362.

Gilbert, L.A. (1994) Reclaiming and returning gender to context: Examples from studies of heterosexual dual-earner families. *Psychology of Women Quarterly*, *18*, 539–558.

Gilligan, C. (1982) *In a different voice.* Cambridge, MA: Harvard University Press.

Ginorio, A., Gutierrez, L., Cauce, A.M. and Acosta, M. (1995) Psychological issues for Latinas. In H. Landrine (ed.) *Bringing cultural diversity to feminist psychology.* Washington, DC: American Psychological Association (pp. 241–264).

Gleitman, H. (1992) *Psychology.* New York: Norton.

Glenn, E.N. (1992) From servitude to service work: Historical continuities in the racial division of paid reproductive labor. *Signs*, *18*, 1–43.

Glick, P. and Fiske, S.T. (1997) The ambivalent sexism inventory: Differentiating hostile and benevolent sexism. *Journal of Personality and Social Psychology*, *70*, 491–512.

Goldberg, P.A. (1968) Are women prejudiced against women? *Transaction*, April, 28–30.

Goldberg, P.A. (1974) Prejudice toward women: Some personality correlates. *International Journal of Group Tensions*, *4*, 53–63.

Goldberg, P.A., Gottesdiener, M. and Abramson, P.R. (1975) Another put-down of women? Perceived attractiveness as a function of support for the feminist movement. *Journal of Personality and Social Psychology*, *32*, 113–115.

Golub, S. (1976) The effect of premenstrual anxiety and depression on cognitive function. *Journal of Personality and Social Psychology*, *34*, 99–104.

Gould, S.J. (1981) *The mismeasure of man.* New York: Norton.

Gould, S.J. (1989) *Wonderful life: The Burgess shale and the nature of history.* New York: Norton.

Grady, K.E. (1975) Androgyny reconsidered. Paper presented at the meeting of the Eastern Psychological Association, New York City. Reprinted in J.H. Williams (ed.) (1979) *Psychology of women: Selected readings.* New York: Norton.

Grady, K.E. (1977) The belief in sex differences. Paper presented at the meeting of the Eastern Psychological Association, Boston.

Grady, K.E. (1981) Sex bias in research design. *Psychology of Women Quarterly*, *5*, 628–636.

Greenwald, A.G. (1975) Consequences of prejudice against the null hypothesis. *Psychological Bulletin*, *82*, 1–20.

Griscom, J.L. (1992) Women and power: Definition, dualism, and difference. *Psychology of Women Quarterly*, *16*, 389–414.

Guinier, L., Fine, M. and Balin, J. (1994) Becoming gentlemen: Women's experiences at one Ivy League law school. *University of Pennsylvania Law Review*, *143*(1), 1001–1082.

Gutek, B.A. and Cohen, A.G. (1987) Sex ratios, sex role spillover, and sex at work: A comparison of men's and women's experience. *Human Relations*, *40*, 97–115.

Hacker, H.M. (1951) Women as a minority group. *Social Forces*, *30*, 60–69.

Haddock, G. and Zanna, M.P. (1994) Preferring 'housewives' to 'feminists': Categorization and the favorability of attitudes toward women. *Psychology of Women Quarterly*, *18*, 25–52.

Hagen, R.I. and Kahn, A.S. (1975) Discrimination against competent women. *Journal of Applied Social Psychology*, *5*, 362–376.

Hall, D.L. (1977) Social implications of the scientific study of sex. Paper presented at the symposium 'The Scholar and the Feminist IV', Barnard College, 23 April.

Halpern, D.F. (1994) Stereotypes, science, censorship and the study of sex differences. *Feminism & Pscyhology*, *4*, 523–530.

Hamilton, D.L. (1979) A cognitive-attributional analysis of stereotyping. In L. Berkowitz (ed.) *Advances in experimental social psychology*, vol. 12. New York: Academic Press.

Hamilton, D.L. and Gifford, R. (1976) Illusory correlations in interpersonal perception: A cognitive basis of stereotypic judgments. *Journal of Experimental Social Psychology*, *12*, 392–404.

Hansen, R.D. (1980) Commonsense attribution. *Journal of Personality and Social Psychology*, *39*, 996–1009.

Hare-Mustin, R.T. and Marecek, J. (1988) The meaning of difference: Gender theory, postmodernism, and psychology. *American Psychologist*, *43*, 455–464.

Hare-Mustin, R.T. and Marecek, J. (eds) (1990) *Making a difference: Psychology and the construction of gender*. New Haven, CT: Yale University Press.

Harris, M.B. (1976) The effects of sex, sex-stereotyped descriptions, and institution on evaluation of teachers. *Sex Roles*, *2*, 15–21.

Harris, S. (1971) Influence of subject and experimenter sex in psychological research. *Journal of Consulting and Clinical Psychology*, *37*, 291–294.

Haug, M., Whalen, R., Aron, C. and Olson, K. (eds) (1993) *The development of sex differences and similarities in behavior*. Dordrecht: Kluwer.

Heilman, M.E. and Saruwatari, L.R. (1979) When beauty is beastly: The effect of appearance and sex on evaluations of job applicants for managerial and nonmanagerial jobs. *Organizational Behavior and Human Performance*, *23*, 360–372.

Helson, R.M. (1978) Creativity in women. In J. Sherman and F. Denmark (eds) *The psychology of women: Future directions of research*. New York: Psychological Dimensions.

Helson, R. (1984–85) E. Nesbit's forty-first year: Her life, times, and symbolization of personality growth. *Imagination, Cognition, and Personality*, *4*, 53–68.

Henley, N.M. (1973) Status and sex: Some touching observations. *Bulletin of the Psychonomic Society*, *3*, 91–93.

Henley, N.M. (1977) *Body politics: Power, sex, and nonverbal communication*. Englewood Cliffs, NJ: Prentice-Hall.

Henley, N.M. (1995) Ethnicity and gender issues in language. In H. Landrine (ed.) *Bringing cultural diversity to feminist psychology*. Washington, DC: American Psychological Association (pp. 361–396).

Henley, N.M. and Freeman, J. (1975) The sexual politics of interpersonal behavior. In J. Freeman (ed.) *Women: A feminist perspective*. Palo Alto, CA: Mayfield.

Hoffman, L.R. and Maier, N.R.F. (1966) Social factors influencing problem solving in women. *Journal of Personality and Social Psychology*, *4*, 382–390.

Hogan, J.D. and Sexton, V.S. (1991) Women and the American Psychological Association. *Psychology of Women Quarterly*, *15*, 623–634.

Holland, D. and Skinner, D. (1987) Prestige and intimacy: The cultural models behind Americans' talk about gender types. In D. Holland and N. Quinn (eds) *Cultural models in language and thought*. New York: Cambridge University Press.

Hollway, W. (1994) Beyond sex differences: A project for feminist psychology. *Feminism & Psychology*, *4*, 538–546.

Holmes, D.S. and Jorgenson, B.W. (1971) Do personality and social psychologists study men more than women? *Representative Research in Social Psychology*, 2, 71–76.

hooks, b. (1984) *Feminist theory: From margin to center*. Boston: South End Press.

Horner, M.S. (1972) Toward an understanding of achievement-related conflicts in women. *Journal of Social Issues*, 28, 157–176.

Howe, K.G. (1985) The psychological impact of a women's studies course. *Women's Studies Quarterly*, 13, 23–24.

Hubbard, R. (1978) Have only men evolved? In R. Hubbard, M.S. Henifin and B. Fried (eds) *Women look at biology looking at women*. Cambridge: Schenkman.

Hyde, J.S. (1991) *Half the human experience: The psychology of women* (4th edn). Lexington, MA: D.C. Heath.

Hyde, J.S. (1994) Should psychologists study gender differences? Yes, with some guidelines. *Feminism & Psychology*, 4, 507–512.

Hyde, J.S. and Linn, M.C. (eds) (1986) *The psychology of gender: Advances through meta-analysis*. Baltimore, MD: Johns Hopkins Press.

Hyde, J.S. and Plant, E.A. (1995) Magnitude of psychological gender differences: Another side to the story. *American Psychologist*, 50, 159–161.

Israel, J. (1979) From level of aspiration to dissonance. In A. R. Buss (ed.) *Psychology in social context*. New York: Irvington.

Izraeli, D.N. (1993) 'They have eyes and see not': Gender politics in the Diaspora Museum. *Psychology of Women Quarterly*, 17, 515–523.

Jaggar, A.M. (1983) *Feminist politics and human nature*. Totowa, NJ: Rowman and Allanheld.

Janeway, E. (1974) *Between myth and morning: Women awakening*. New York: William Morrow.

John, B.A. and Sussman, L.E. (1984–85) Initiative taking as a determinant of role-reciprocal organization. *Imagination, Cognition, and Personality*, 4, 277–291.

Johnson, P. (1974) Social power and sex role stereotypes. Paper presented at the meeting of the Western Psychological Association, San Francisco.

Johnson, P. (1976) Women and power: Toward a theory of effectiveness. *Journal of Social Issues*, 32, 99–110.

Kagan, J. (1976) Emergent themes in human development. *American Scientist*, 64, 186–196.

Kahn, A.S., Mathie, V.A. and Torgier, C. (1994) Rape scripts and rape acknowledgement. *Psychology of Women Quarterly*, 18, 53–66.

Kahn, A.S. and Yoder, J.D. (1989) The psychology of women and conservatism: Rediscovering social change. *Psychology of Women Quarterly*, 13, 417–432.

Kahn, A.S. and Yoder, J.D. (eds) (1992) Women and power. *Psychology of Women Quarterly*, 16(4).

Kanter, R.M. (1977) *Men and women of the corporation*. New York: Basic Books.

Katz, P.A. (1986) Modification of children's gender-stereotyped behavior: General issues and research considerations. *Sex Roles*, 14, 591–602.

Keller, E.F. and Moglen, H. (1987) Competition: A problem for academic women. In V. Minor and H. Longino (eds) *Competition: A feminist taboo*. New York: Feminist Press (pp. 21–37).

Kessler, S.J. and McKenna, W. (1978) *Gender: An ethnomethodological approach*. New York: Wiley.

Kidder, L.H., Belletirie, G. and Cohn, E.S. (1977) Secret ambitions and public performance: The effect of anonymity on reward allocations made by men and women. *Journal of Experimental Social Psychology*, 13, 70–80.

Kieffer, M.G. and Cullen, D.M. (1974) Women who discriminate against other women: The process of denial. *International Journal of Group Tensions, 4*, 21–33.

Kimble, G.A. (1984) Psychology's two cultures. *American Psychologist, 39*, 833–839.

Kimura, D. (1973) The asymmetry of the human brain. *Scientific American, 228*(3), 70–78.

King, D.J. (1980) Values of undergraduate students and faculty members on theoretical orientations in psychology. *Teaching of Psychology, 7*, 236–237.

Kirkpatrick, C. (1936) The construction of a belief pattern scale for measuring attitudes toward feminism. *Journal of Social Psychology, 7*, 421–437.

Kitzinger, C.C. (1987) *The social construction of lesbianism.* London: Sage.

Kitzinger, C.C. (1990) Resisting the discipline. In E. Burman (ed.) *Feminists and psychological practice.* London: Sage.

Kitzinger, C.C. (1991) Feminism, psychology, and the paradox of power. *Feminism & Psychology, 1*, 111–129.

Kitzinger, C.C. (1994) Sex differences: Feminist perspectives. *Feminism & Psychology, 4*, 501–506.

Kitzinger, C.C. (1996) The token lesbian chapter. In S. Wilkinson (ed.) *Feminist social psychologies: International perspectives.* Milton Keynes: Open University Press (pp. 119–144).

Kocel, K.M. (1977) Cognitive abilities: Handedness, familial sinistrality, and sex. *Annals of the New York Academy of Sciences, 299*, 233–243.

Koch, S. (1981) The nature and limits of psychological knowledge: Lessons of a century qua 'Science'. *American Psychologist, 36*, 257–269.

Koeske, R.K. and Koeske, G.F. (1975) An attributional approach to moods and the menstrual cycle. *Journal of Personality and Social Psychology, 31*, 473–478.

Konner, M. (1981) *The tangled wing: Biological constraints on the human spirit.* New York: Harper & Row.

Koss, M.P. (1990) The women's mental health research agenda: Violence against women. *American Psychologist, 45*, 374–380.

Koss, M.P., Heise, L. and Russo, N.F. (1994) The global health burden of rape. *Psychology of Women Quarterly, 18*, 509–537.

Krasner, L. and Houts, A.C. (1984) A study of the 'value' systems of behavioral scientists. *American Psychologist, 39*, 840–850.

Kuhn, T.S. (1970) *The structure of scientific revolutions.* Chicago: University of Chicago Press.

Ladd, E.C., Jr. and Lipset, S.M. (1976) Sex differences in academe. *Chronicle of Higher Education*, 10 May, 18.

LaFrance, M. (1985) Women and mentoring: Problems and paradoxes. Paper presented at the Second Interdisciplinary Conference on Sex and Gender, Nags Head, North Carolina.

LaFrance, M. (1990) Clara Mayo: 1931–1981. In A.N. O'Connell and N.F. Russo (eds) *Women in psychology: A bio-bibliographic sourcebook.* Westport, CT: Greenwood Press (pp. 238–245).

LaFrance, M. (1992) Gender and interruptions: Individual infraction or violation of the social order? *Psychology of Women Quarterly, 16*, 497–512.

LaFrance, M. and Mayo, C. (1978) *Moving bodies: Nonverbal communication in social relationships.* Monterey, CA: Brooks/Cole.

LaFromboise, T., Bennett, S., Running Wolf, P. and James, A. (1995) American Indian women and psychology. In H. Landrine (ed.) *Bringing cultural diversity to feminist psychology: Theory, research, and practice.* Washington, DC: APA.

Lake, D.A. and Bryden, M.P. (1976) Handedness and sex differences in hemispheric asymmetry. *Brain and Language, 3,* 266–282.

Lana, R.E. (1976) *The foundations of psychological theory.* Hillsdale, NJ: Lawrence Erlbaum.

Landrine, H. (ed.) (1995) *Bringing cultural diversity to feminist psychology: Theory, research, practice.* Washington, DC: American Psychological Association.

Landrine, H., Klonoff, E.A. and Brown-Collins, A. (1992) Cultural diversity and methodology in feminist psychology: Critique, proposal, empirical example. *Psychology of Women Quarterly, 16,* 145–163.

Langer, E.J. and Imber, L. (1980) Role of mindlessness in the perception of deviance. *Journal of Personality and Social Psychology, 39,* 360–367.

Lansdell, H. (1962) A sex difference in the effect of temporal lobe neurosurgery on design preference. *Nature, 194,* 852–854.

Larkin, J. and Popaleni, K. (1994) Heterosexual courtship violence and sexual harassment: The public and private control of young women. *Feminism & Psychology, 4,* 213–227.

Laws, J.L. (1975) The psychology of tokenism: An analysis. *Sex Roles, 1,* 51–67.

Laws, J.L. (1979) *The second X: Sex role and social role.* New York: Elsevier.

Lemay, M. and Unger, R.K. (1982) The perception of females and males: The relationship between attractiveness and gender. Paper presented at the Meeting of the Eastern Psychological Association, Baltimore.

Lerman, H. (1986) *A mote in Freud's eye: From psychoanalysis to the psychology of women.* New York: Springer.

Lerman, H. and Porter, N. (eds) (1990) *Feminist ethics in psychotherapy.* New York: Springer.

Levay, S. (1993) *The sexual brain.* Cambridge, MA: MIT Press.

Levine, M. (1974) Scientific method and the adversary model. *American Psychologist, 29,* 661–677.

Lewin, M. (ed.) (1984) *In the shadow of the past: Psychology portrays the sexes.* New York: Columbia University Press.

Locher, P., Unger, R.K., Sociedade, P. and Wahl, J. (1993) At first glance: Accessibility of the physical attractiveness stereotype. *Sex Roles, 28,* 729–743.

Looft, W.R. (1971) Sex differences in the expression of vocational aspirations by elementary school children. *Developmental Psychology, 5,* 366.

Lorde, A. (1984) *Sister Outsider.* Trumansberg, NY: Crossing Press.

Lott, B. (1994) *The psychology of women* (2nd edn). Monterey, CA: Brooks/Cole.

Lott, B. (1995) 'Who ever thought I'd grow up to be a feminist foremother?' In Phyllis Chesler, Esther D. Rothblum and Ellen Cole (eds) *Feminist foremothers in women's studies, psychology, and mental health.* New York: Haworth Press.

Lykes, M.B. (1985) Gender and individualistic vs. collectivist bases for notions about the self. *Journal of Personality, 53,* 357–383.

Lykes, M.B. (1989) Dialogue with Guatemalan Indian women: Critical perspectives on constructing collaborative research. In R.K. Unger (ed.) *Representations: Social constructions of gender.* Amityville, NY: Baywood Press (pp. 167–185).

Lykes, M.B., Brabeck, M.M., Ferns, T. and Radan, A. (1993) Human rights and mental health among Latin American women in situations of state-sponsored violence: Bibliographic resources. *Psychology of Women Quarterly, 17,* 525–544.

Lykes, M.B. and Stewart, A.S. (1986) Evaluating the feminist challenge to research in personality and social psychology: 1963–1983. *Psychology of Women Quarterly, 10,* 393–412.

Maccoby, E.E. and Jacklin, C.N. (1974) *The psychology of sex differences.* Palo Alto, CA: Stanford University Press.

McCombs, H.G. (1986) The application of an individual/collective model to the psychology of black women. In D. Howard (ed.) *The dynamics of feminist therapy.* New York: Haworth Press (pp. 67–80).

McGlone, J. and Kertesz, A. (1973) Sex differences in cerebral processing of visuospatial tasks. *Cortex, 9,* 313–320.

McGuire, W.C., McGuire, C.V. and Winton, W. (1979) Effects of household sex composition on the salience of one's gender in the spontaneous self concept. *Journal of Experimental Social Psychology, 15,* 77–90.

McGrath, J.E. (1986) Continuity and change: Time, method, and the study of social issues. *Journal of Social Issues, 42,* 5–19.

McHugh, M., Koeske, R. and Frieze, I.H. (1986) Issues to consider in conducting nonsexist psychological research: A guide for researchers. *American Psychologist, 41,* 879–890.

McKee, J.P. and Sheriffs, A.C. (1957) The differential evaluation of males and females. *Journal of Personality, 25,* 356–371.

McKenna, W. and Kessler, S.J. (1977) Experimental design as a source of sex bias in social psychology. *Sex Roles, 3,* 117–128.

Major, B. (1980) Information acquisition and attribution processes. *Journal of Personality and Social Psychology, 39,* 1010–1023.

Major, B. (1994) From social inequality to personal entitlement: The role of social comparisons, legitimacy appraisals, and group membership. In M.P. Zanna (ed.) *Advances in experimental social psychology,* vol. 26. New York: Academic Press (pp. 293–355).

Marecek, J. (1995) Gender, politics, and psychology's ways of knowing. *American Psychologist, 50,* 162–163.

Marshall, J. (1986) Exploring the experiences of women managers: Towards rigour in qualitative methods. In S. Wilkinson (ed.) *Feminist social psychology: Developing theory and practice.* Milton Keynes: Open University

Masica, D.N., Money, J., Ehrhardt, A.A. and Levis, V.S. (1969) IQ, fetal sex hormones and cognitive patterns: Studies in the testicular feminizing syndrome of androgen insensitivity. *Johns Hopkins Medical Journal, 124,* 34–43.

Mayo, C. and Henley, N.M. (eds) (1981) *Gender and nonverbal behavior.* New York: Springer-Verlag.

Mednick, M.T.S. (1976) Comments on review essay: Psychology. *Signs, 1,* 763–770.

Mednick, M.T.S. (1978) Now we are four: What should we be when we grow up? *Psychology of Women Quarterly, 3,* 123–138.

Mednick, M.T.S. (1989) On the politics of psychological constructs: Stop the bandwagon, I want to get off. *American Psychologist, 44,* 1118–1123.

Mednick, M.T.S. and Tangri, S.S. (eds) (1972) New perspectives on women. *Journal of Social Issues, 28*(2).

Mednick, M.T. and Urbanski, L.L. (1991) The origins and activities of APA's Division of the Psychology of Women. *Psychology of Women Quarterly, 15,* 651–663.

Merton, R.K. (1968) The Matthew effect in science: The reward and communication systems of science are considered. *Science, 199,* 55–63.

Miller, F. (1990) Toward an understanding of adolescents' attitudes about reality. Paper presented at the meeting of the American Psychological Association, Boston, MA.

Miller, J.B. (1976) *Toward a new psychology of women*. Boston: Beacon Press.

Miller, T.W. (1974) Male attitudes towards women's rights as a function of their level of self esteem. *International Journal of Group Tensions*, *4*, 35–44.

Money, J. and Ehrhardt, A.A. (1972) *Man and woman, boy and girl*. Baltimore, MD: Johns Hopkins University Press.

Murray, S.R. and Mednick, M.T.S. (1977) Black women's achievement orientation: Motivational and cognitive factors. *Psychology of Women Quarterly*, *1*, 247–259.

Myers, D.G. (1992) *Psychology* (3rd edn). New York: Worth Publishers.

Nadelman, L. (1974) Sex identity in American children: Memory, knowledge, and preference tests. *Developmental Psychology*, *10*, 413–417.

Nash, S.C. (1975) The relationship among sex-role stereotyping, sex-role preference, and the sex difference in spatial visualization. *Sex Roles*, *1*, 15–32.

Neisser, U. (1967) *Cognitive Psychology*. New York: Appleton-Century-Croft.

Neuborne, E. (1995) Imagine my surprise. In B. Findlen (ed.) *Listen up: Voices of the next feminist generation*. Seattle, WA: Seal Press.

Newcombe, N. (1980) Beyond nature and nurture. *Contemporary Psychology*, *25*, 807–808.

O'Connell, A.N., Alpert, J.L., Richardson, M.S., Rotter, N.G., Ruble, D.N. and Unger, R.K. (1978) Gender-specific barriers to research in psychology. *JSAS Catalog of Selected Documents in Psychology*, *8*, 80 (MS. No. 1753).

O'Leary, V.E. (1977) *Toward understanding women*. Monterey, CA: Brooks/Cole.

O'Leary, V.E., Unger, R.K. and Wallston, B.S. (eds) (1985) *Women, gender, and social psychology*. Hillsdale, NJ: Erlbaum.

Paige, K.E. (1973) Women learn to sing the menstrual blues. *Psychology Today*, September, 41–46.

Parlee, M.B. (1975) Review essay: Psychology. *Signs*, *1*, 119–138.

Parlee, M.B. (1978) Psychological aspects of menstruation, childbirth, and menopause. In J. Sherman and F. Denmark (eds) *Psychology of women: Future directions of research*. New York: Psychological Dimensions.

Parlee, M.B. (1979) Psychology and women: Review essay. *Signs*, *5*, 121–133.

Parlee, M.B. (1981) Appropriate control groups in feminist research. *Psychology of Women Quarterly*, *5*, 637–644.

Payer, M.E. (1977) Is traditional scholarship value free? Toward a critical theory. Paper presented at the symposium 'The Scholar and the Feminist IV', Barnard College, 23 April.

Pedersen, D.M., Shinedling, M.M. and Johnson, D.L. (1968) Effects of sex of examiner and subject on children's quantitative test performance. *Journal of Personality and Social Psychology*, *10*, 251–254.

Peplau, L.A. and Conrad, E. (1989) Beyond nonsexist research: The perils of feminist methods in psychology. *Psychology of Women Quarterly*, *13*, 379–400.

Perlman, D. (1979) Rear-end analysis: The use of social psychology textbook citation data. *Teaching of Psychology*, *6*, 101–104.

Peters, D.P. and Ceci, S.J. (1982) Peer-review practices of psychological journals: The fate of published articles, submitted again. *The Behavioral and Brain Sciences*, *5*, 187–195.

Peterson, S.B. and Kroner, T. (1992) Gender biases in textbooks for introductory psychology and human development. *Psychology of Women Quarterly*, *16*, 17–36.

Pheterson, G.I., Kiesler, S.B. and Goldberg, P.A. (1971) Evaluation of the performance of women as a function of their sex, achievement, and personal history. *Journal of Personality and Social Psychology*, *19*, 114–118.

Piliavin, J.A. and Unger, R.K. (1985) The helpful but helpless female: Myth or reality? In V.E. O'Leary, R.K. Unger and B.S. Wallston (eds) *Women, gender, and social psychology*. Hillsdale, NJ: Erlbaum.

Pope, K.V. (1984–1985) The divided lives of women in literature. *Imagination, Cognition, and Personality*, 4, 161–169.

Powell, G.N. (1987) The effects of sex and gender on recruitment. *Academy of Management Review*, 12, 731–743.

Rabinowitz, V.C. and Sechzer, J.A. (1993) Feminist perspectives on research methods. In F.L. Denmark and M.A. Paludi (eds) *Psychology of women: A handbook of issues and theories*. Westport, CT: Greenwood Press (pp. 23–66).

Raymond, B.J. and Unger, R.K. (1972) 'The apparel oft proclaims the man': Cooperation with deviant and conventional youths. *Journal of Social Psychology*, 87, 75–82.

Raymond, B.J., Unger, R.K. and Stone, S. (1972) To demand or not to demand. *American Psychologist*, 27, 577–579.

Reid, P.T. (1988) Racism and sexism: Comparisons and conflicts. In P.A. Katz and D.A. Taylor (eds) *Eliminating racism: Profiles in controversy*. New York: Plenum (pp. 203–221).

Reid, P.T. (1993) Poor women in psychological research: Shut up and shut out. *Psychology of Women Quarterly*, 17, 133–150.

Reinharz, S. (1992) *Feminist methods in social research*. New York: Oxford University Press.

Rheingold, H.L. and Cook, K.V. (1975) The contents of boys' and girls' rooms as an index of parents' behavior. *Child Development*, 46, 459–463.

Ricketts, M. (1989) Epistemological values of feminists in psychology. *Psychology of Women Quarterly*, 13, 401–415.

Riegel, K.F. (1979) *Dialectical psychology*. New York: Academic Press.

Robinson, D. and Unger, R.K. (1983) Attitudes towards the pregnant professional. Paper presented at the meeting of the Eastern Psychological Association, Philadelphia.

Rodin, J. (1976) Menstruation, reattribution, and competence. *Journal of Personality and Social Psychology*, 33, 345–353.

Roman, L.G. (1993) White is a color! White defensiveness, postmodernist, and anti-racist pedagogy. In C. McCarthy and W. Crichlow (eds) *Race identity and representation in education*. New York: Routledge (pp. 71–88).

Rosaldo, M.Z. and Lamphere, L. (eds) (1974) *Woman, culture and society*. Palo Alto, CA: Stanford University Press.

Rosenberg, R. (1982) *Beyond separate spheres: Intellectual roots of modern feminism*. New Haven, CT: Yale University Press.

Rosenkrantz, P.S., Vogel, S.R., Bee, H., Broverman, I.K. and Broverman, D.M. (1968) Sex-role stereotypes and self-concepts in college students. *Journal of Consulting and Clinical Psychology*, 32, 287–295.

Rosenthal, N.B. (1984) Consciousness-raising: From revolution to re-evaluation. *Psychology of Women Quarterly*, 8, 309–326.

Roth, W. (1983) Handicap as a social construct. *Society* (March–April), 51–56.

Rotter, N.G. (1978) Tripping up from girl to colleague: Training barriers to women doing research. In A.N. O'Connell et al., Gender-specific barriers to research in psychology. JSAS *Catalog of Selected Documents in Psychology*, 8, 80 (Ms. No. 1753).

Rubin, L.B. (1976) *Worlds of pain: Life in the working class family.* New York: Basic Books.

Ruble, D.N. (1978) Report on gender-specific expectations. In A.N. O'Connell et al., Gender-specific barriers to research in psychology. JSAS *Catalog of Selected Documents in Psychology, 8,* 80 (Ms. No. 1753).

Ruble, T.L. (1983) Sex stereotypes: Issues of change in the 1970s. *Sex Roles, 9,* 397–402.

Russell, B. (1943) *A history of western philosophy.* New York: Simon & Schuster.

Russell, K., Wilson, M. and Hall, R. (1992) *The color complex: The politics of skin color among African Americans.* New York: Harcourt Brace Jovanovich.

Russett, C.E. (1989) *Sexual science.* Cambridge, MA: Harvard University Press.

Russo, N.F. (1982) Psychology of women: Analysis of the faculty and courses of an emerging field. *Psychology of Women Quarterly, 7,* 18–31.

Russo, N.F. and duMont, A. (1997) Division 35: Origins, activities, future. In D. Dewsbury (ed.) *A history of the divisions in the American Psychological Association.* Washington, DC: American Psychological Association.

Sadker, M. and Sadker, D. (1994) *Failing at fairness: How America's schools cheat girls.* New York: Scribner.

Samelson, F. (1978) From 'race psychology' to 'studies in prejudice': Some observations on the thematic reversals in social psychology. *Journal of the History of the Behavioral Sciences, 14,* 265–278.

Sampson, E.E. (1978) Scientific paradigms and social values: Wanted – a scientific revolution. *Journal of Personality and Social Psychology, 36,* 1332–1343.

Sampson, E.E. (1981) Cognitive psychology as ideology. *American Psychologist, 36,* 730–743.

Sanders, A., Steil, J. and Weinglass, J. (1984–85) Taking the traditional route: Some covert costs of decisions for the married career woman. *Imagination, Cognition, and Personality, 3,* 327–336.

Sanger, S.P. and Alker, H.A. (1972) Dimensions of internal–external locus of control and the women's liberation movement. *Journal of Social Issues, 28,* 115–129.

Sarason, S.B. (1973) Jewishness, Blackishness, and the nature-nurture controversy. *American Psychologist, 28,* 962–971.

Scarborough, E. and Furumoto, L. (1987) *Untold lives: The first generation of American women psychologists.* New York: Columbia University Press.

Scott, J. (1991) Deconstructing equality vs difference: On the use of post-structionalist theory for feminism. In M. Hirsch and E. Keller (eds) *Conflicts in feminism.* New York: Routledge.

Serbin, L.A., Connor, J.M. and Citron, C.C. (1978) Environmental control of independent and dependent behaviors in preschool boys and girls: A model for early independence training. *Sex Roles, 4,* 867–875.

Sherif, C.W. (1976) *Orientation in social psychology.* New York: Harper & Row.

Sherif, C.W. (1979) Bias in psychology. In J.A. Sherman and E.T. Beck (eds) *The prism of sex: Essays in the sociology of knowledge.* Madison, WI: University of Wisconsin Press (pp. 93–133).

Sherif, C.W. (1982) Needed concepts in the study of gender identity. *Psychology of Women Quarterly, 6,* 375–398.

Sherman, J.A. (1971) *On the psychology of women: A survey of empirical studies.* Springfield, IL: C.C. Thomas.

Sherman, J.A. and Beck, E.T. (eds) (1979) *The prism of sex: Essays in the sociology of knowledge.* Madison, WI: University of Wisconsin Press.

Sherman, J.A. and Denmark, F.L. (eds) (1978) *The psychology of women: Future directions of research*. New York: Psychological Dimensions.

Sherwood, J.J. and Nataupsky, M. (1968) Predicting the conclusions of Negro–White intelligence research from biographic characteristics of the investigator. *Journal of Personality and Social Psychology, 8*, 53–58.

Shields, S.A. (1975a) Functionalism, Darwinism, and the psychology of women: A study in social myth. *American Psychologist, 30*, 739–753.

Shields, S.A. (1975b) Ms. Pilgrim's progress: The contribution of Leta Stetter Hollingworth to the psychology of women. *American Psychologist, 30*, 852–857.

Shields, S.A. (1994) Blindsight: Overcoming mainstream psychology's resistance to feminist theory and research. *Psychological Inquiry, 5*, 92–96.

Shields, S.A. and Crowley, J.J. (1996) Appropriating questionnaires and rating scales for a feminist psychology: A multi-method approach to gender and emotion. In S. Wilkinson (ed.) *Feminist social psychologies: International perspectives*. Milton Keynes: Open University Press (pp. 218–232).

Siiter, R. and Unger, R.K. (1975) Ethnic differences in sex role stereotypes. Paper presented at the meeting of the American Psychological Association, Chicago.

Sluzki, C. and Ransom, D. (eds) (1976) *Double bind: The foundation of a communications approach to the family*. New York: Grune and Stratton.

Smith, A. and Stewart, A.J. (eds) (1983) Racism and sexism in black women's lives. *Journal of Social Issues, 39*(3).

Smith, C.A. and Ellsworth, P.C. (1985) Patterns of cognitive appraisal in emotion. *Journal of Personality and Social Psychology, 48*, 813–838.

Smith, D.E. (1979) A sociology for women. In J.A. Sherman and E.T. Beck (eds) *The prism of sex*. Madison, WI: University of Wisconsin Press.

Smith, M.B. (1980) Attitudes, values, and selfhood. In H.E. Howe Jr. and M.M. Page (eds) *Nebraska symposium on motivation, 1979*. Lincoln, NE: University of Nebraska Press.

Smith-Brinton, M. and Unger, R.K. (1992–93) Ideological differences in the construction of meaning. *Imagination, Cognition, and Personality, 12*, 395–412.

Snyder, M., Tanke, E.D. and Berscheid, E. (1977) Social perception and interpersonal behavior: On the self-fulfilling nature of social stereotypes. *Journal of Personality and Social Psychology, 35*, 656–666.

Snyder, M. and Uranowitz, S.W. (1978) Reconstructing the past: Some cognitive consequences of person perception. *Journal of Personality and Social Psychology, 36*, 941–950.

Spelman, E. (1988) *Inessential woman: Problems of exclusion in feminist thought*. Boston: Beacon Press.

Spence, J.T. and Helmreich, R.L. (1978) *Masculinity and femininity: Their dimensions, correlates, and antecedents*. Austin, TX: University of Texas Press.

Spence, J.T., Helmreich, R. and Stapp, J. (1975) Likability, sex-role congruence of interest, and competence: It all depends upon how you ask. *Journal of Applied Social Psychology, 5*, 93–109.

Spence, J.T. and Sawin, L.L. (1985) Images of masculinity and femininity: A reconceptualization. In V.E. O'Leary, R.K. Unger and B.S. Wallston (eds) *Women, gender, and social psychology*. Hillsdale, NJ: Erlbaum.

Starer, R. and Denmark, F. (1974) Discrimination against aspiring women. *International Journal of Group Tensions, 4*, 65–70.

Steffen, V.J. and Eagly, A.H. (1985) Implicit theories about influence style: The effect of status and sex. *Personality and Social Psychology Bulletin, 11*, 191–205.

Steil, J.M. and Hillman, J.L. (1993) The perceived value of direct and indirect influence strategies: A cross-cultural comparison. *Psychology of Women Quarterly*, *17*, 457–462.

Stewart, A.J. (1987) Some consequences of the things our mothers did and didn't teach us: Social and individual change in women's lives. Invited address at the Meeting of the Eastern Psychological Association, Crystal City, Virginia.

Stewart, A.J. and Healy, J.M. Jr. (1989) Linking individual development and social changes. *American Psychologist*, *44*, 30–42.

Stewart, A.J. and Ostrove, J.M. (1993) Social class, social change, and gender: Working-class women at Radcliffe and after. *Psychology of Women Quarterly*, *17*, 475–497.

Stimpson, C.R. (1979) The power to name: Some reflections on the avant-garde. In J. Sherman and E.T. Beck (eds) *The prism of sex: Essays in the sociology of knowledge*. Madison, WI: University of Wisconsin Press.

Tavris, C. (1993) Good intentions and wrong turns: A critique of modern feminism. Invited address to Division 35 at the meeting of the American Psychological Association, Toronto, August.

Taylor, S.E. and Fiske, S.T. (1978) Salience, attention and attribution: Top of the head phenomena. In L. Berkowitz (ed.) *Advances in experimental social psychology*, vol. 11. New York: Academic Press.

Taylor, S.E. and Langer, E.J. (1977) Pregnancy: A social stigma? *Sex Roles*, *3*, 27–35.

Taylor, S.E., Fiske, S.T., Etcoff, N.L. and Ruderman, A.J. (1978) Categorical and contextual bases of person memory and stereotyping. *Journal of Personality and Social Psychology*, *36*, 778–793.

Tennov, D. (1975) *Psychotherapy: The hazardous cure*. New York: Abelard-Schuman.

Thompson, S.K. (1975) Gender labels and early sex role development. *Child Development*, *46*, 339–347.

Thorne, B. (1986) Girls and boys together, but mostly apart. In W.W. Hartup and Z. Rubin (eds) *Relationships and development*. Hillsdale, NJ: Erlbaum.

Thorne, B. and Henley, N.M. (eds) (1975) *Language and sex: Difference and dominance*. Rowley, MA: Newbury House.

Tiefer, L. (1991) A brief history of the Association for Women in Psychology: 1969–1991. *Psychology of Women Quarterly*, *15*, 635–649.

Tobach, E. (1971) Some evolutionary aspects of human gender. *American Journal of Orthopsychiatry*, *41*, 710–715.

Tomarelli, M. (1996) Review of Mary Crawford's 'Talking Difference'. *Contemporary Psychology*, *42*, 19–21.

Torres, L. (1992) Women and language: From sex differences to power dynamics. In C. Kramarae and D. Spender (eds) *The knowledge explosion: Generations of feminist scholarship*. New York: Teachers College Press (pp. 281–290).

Tromel-Ploetz, S. (1991) Selling the apolitical. *Discourse & Society*, *2*, 489–502.

Turner, B.F. and McCaffrey, J.H. (1974) Socialization and career orientation among black and white college women. *Journal of Vocational Behavior*, *55*, 307–319.

Unger, R.K. (1975) *Sex role stereotypes revisited: Psychological perspectives on women's studies*. New York: Harper & Row.

Unger, R.K. (1976) Male is greater than female: The socialization of status inequality. *The Counseling Psychologist*, *6*, 2–9.

Unger, R.K. (1977) The rediscovery of gender. Paper presented at the Meeting of the Eastern Psychological Association, Boston.

Unger, R.K. (1978a) The politics of gender. In J. Sherman and F. Denmark (eds) *Psychology of women: Future directions of research.* New York: Psychological Dimensions (pp. 463–517).

Unger, R.K. (1978b) Structural barriers to women doing research. In A.N. O'Connell et al., Gender-specific barriers to research in psychology. JSAS *Catalog of Selected Documents in Psychology, 8,* 80 (Ms. No. 1753).

Unger, R.K. (1979a) *Female and male: Psychological perspectives.* New York: Harper & Row.

Unger, R.K. (1979b) Sexism in teacher evaluation: The comparability of real life and laboratory analogs. *Academic Psychology Bulletin, 1,* 163–170.

Unger, R.K. (1979c) Toward a redefinition of sex and gender. *American Psychologist, 34,* 1085–1094.

Unger, R.K. (1981) Sex as a social reality: Field and laboratory research. *Psychology of Women Quarterly, 5,* 645–653.

Unger, R.K. (1982) Advocacy versus scholarship revisited: Issues in the psychology of women. *Psychology of Women Quarterly, 7,* 5–17.

Unger, R.K. (1983) Through the looking glass: No Wonderland yet! (The reciprocal relationship between methodology and models of reality). *Psychology of Women Quarterly, 8,* 9–32.

Unger, R.K. (1983–1984) Sex in psychological paradigms – from behavior to cognition. *Imagination, Cognition, and Personality, 3,* 227–234.

Unger, R.K. (1984–1985) Explorations in feminist ideology: Surprising consistencies and unexamined conflicts. *Imagination, Cognition, and Personality, 4,* 387–405.

Unger, R.K. (1985a) Epistemological consistency and its scientific implications. *American Psychologist, 40,* 1413–1414.

Unger, R.K. (1985b) Personal appearance and social control. In M. Safir, M. Mednick, D. Izraeli and J. Bernard (eds) *Women's worlds: The new scholarship.* New York: Praeger.

Unger, R.K. (1986a) Looking toward the future by looking at the past: Social activism and social history. *Journal of Social Issues, 42*(1), 215–227.

Unger, R.K. (1986b) SPSSI Council: A collective biography. *Journal of Social Issues, 42*(4), 81–88.

Unger, R.K. (1988a) Myths we choose to live by: Feminist lives as speculative fiction. Paper presented at the meeting of the American Psychological Association, Atlanta, Georgia.

Unger, R.K. (1988b) Psychological, feminist, and personal epistemology: Transcending contradiction. In M. Gergen (ed.) *Feminist thought and the structure of knowledge.* New York: New York University Press (pp. 124–141).

Unger, R.K. (1988c) The psychology of social issues: Commonalities from specifics. In K. Quina and P. Bronstein (eds) *Teaching about a psychology of people.* Washington, DC: American Psychological Association (pp. 184–191).

Unger, R.K. (ed.) (1989a) *Representations: Social constructions of gender.* Sponsored by SPSSI. Amityville, NY: Baywood.

Unger, R.K. (1989b) Sex, gender, and epistemology. In M. Crawford and M. Gentry (eds) *Gender and thought.* New York: Springer-Verlag (pp. 17–35).

Unger, R.K. (1990) Imperfect reflections of reality: Psychology and the construction of gender. In R. Hare-Mustin and J. Marecek (eds) *Making a difference:*

Representations of gender in psychology. New Haven: Yale University Press (pp. 102–149).

Unger, R.K. (1992) Will the 'real' sex difference please stand up? *Feminism & Psychology*, 2, 231–238.

Unger, R.K. (1993a) Alternative conceptions of sex (and sex differences). In M. Haug, R. Whalen, C. Aron and K.L. Olsen (eds) *The development of sex differences and similarities in behavior*. Dordrecht: Kluwer (pp. 457–476).

Unger, R.K. (1993b) The personal is paradoxical: Feminists construct psychology. *Feminism & Psychology*, 3, 211–218.

Unger, R.K. (1995a) Cultural diversity and the future of feminist psychology. In H. Landrine (ed.) *Bringing cultural diversity to feminist psychology*. Washington, DC: American Psychological Association (pp. 413–431).

Unger, R.K. (1995b) Nancy Datan: Her many unique voices. *Feminism & Psychology*, 5, 441–448.

Unger, R.K. (1996) Using the master's tools: Epistemology and empiricism. In S. Wilkinson (ed.) *Feminist social psychologies: International perspectives*. Milton Keynes: Open University Press (pp. 165–181).

Unger, R.K. (1997) A just noticeable difference: The impact of gender, race, ethnicity, and social class on psychology. In D. Helly (ed.) *Psychology*. Baltimore: National Center for Curriculum Transformation Resources on Women.

Unger, R.K. (1998) Positive marginality: Antecedents and consequences. *Journal of Adult Development*, 5, 163–170.

Unger, R.K. and Crawford, M. (1989) Review of *Sex differences in social behavior: A social-role interpretation* by A.H. Eagly. *Contemporary Psychology*, 34, 122–123.

Unger, R.K. and Crawford, M. (1993) Sex and gender: The troubled relationship between terms and concepts. *Psychological Science*, 4, 122–124.

Unger, R.K. and Crawford, M. (1996) *Women and gender: A feminist psychology* (2nd edn). New York: McGraw-Hill.

Unger, R.K. and Denmark, F.L. (1975) *Woman: Dependent or independent variable?* New York: Psychological Dimensions.

Unger, R.K., Draper, R.D. and Pendergrass, M.L. (1986) Personal epistemology and personal experience. *Journal of Social Issues*, 42, 67–79.

Unger, R.K. and Fishbein, C. (1973) Making value judgments: Self vs peer vs parent ratings. Paper presented at the meeting of the Eastern Psychological Association, Washington, DC.

Unger, R.K., Hilderbrand, M. and Madar, T. (1982) Physical attractiveness and assumptions about social deviance: Some sex by sex comparisons. *Personality and Social Psychology Bulletin*, 8, 293–301.

Unger, R.K. and Jones, J. (1988) Personal epistemology and its correlates: The subjective nature of sex and race. Paper presented at the meeting of the International Society of Political Psychology, Meadowlands, NJ.

Unger, R.K. and Kahn, A.S. (1998) Carolyn Wood Sherif: A prescient wisdom. *Feminism & Psychology*, 8, 51–57.

Unger, R.K. and Lemay, M. (1991) Who's to blame? The relationship between political attributions and assumptions about reality. *Contemporary Social Psychology*, 15, 144–149.

Unger, R.K., O'Leary, V.E. and Fabian, S. (1977) *Membership characteristics of the Division of the Psychology of Women of the American Psychological Association*. Unpublished report to Division 35 executive committee.

Unger, R.K. and Raymond, B.J. (1974) External criteria as predictors of values: The importance of race and attire. *Journal of Social Psychology, 93*, 295–296.

Unger, R.K., Raymond, B.J. and Levine, S. (1974) Are women discriminated against? Sometimes! *International Journal of Group Tensions, 4*, 71–81.

Unger, R.K. and Safir, M. (1990) Cross cultural aspects of the Attitudes about Reality Scale. Paper presented at the annual meeting of the American Psychological Association, Boston, MA, 13 August.

Unger, R.K. and Sanchez-Hucles, J. (ed.) (1993) Gender and culture. *Psychology of Women Quarterly, 17*(4).

Unger, R.K. and Saundra (1993) Sexism: An integrated perspective. In F.L. Denmark and M. Paludi (eds) *Psychology of women: A handbook of issues and theories.* New Jersey: Greenwood Press (pp. 141–188).

Unger, R.K. and Serbin, L. (eds) (1986) Sex, gender, and social change. *Sex Roles, 14*(11/12).

Unger, R.K. and Siiter, R. (1974) Sex role stereotypes: The weight of a 'grain of truth'. Paper presented at the meeting of the Eastern Psychological Association, Philadelphia. Reprinted in B.B. Watson (ed.) (1976) *Women's Studies: The Social Realities.* New York: Harper & Row.

Unger, R.K. and Sussman, L.E. (1986) 'I and thou': Another barrier to societal change? *Sex Roles, 14*, 629–636.

Vaughter, R.M. (1976) Review essay: Psychology. *Signs, 2*, 120–146.

von Baeyer, C.L., Sherk, D.L. and Zanna, M.P. (1981) Impression management in the job interview: When the female applicant meets the male (chauvinist) interviewer. *Personality and Social Psychology Bulletin, 7*, 45–51.

Walkerdine, V. (1996) Special issue on social class. *Feminism & Psychology, 6*(3).

Wallston, B.S. (1981) What are the questions in the psychology of women? A feminist approach to research. *Psychology of Women Quarterly, 5*, 597–617.

Wallston, B.S. and Grady, K.E. (1985) Synthesizing the feminist critique. In V.E. O'Leary, R.K. Unger and B.S. Wallston (eds) *Women, gender, and social psychology.* Hillsdale, NJ: Erlbaum (pp. 7–33).

Wallston, B.S. and O'Leary, V.E. (1981) Sex makes a difference: Differential perceptions of women and men. In L. Wheeler (ed.) *Review of personality and social psychology,* vol. 2. Beverly Hills, CA: Sage.

Walsh, M.R. (1985) Academic professional women organizing for change: The struggle in psychology. *Journal of Social Issues, 41*, 17–28.

Weisstein, N. (1968) *Kinder, Küche, Kirche as scientific law: Psychology constructs the female.* Boston, MA: New England Free Press.

Weisstein, N. (1970) Neural symbolic activity: A psychophysical measure. *Science, 168*, 1489–1491.

Weisstein, N. (1977) 'How can a little girl like you teach a great big class of men?', the chairman said, and other adventures of a woman in science. In S. Ruddick and P. Daniels (eds) *Working it out.* New York: Pantheon (pp. 241–250).

Weisstein, N. (1993) Power, resistance, and science: A call for a revitalized feminist psychology. *Feminism & Psychology, 3*, 239–245.

Weiten, W. (1994) *Psychology: Themes and variations* (2nd edn). Pacific Grove, CA: Brooks/Cole.

Weitz, S. (ed.) (1976) *Nonverbal communication.* New York: Oxford University Press.

West, C. and Zimmerman, D.H. (1987) Doing gender. *Gender & Society, 1*, 125–151.

White, A.M. (1994) A course in the psychology of oppression: A different approach to teaching about diversity. *Teaching of Psychology, 21*, 17–23.

Wicker, A.W. (1969) Attitudes versus actions: The relationship of verbal and overt behavioral responses to attitude objects. *Journal of Social Issues, 25,* 41–78.

Wilkinson, S. (ed.) (1986) *Feminist social psychology: Developing theory and practice.* Milton Keynes: Open University.

Wilkinson, S. (ed.) (1996) *Feminist social psychologies: International perspectives.* Milton Keynes: Open University Press.

Wilkinson, S. and Kitzinger, C.C. (eds) (1993) *Heterosexualty: A feminism and psychology reader.* London: Sage.

Williams, J.H. (ed.) (1979) *Psychology of women: Selected readings.* New York: Norton.

Wittig, M.A. (1985) Metatheoretical dilemmas in the psychology of gender. *American Psychologist, 40,* 800–811.

Wolf, N. (1991) *The beauty myth: How images of beauty are used against women.* New York: William Morrow.

Wolman, C. and Frank, H. (1975) The solo woman in a professional peer group. *American Journal of Orthopsychiatry, 45,* 164–171.

Women's Program Office (1991) *Graduate faculty interested in the psychology of women.* Washington, DC: American Psychological Association.

Women's Program Office (1993) *Women in the American Psychological Association.* Washington, DC: American Psychological Association.

Wong, E. and Weisstein, N. (1982) A new perceptual context-superiority effect: Line segments are more visible against a figure than against a ground. *Science, 218,* 587–589.

Wood, J.T. and Conrad, C. (1983) Paradox in the experiences of professional women. *Western Journal of Speech Communication, 47,* 305–322.

Wrightsman, L.S. (1992) *Assumptions about human nature: Implications for researchers and practitioners* (2nd edn). Newbury Park, CA: Sage.

Wyche, K.F. and Graves, S.B. (1992) Minority women in academia: Access and barriers to professional participation. *Psychology of Women Quarterly, 16,* 429–437.

Yoder, J.D. and Kahn, A.S. (1992) Toward a feminist understanding of women and power. *Psychology of Women Quarterly, 16,* 381–388.

Zimbardo, P.G. (1992) *Psychology and life* (13th edn). New York: HarperCollins.

Zinn, M.B. (1994) Feminist rethinking from racial-ethnic families. In M.B. Zinn and B.T. Dill (eds) *Women of color in U.S. society.* Philadelphia: Temple University Press (pp. 303–314).

Index